Mistress of Herself

DIANA WHITEHILL LAING, a daughter
of Walter Muir Whitehill, Director of the
Boston Athenaeum, grew up in North An-
dover, Massachusetts. She attended the
Thomas School in Rowayton, Connecticut,
and Bryn Mawr College. In 1954 she married C. Christopher Laing, a British tea
planter's son from Ceylon who had come
to Harvard. Their first years were peripa-
tetic, for immediately after their marriage
he became an American citizen and entered
Officer Candidate School at Newport, Rhode
Island. While he was at sea in an aircraft
carrier, the idea of this biography arose.
Mrs. Laing had known her subject both in
Massachusetts and England, and amplified
her own recollections by intensive study of
papers in the Massachusetts Historical Society and the University of Birmingham.
She started the writing on Beacon Hill in
Boston. The book was completed in a stone
farmhouse in Chadds Ford, Pennsylvania,
where Mr. and Mrs. Laing have lived since
1962 when he joined E. I. du Pont de Ne-
mours and Company. There, with three children, a cat, a pony, and a dozen beagles to
interrupt her, Diana Whitehill Laing is,
like Mary Endicott, "Mistress of Herself".

Mistress
of Herself

DIANA
WHITEHILL
LAING

Barre Publishers

BARRE · MASSACHUSETTS · 1965

Library of Congress Catalogue No. 65–24404
Printed by The Stinehour Press, Lunenburg, Vermont
Illustrations by The Meriden Gravure Company, Meriden, Connecticut

For Kit with love

CONTENTS

	Preface	9
I	The Marriage of True Minds	13
II	Salem Liverpool	18
III	London Men and English Men	24
IV	At Home in Washington	32
V	The Lion Rampant	37
VI	"And Leave Thee for Awhile"	50
	Illustrations *following page*	64
VII	"Dear Lady, Welcome Home"	65
VIII	The Road to Office	80
IX	"To Visit the Queen"	94
X	"To Thy Jubilee Throng"	111
XI	"We Are Marching to Pretoria"	126
XII	"Much Have I Travelled in the Realms of Gold"	150
XIII	In Sight of the Promised Land	168
XIV	"Others I Doubt Not, If Not We"	187
XV	"Je Tiens Ferme"	210
	Notes	229
	Bibliography	236
	Index	238

THROUGHOUT the writing of this book I have had the
enthusiastic help of family and friends in England and
America. Mary Endicott and my grandfather, Julian Lowell
Coolidge, were second cousins; through my childhood I heard occasionally of "Cousin Mary", who lived in London. I had been born
in London, and christened by Canon Carnegie at St. Margaret's,
Westminster. Afterwards, Cousin Mary gave me a party; but as we
all returned to Massachusetts when I was still a baby, my connec-
tion with her later seemed rather distant. Wandering through a
maze of Boston relatives, I had to sort out Peabodys, Gardners, and
Coolidges. This kept me busy enough without considering an Endicott who lived abroad.

After the war, when Cousin Mary resumed her annual visits to
America, I grew to know her better. Everyone said how wonderful
she was at her age; alert and charming, she had been quite undaunted by the Blitz. In 1953, while on a trip to England, I went to
visit St. Margaret's. There was the christening recorded: Diana,
daughter of Jane and Walter Whitehill. Cousin Mary had asked
me to lunch, and my thoughts were already in the past when I
reached her house at one-fifteen. We exchanged family news
through the meal, then she began to speak of London long ago. We
went to see her fan collection, Mr. Chamberlain's china collection,
the brocade from her Presentation dress, and other special treas-
ures. Ever graceful, completely charming, Cousin Mary touched on
politics and parties of sixty years before. Lost among her recollections, I finally came to and realized it was four-thirty! Regretfully,
I said good-bye, and hoped that we would meet again.

The next year, when Christopher Laing and I were about to be
married, we went round to tea with Cousin Louise Endicott in
Boston. Cousin Mary was visiting her sister-in-law—impossible to
believe she had passed ninety! She smiled and spoke so winningly,
we were both enthralled. In succeeding months both my husband
and my father murmured about "putting Cousin Mary down on

paper". The next summer, when Cousin Mary came to Danvers, I walked with her through gardens Joseph Chamberlain had laid out. We sat and watched the sunset from the McIntire summerhouse on Cousin Louise's place; Cousin Mary laughed to think of writing memoirs. She was much too busy; how could she spend all her time looking backwards at the past? And so we parted, and my plans lay dormant. She died in 1957 and Cousin Louise followed her in the spring of 1958.

Meanwhile my husband and I, after his service in the Navy, returned to Boston. We found an old house on Beacon Hill and with our daughters, Diana and Julia, gradually settled in. Father would turn up from time to time with presents for the house—books and vases from the Endicott houses, now broken up, appeared, and with them came the thought of writing Cousin Mary's life. Boxes and bales of Endicott papers had gone off to the Massachusetts Historical Society. Our house was now re-modelled; why, my husband asked, should I not begin this other work?

It was 1960, and for the next two and a half years my parents generously abetted my project. They underwrote my baby-sitting and travel costs, cheered when new material came to light, read draft after draft of manuscript, and were always encouraging. My thanks to them, and to Miss Annette Corriveau, whose able and loving care of our children made the book possible, cannot be often enough repeated. Both the girls and their father cheerfully adopted Cousin Mary into the family. Endicott photographs, letters, and file-cases littered the house. My grocery lists got mixed with index cards, and all too often the crises of the 1960's were shunted aside by those of the 1880's. No one complained. To my husband, who criticized, edited, exhorted, and applauded, I am especially grateful.

Thomas Boylston Adams, President, and Stephen T. Riley, Director, of the Massachusetts Historical Society, kindly gave me free rein among the Endicott Papers. The staff of the Society, and of the Boston Athenaeum, where I also worked, were helpful and sympathetic. Among the many people who talked or wrote to me about the book I want also to thank Julian Amery, G. Peabody Gardner, Professor Mason Hammond, James Lawrence, Jr., Francis B. Lo-

throp, Harriet Rantoul, R. Minturn Sedgwick, Miriam Shaw, and
Sir John Wheeler-Bennett, K.C.V.O.

Mary Endicott's extended family in England were patient in an-
swering my letters, and sent me favourite clippings, photographs,
and anecdotes as well. K. W. Humphries, B.Litt., M.A., Librarian
of the University of Birmingham, put the Chamberlain Collection
at my disposal when I visited England in the autumn of 1960, and
I am grateful to him and his staff.

While abroad I called on or visited most of the people I had been
besieging by mail. Their hospitality and interest, as well as their
considerable assistance, are much appreciated. Hilda Chamberlain,
the only surviving child of Joseph Chamberlain, recalled with especial vividness Mary's early life in Birmingham and London. Colonel
Terence Maxwell and his wife Diane, the daughter of Sir Austen
Chamberlain, were both most helpful. Mrs. Maxwell arranged for
me to talk with Dance, Mary's maid in her last years. Stephen
Lloyd and his wife Dorothy, the daughter of Neville Chamberlain,
also shared their recollections.

Miss Maud Austen assisted greatly with her accurate memories
of life in the Carnegie family. Sidney Pink, who was for over half a
century in Mary's service, answered hosts of household questions,
and told me favourite anecdotes as well.

Canon Carnegie's daughters—Frances, May, Kathleen, Jocosa,
and Rachel—all welcomed me warmly, and gave me help and encouragement. I want to thank them and their families: Sir Michael
and Lady Peto, Mrs. G. P. Slade, Mr. and Mrs. Raymond Gibbs,
Captain and Mrs. Casper Silas Balfour Swinley, and Mr. and Mrs.
A. Drewett Chaytor.

Finally, the unsung hero of these pages is my son Christopher,
who raised no objections to a strenuous prenatal career of hours at
the typewriter, hurried meals, and journeys by bus, train, and jet
plane. He was born uneventfully three months after my return from
England, and shared his mother most obligingly with Mary Endicott. Perhaps he knows her best of all.

DIANA WHITEHILL LAING

Chadds Ford, Pennsylvania
June, 1965

Oh! blest with Temper, whose unclouded ray
Can make to-morrow cheerful as to-day;
She, who can love a Sister's charms, or hear
Sighs for a daughter with unwounded ear;
She, who ne'er answers till a Husband cools,
Or, if she rules him, never shews she rules;
Charms by accepting, by submitting sways,
Yet has her humour most, when she obeys; . . .
Disdains all loss . . . above them all,
And mistress of herself, tho' China fall.

ALEXANDER POPE, *Moral Essays*,
Epistle II.

CHAPTER I

The Marriage of True Minds

"I REQUIRE intelligent sympathy from women," declared the man from the Midlands. Frock-coated and clean-shaven, an orchid in his buttonhole, and monocle enhancing his piercing gaze, the Right Honourable Joseph Chamberlain might have been declaiming a party platform.

"It pains me to have any of my views controverted," he continued.

"You don't like division of opinion in your household," said his companion.

"I can't help people thinking differently from me."

"But you don't allow the expression of the difference."

"No."[1]

On this point the Radical statesman, forty-seven and twice widowed, rested and lost his case. Exhausted, as after a major speech, the Member for Birmingham had filibustered for two days on matrimony. It was early January of 1884, and walking beside him in an English country garden was a gifted and ambitious young woman who might have become his third wife. Beatrice Potter,[2] daughter of a successful London capitalist, had for years taken an active part in her father's business and social affairs. Anxious for a useful career, and accustomed to independence of thought, she was infuriated by Chamberlain's tactics as a lover. "Not a suspicion of feeling did he show towards me. He was simply determined to assert his convictions . . . to ascertain whether I yielded to his absolute supremacy."[3] It was servility, she felt, and not sympathy, that Chamberlain required from women.[4]

It is hard to imagine any spirited woman being tempted by such wooings; but four years later, on a snowy afternoon in America, Joseph Chamberlain proposed marriage under quite different circumstances, and this time was accepted.

Mary Crowninshield Endicott, daughter of Grover Cleveland's Secretary of War, had little in common with Beatrice Potter. She was intelligent, but not intellectual; fond of listening to men talk, she also liked to dance with them. Never shy, Mary moved with ease in all surroundings: with childhood friends in Massachusetts, or out to dinner in the Capital, she seemed equally at home. In Washington she met many interesting men, but Mary Endicott had, in 1887, no thought of marrying in haste.

That autumn Joseph Chamberlain arrived from England on an important diplomatic mission: the settlement of Canadian-American fisheries disputes. Official Washington rallied round the visitor, and Mary was asked several times "to meet Mr. Chamberlain". As a Cabinet member, Mary's father dined out with the visiting statesman, and asked him in due course to his own house. To her surprise, and bewilderment, Mary found her friendship with Mr. Chamberlain developing along no ordinary lines. She liked to sit up late, writing letters to her cousins about the parties she had been to, and the people she had seen. But it was hard to describe her feelings about this man, said to be the best speaker in England, who now addressed himself to her. At Christmas-time, when she had known him for a month, Mary wrote reassuringly to New England, "I feel like a safety match warranted not to go off—till struck on the right box . . . I am in a very cool frame of mind."[5] Only seven weeks later Mary Endicott had promised to marry Joseph Chamberlain. And she confided, "Every now and then I wonder if I am in a dream, for I scarcely recognize myself. Certainly it was about as improbable a thing as could have happened."[6]

The Endicotts emphatically agreed. Mary Endicott was twenty-three years old, a forthright and clear-headed young lady. She had been raised in conservative and dignified traditions; her Salem family's proudest claim was its descent from John Endecott, Puritan governor of the Massachusetts Bay Colony. Questions of taste and behaviour were paramount; though the Endicotts' financial position was more than comfortable, it was always understated. Simple and direct in manner, Mary Endicott was an aristocrat in outlook.

By contrast, Joseph Chamberlain was fifty-one years old, a widower twice over, and the father of six children, two of whom were

older than Mary. His background was solidly middle-class, and he
grew up accustomed to hard work. He left London at eighteen, and
went to Birmingham to supervise his father's investment in a screw
factory; in twenty years there he had gained a fortune. Leaving business for politics, Chamberlain spoke and acted for a better life for
the masses, and earned himself the reputation of a dangerous Radical. Spurning the intellectualism of the London drawing room, he
played upon the enthusiasms of the workers of Birmingham. As
mayor there he fought dirt and corruption untiringly, and by letting in the light of reform caused his own star to rise. Joseph Chamberlain passed into contemporary legend as "Good Old Joe", the
"Brummagem Lion".

A decade after these civic triumphs, though the lion's mane was
trimmed, he would not consent to lie down with the lamb. After
only four years in Parliament, he had spent six years in Cabinet
positions. The Radical turned Liberal seemed to have a promising
future, for the Grand Old Man of British politics, Mr. Gladstone,
was growing old, and Chamberlain might reasonably inherit his
mantle. His vision was extended, though, beyond the nation to the
larger scene of Empire. With his followers, the Liberal Unionists,
Chamberlain looked for a day of federation between England and
her dependencies; he felt he had no choice but to vote against
Mr. Gladstone on the question of Irish Home Rule.

The Liberal Party split, the Conservatives came to power, and
Chamberlain was everywhere vilified. It was said he had wrecked
the Liberals, and betrayed Irish nationalism. The new Prime Minister, Lord Salisbury, hoping to bring the Liberal Unionists into a
firm Conservative alliance, and appreciating both Chamberlain's
difficult position, and his marked talents for business, was not long
in finding him employment. He sent him to America as Chief Plenipotentiary to the Fisheries Conference.

There the magnetic statesman carried the field from the day of
his arrival. He was discreet with reporters, hard-headed in business,
a bon vivant of incredible energy. Washington watched him dine
out tirelessly, and return hospitality with lavish banquets of his
own. Apparently Chamberlain enjoyed equally an evening at a
play, a serious talk with some Senators, or a tête-à-tête with an

American belle. Despite the variety of his social encounters, the papers swiftly surmised his attachment to Mary Endicott, and the gossip columnists seized eagerly on the match.

In 1888 marriages between American girls and Englishmen were not at all uncommon—but the girls were generally rich and aspiring, the husbands poor but noble. The resulting alliances, if not romantic, often served a practical purpose. For his daughter's engagement, however, Secretary Endicott could find no precedent. Mary's family was the old and distinguished one; while to Chamberlain fell the honours in worldly achievement. The man was brilliant, obviously, and destined for a dramatic future; but it was hard to think of Mary, brought up as she had been, sharing the glare of public life. London was a wider world than Washington; and the Endicotts, though used to official entertaining, and doing their social duty, still preferred to live modestly, in accordance with Salem custom. At last, convinced that Mary's feelings would not change, the Endicotts braced themselves, and consented to her marriage.

Mary Endicott lived for the next seventy years in London, saw five monarchs succeed to Queen Victoria's throne, and knew the important political and social figures in every era. For a quarter of a century she stood beside Joseph Chamberlain, helping him through discouragements, sharing all his hopes and projects, and rejoicing in his success. Though he never held office as Prime Minister, as Colonial Secretary Chamberlain wielded an unprecedented power, and saw his dream of a federated British Empire come slowly to reality. In the last years of Queen Victoria's reign, he carried forward the banner of imperialism, and became a favourite Minister. Both friends and opponents felt he had had an influence rare in any generation, which must always give him a place in the first rank of English statesmen.[7] The Chamberlain tradition was carried on by his sons: Austen, most famous as Foreign Secretary, for achieving the 1925 Treaty of Locarno; and Neville, the Prime Minister, who tried whole-heartedly to forestall the Second World War.

Mary was not made to live alone with her memories. In the forty-three years of life left to her after Joseph Chamberlain's death, her chief complaint was there was not time enough for all she wished to do. Maintaining the same closeness and interest in the Chamberlains' lives she always had, she presently remarried, helped her husband in his career, and was mother to the five children of his previous marriage. Widowed a second time, she bought a house in London to serve as centre for all her families, English and American.

Every year it could be managed she made what others called a farewell visit to New England. Mary never saw it that way; she felt at home on either side of the Atlantic. The miles that parted her from those she loved were as irrelevant as years. In the spring of 1957 she was still giving dinner-parties, telling stories about London as it used to be. She had laughed at the thought of memoirs—how could she spare the time to work on them? she asked. And so her story has been gathered here and there; as she wrote, and spoke, or simply smiled, entering a room, one glimpsed her charm; to know her better we must travel back to Salem, a century ago.

CHAPTER II

Salem Liverpool

O N the 15th of March, 1864, William Crowninshield Endicott left for his law office in some anxiety of mind. He and
his cousin Ellen Peabody had been married four years;
they were comfortably settled in a yellow clapboard house on Essex
Street, with both their families nearby. But Ellen had woken at six
that day, complaining she did not feel well; perhaps the new baby
was on its way. Three year old Willy had a large garden to romp in;
Salem was full of relatives to help look after him. But his father was
fretful. Ellen had always enjoyed "delicate" health, though she had
seemed strong and cheerful lately. Her husband sent messages to
doctor and midwife, just in case, was assured nothing could happen
before evening, so went to work as usual. The soothing routine of
the morning letters was abruptly interrupted.

"Immediately after I left, pains commenced, they sent for the
doctors, the child was born, shot into the world before any of them
got here . . . Somewhat astounded, I went home, found Aunt Eliza[1]
in the kitchen with the smallest of babys wrapped in cotton, holding it over the stove. The little thing was white with pale lips, eyes
closed, and its little mouth gasping as for breath. Except for Aunt
E. it would never have lived. The doctor thought it was an even
chance if it lived. [The midwife] said from the first 'twas a vigorous,
tho' small child, and would live. I was so anxious about Ellen did
not think much about the child."[2]

The new baby, who gave her first cry nearly two hours after her
precipitate arrival, was named for her father's mother, Mary
Crowninshield. She proved as vigorous and determined to live as
the midwife and her resourceful aunt predicted. Her father was
kept busy in the months following Mary's birth, and had no time
for his diary. His entries there, though never dashing, had at least

been regular; after this hectic Ides of March they ceased entirely for the balance of the year.

The Endicotts, like others round them, felt closer to their own concerns than to the Civil War. Ulysses Grant had just been appointed General-in-Chief of the armies of the United States, but the news did not excite much comment in town. Tradition and family customs abounded in Salem; people were proud of being somewhat apart from the currents of daily life.

Though born in the shadow of war, Mary passed a childhood free from tumult and alarm. The tenor of her parents' lives was a calm one: they had occupied the evening after their wedding in their Salem parlour, reading the newspaper aloud. For many years afterward even Christmas was quietly observed. Puritan sentiments passed slowly from Salem, and when Mary was tiny her father went to the office then, as on any other day, small presents and family visits being exchanged on New Year's Day.

The Endicott children spent a lot of time with their grandparents and cousins. At Thanksgiving the clans rallied in force; Mary's first memory was of Thanksgiving dinner in Grandma Peabody's dining room. Aged two, and dressed in her best, Mary was the youngest person at the celebration, and thus required to execute an old ceremony. She was lifted up and placed in front of Grandpa, then sent toddling along the table's length to Grandma. She managed this maneuver without breaking a dish, or snatching for a sweetmeat. The grown-ups exclaimed over her, and Mary, pleased and excited, was wafted away.

Houses were large, and servants plentiful; as a little girl Mary took part in many such reunions. Thirty or forty of her relations might gather in Salem or Boston for a wedding anniversary or Fourth of July party. Both Mary and her brother were early used to sitting in on grown-up conversation. When she was six, she heard much talk about the Franco-Prussian War. There was an easy shift in conversation from the international to the local scene. The Endicotts felt it was really only yesterday that John Endecott had arrived at Naumkeag (the early name for Salem) in 1628, and become Governor of the Bay Colony. Asked in later years about her apparently English voice, Mary ingenuously remarked that though her family came from near Boston, their ancestors had been English; and she supposed that they retained many of the English ways of thought and speech.

Preservation, and an absorption in genealogy, were characteristic of many in Essex County. Mary's brother spent much of his life in these pursuits, in the ample leisure afforded him by the financial acumen of his great-grandfather Peabody.

Joseph Peabody, who sprang from a small farm in Middleton, had done little more remarkable than keeping pigs until a happy venture into privateering during the Revolution brought him, in his late teens, into possession of a sum sufficient to free him from farm duties, and go to board with the local minister. There he improved not only his book learning, but his social contacts. After a year of study, he returned to sea; ten years later, in 1791, he married first one, and when she died, the second of the Reverend Elias Smith's daughters, and removed to nearby Salem.

Though most of his own voyages were coastal ones, or only as far afield as the West Indies, a native shrewdness in Joseph Peabody brought him first part, then sole ownership in a substantial and far-ranging trading fleet. His most successful ventures were made in the Sumatra pepper trade: his captains, being on to a good source of supply, kept their counsel and exploited it, and their employer by the time of his death in 1844 was accounted Salem's principal merchant.

His closeness to money did not go unremarked. In the early years of the present century a great-grandson, Augustus Peabody Gardner, was campaigning for Congressman, and returned to Essex County for some speech-making and socializing. In one town the oldest inhabitant came forth and quavered, "Be you the grandson of Joseph Peabody?"

"No, sir, I'm his great-grandson," the candidate smilingly replied.

"Be you as mean as he was?"

Eccentricity about money was typical not only around Salem, but throughout New England. Still, by anyone's standards the Endicott family were distinctly comfortable when, in 1873, Mary's father was called to serve as Justice in the Massachusetts Supreme Court.

His manner was charming, and dignified; William Endicott, gruff and bewhiskered, looked like a judge and played the part well. For nine years he was strenuously employed; he did his own research, and as the typewriter was not then in common use prepared most of his opinions tediously in longhand. His exactitude and devotion to duty exhausted his health, and in 1882 Judge Endicott was obliged to retire from the bench.

These years, though wearing to her father, were exceptionally happy for Mary. She summered with the elder Endicotts on their farm at Milford, New Hampshire, or with the Peabodys on the island of Nahant. Farm life was quiet for her, but at Nahant there were successions of picnics, charades, and parties to enjoy.

Her schooling was sketchy. Miss Jenny Phillips conducted classes on the top floor of a Chestnut Street house, during most of which the girls played pranks on their long-suffering mistress. Mary was no star pupil, and caused her share of mischief. She would much rather have been climbing trees than bending to her books. At home on Sunday evenings the Endicotts would gather round the piano to sing, Mary quavering happily away, young William sounding forth lustily, and their mother in between, with a soft, lovely voice. Church was a familiar place to Mary; Grace Episcopal Church was only a stone's throw from their own front door, and she had known the minister, the Reverend J. P. Franks, since the age of six, when she climbed into his lap and gave him a thorough looking-over. Thereafter Mary would pop in and out of his house, chattering to his wife, and admiring the Franks babies as they came along. Mary enjoyed trotting round the church to spread the Christmas greens, and going to carol-singing services. Though no more thrilled with sermons than any other little girl, Mary was not a wriggler; she had been too well trained for this.

High-spirited and intelligent, somewhat petted and indulged, a bit of a tomboy—Mary was all of these, but from an early age she was learning from mother and grandparents important attitudes about "being a lady". As a very young girl she was escorted on an afternoon call by a family friend, Colonel Livermore. Upon returning her home he left her at the gate, whereupon she drew herself up and declared sweetly, "A gentleman should open the gate for a lady." She walked in like a queen, and thanked the Colonel in such a way that he said years after he felt he could have gone on opening and shutting the gate for her forever.

At twelve, when she was both rotund and romantic, Mary shared with several cousins a crush on a handsome man eight years older than herself, who regrettably married another. Attending the wedding of Lucius Manlius Sargent to Marian Coolidge in the fall of 1876, she afterwards lamented for pages in the "very private" depths of her diary, and helped compose a poem in mournful celebration of the event. To the diary, meant only for the eyes of her cousin Clara Sears, she gloomily emoted, "Oh dear, oh dear, no more tales of Lucius, no more walks down Beacon Street in hopes of meeting him, no more exciting times about him. Lucius is gone forever . . . We pressed the roses we had at the wedding and are going to keep them as remembrances of a happy secret of the past."[3]

Clearly Mary was growing up. At Christmas-time she had for presents a Russian leather travelling bag, an ivory brush, an opera glass ("Pretty swell!") and the "most superb" hat one could imagine ("Sweller still!"). After a huge dinner she spent the holiday evening in Grandma Peabody's parlour reading love poetry, dancing, and nibbling away on oysters and ice cream. Next day she came down to earth, and told her diary proudly she and Clara had prepared to cook, and made a splendid stew of applesauce. Though her excursions were infrequent, Mary had at least a nodding knowledge of her mother's kitchen, and sometimes tried her hand at making bread. She knew how things ought to be, even if she could not make them that way herself. Mary claimed years later that her culinary gifts were confined to being a "competent critic".

The years went along peacefully: Mary wrote occasionally for *St. Nicholas* magazine, browsed through Byron and Tennyson, and sometimes went to Boston for a picture exhibition. Her teeth had been straightened, and she found with satisfaction she was losing childhood fat, and filling out becomingly. She had spent long hours at Nahant drilling her posture under Grandma Peabody's tutelage. Up and down she went, a backgammon board upon her head, arms in back, looped round a croquet mallet: her carriage now was perfectly erect. To her great pride her cousin Fanny Peabody, eight years older than herself, lent her a sprigged silk dress for a family wedding in 1879. With her braces gone, Mary had a winning smile; she smoothed her rustling skirts and felt they "lent dignity to the occasion, and perhaps helped to account for the gratifying enquiry of Mrs. Lawrence whether [I] was coming out the next winter. Being about fifteen I felt much buoyed up."[4]

Between 1879 and 1883 young William Endicott was a Harvard undergraduate; and so his sister's horizons gradually broadened to include theatre trips, dances, and evening receptions. Yet she was not formally "out" in the world, so most of Mary's evenings were passed more quietly. She would sit tucked into one corner of Judge Endicott's library, listening to his talk with legal and political friends. From this long-standing custom she came to understand what really interested gentlemen. She learned to ask a man just the right questions so that, in airing his own views, he felt he was addressing a most delightful and informed companion.

Mary was independent and strong-minded from the moment she was born. Through her growing-up she constantly ran into life's formalities: this was nice, and that was not; this lay within propriety, but that without. Conventions of the day were sternly fixed, but she was seldom oppressed by them. Returning from a visit to Newport Mary assured her mother there would be no young men on the train; but should she meet any, she would know how to deal with them. Mary's vocabulary was flowery and romantic, filled with contemporary catchwords and phrases. "Too delicious" might apply to trees, breezes, or dancing partners; while "superb" applied alike to hats and scenery. Family meetings and partings she spoke of in the most elaborate terms. Victorian society placed great restrictions on her speech and thought, but as she grew to womanhood Mary's warmth and sympathy shone out for all to see. Eagerly she awaited the adventure of her formal debut in the world.

CHAPTER III

London Men and English Men

ABRUPTLY all Mary's daydreams dissolved, and she found herself in the spring of 1882 companion to her parents on a trip to Europe. Through his conscientiousness, Judge Endicott had tried his nerves too far; his doctor had ordered him off on a voyage of indefinite length. He was gloomy and depressed, Mary's mother anxious and discouraged. Since the Endicotts were being economical, and taking along no courier maid or valet to pack, buy tickets, and do errands, Mary found herself in this role. All her friends would come out without her; she would miss the parties, pretty dresses, and new excursions to Boston and to Cambridge. This was bad enough, but it was worse still not to have any idea how long the exile would last. Mary was completely wretched, and obviously showed it, though she did all her chores dutifully enough. Her uncle, Powell Mason, seeing the Endicotts off in New York, provided her with a new nick-name, with the avuncular advice, "Keep a stiff upper lip, Miserable!"

Once aboard R.M.S. *Republic*, Mary's parents shuttled methodically between cabin and deck chairs; having settled them in one place or another, Mary was on her own. She promptly made two rival conquests: Mr. Wilkinson and Mr. Wood.

Mr. Wilkinson, anxious to impress, took her aft one bright day, while the sailors were singing at their work, and proceeded to tell her the names of several important-looking lines and sails. Mr. Wood, observing this, followed them and took pains to contradict the information, much to his rival's discomfiture. Mary changed companions smoothly, and found Mr. Wood "much disgusted with the sordid life of businessmen, in fact thinks that is not worth *living*. Such a man is made to be an artist, but his friends don't look at it in the same light that he does."[1] Shipboard duties were not too

24

onerous, for Mary soon observed the Captain striding up and down, and the Purser marching round in obvious search of his favourite lady companion.

A few days later Mr. Wood gave Mary a pretty little Japanese match box; she showed it to the Captain, who to her dismay calmly pocketed it—"the wretch!" Her annoyance was short-lived, for that evening Mary persuaded her mother to come along as chaperone, while she and the Captain paced the deck, and watched the moonlight on the waves. Later in the trip there was a journey to the engine room, again with Mrs. Endicott chaperoning; holding their skirts cautiously, the ladies plunged down into heat and noise and blackness. Then there was the day when Mary was summoned to the wheelhouse and, the Captain hovering over her, allowed to steer the ship for twenty-five minutes. It was pleasant to record these adventures in her new diary; on one occasion the Captain actually scuffled with Mary for the key to this black-and-gold volume, and threatened to keep it! By the last day out he had to give all attention to his ship, and it was time for Mary to say good-bye to new friends. Entirely demure, Mary debarked with her parents at Liverpool on June 5th; on the six-hour rail trip to London she had her first look at England.

Jumping from one window to another, like most tourists, Mary exclaimed at the picture-book cottages. Look at the tiled roofs, the bright gardens; there were flowering hedges everywhere! Then there was Manchester, a large smutty place all chimneys and smoke, dismissed with a sniff as "just one's idea of a manufacturing town." After ship-shape Salem, Mary was distressed by the dirt of large cities; reaching London, "It is all delightful; but such a dingy place it is." A hansom cab bore her away to Brown's Hotel, where her parents had taken rooms for their first night. When they were settled in, she found happily her day was not to end just yet.

With her cousin William Endicott, who had lived in London many years, Mary was whirled about in a cab all through the city. Her impressions were kaleidoscopic: one important building succeeded another, and at the time she was more interested in the people she saw. She was disappointed to find, studying the theatre-going crowds, that they were little different from crowds at home, indeed "Most of them look as we do." But stored away, as a clear series of pictures, were the impressions of her first night in London, and Mary would never forget this introduction to life abroad.

Next day the Endicotts transferred to quarters in the Pulteney Street Hotel; having finished the unpacking, Mary was eager to go walking. When she did she joined the legions of those surprised by English weather. A day might start sunny, go on with three or four rain showers, and finish with a cloudless sky. She noticed that no one at home in England seemed to mind this, so soon adopted the prevailing indifference, umbrellas, and rubber boots.

Setting out one day for a decorous stroll, Mary and her father found themselves in Hyde Park, in the midst of an Irish demonstration against the Coercion Act. To their astonishment they found themselves marching down Piccadilly to the strains of "Wearing of the Green", whereupon they thought it advisable to hail a hansom.[2] On their way home they caught their first glimpse of the lovely Alexandra, Princess of Wales, out driving with her children.

Most of the Endicott sight-seeing was done with the help of friends. Mr. Wilkinson, the shipboard conquest, arranged a tour for them through some precincts of the law: Lincoln's Inn, Middle Temple, and Temple Church. Cousin William Endicott stopped by with frequent bits of good advice. As Mrs. Endicott's first cousin, S. Endicott Peabody, was a partner in the house of Morgan, the Endicotts enjoyed a good deal of hospitality from Mr. Pierpont Morgan. Mary loved to explore London, but found it irksome to have to go about with a chaperone everywhere. Presently her father announced that London was too noisy, and proposed a stay in Tunbridge Wells. This was a highly boring prospect for Mary, who promptly sneaked off alone by hansom cab for a last fling at London shopping. William would be shocked if he knew! Still, once her parents settled into their exceedingly quiet and respectable watering place, Mary found it had one compensation: she could go about alone, on her own excursions. The next family move was to Canterbury; to Mary's disgust they were put in charge of an over-zealous verger, and "it was impossible to mouse around or get out of hearing of his long-winded anecdotes."[3] Like many pilgrims, Mary found considerable sameness in cathedrals; though she was glad to have visited such a superb example she was relieved when they had finished with the sights of Canterbury. Her father declaring himself much restored, they were now all free to return to London.

They heard with excitement about the latest military operations in Egypt. Unrest there had led to the massacre by nationalists of fifty Europeans, and the wounding of the British consul. In mid-July came the retaliatory bombardment of the Alexandria forts by Admiral Seymour. Victory was promptly won, and British control of the Suez Canal re-affirmed.

They had, too, a pleasing vignette of old-fashioned London. Grandpa Peabody's Harvard room-mate, Mr. Russell Sturgis, came calling on the Endicotts, turned out in a close-fitting fawn-coloured overcoat. Courtly and distinguished in manner, he presently invited them to dine with his family in Carlton House Terrace. Mary felt the whole occasion was straight out of a Jane Austen novel: Mrs. Sturgis wore a cap, after the fashion of years gone by, was kind and friendly to them, while her husband conducted a stately and elaborate meal-time conversation.

As the months went along, there were many London invitations for the Endicotts. Mary and her mother were determinedly cheerful, had new clothes made, and concocted bright stories of their adventures when, as was often the case, Judge Endicott remained at home. They were asked to stay wherever they had introductions; and the Endicotts happily accepted the invitations, with a fine disregard for whether they could repay their obligations. This was typical of the age: people were hospitable to them, and as the Endicotts would have been glad to entertain any sympathetic Englishman who turned up in Salem, they felt they could enjoy themselves abroad without further ado.

When they turned to the Continent Mary found the world grown brusque. At Avignon, on a raw January day, "We had coffee under difficulties, as no one paid any attention to us, and we were obliged to drink out of regular bowls standing on the platform."[4] They stopped at Monte Carlo, judged by Mary "the smallest, and I fancy the most depraved principality of the world . . . We turned to that nest of unhappiness the gambling room. Such a crowd! The most horrible-looking women and men, their eyes eager and hands trembling as they watched the play . . . I think it well to see such a place as that, for one ought to know and realize the snares and wickedness of the world."[5] Not all her reflections were on this fervent plane, but Mary wrote up diligently a record of the next four months' sight-seeing. When they returned to London in May of 1883, she felt it was almost like arriving home. A trip she made to Westminster Abbey was like greeting an old friend. No church she had met anywhere impressed her as the Abbey did; she was always drawn by its air of peace and solemnity.

A five-day stay at Dover House, Mr. Morgan's country place, was generally pleasant, but not without incident. Judge Endicott was definitely improving, but he was still easily confused, and distinctly absent-minded. On May 15th, as Mary sat over her diary she was interrupted "by hearing a great noise in Papa's dressing room and hearing him gasp 'Water!' I seized my pitcher, rushed to the room, and found him fighting flames. The curtains had caught on fire in some way, and it seemed as if the whole house would go. I flew for more water, and Mama got up some servants and sent for the butler and housekeeper. By the time they arrived, however, all cause for alarm was over, for Papa had managed to pull down the curtains and had smothered them in blankets. But he had to use the utmost strength and exertion. It is only a wonder more harm was not done, and that he himself was not burned. Happily, no one else was disturbed, but the rooms were so full of smoke it was a long time before we could get to bed. Morning sunshine revealed a black and charred window frame, and a deluged floor—fortunate and miraculous it was that the house itself did not catch. About 11 o'clock we came back to London after a charming visit. Mr. Morgan has been so kind and delightful."

It was a delightful host, indeed, who did not blink when his house was nearly burnt down by his guests. The incident passed without apparent embarrassment; and Mr. Morgan continued to loan the Endicotts his box at the Opera, and to send them tickets for other events he thought they might enjoy. As no further fiery escapades are chronicled, Mary and her mother must have doubled their vigilance on Papa and his evening candle.

The two Endicott ladies had to spend many days in the assembly of fine plumage. Though no one was more conscious than Mary of a becoming fit, colour, or piece of material, she loathed the long, drawn-out fitting sessions. The final result was what she cared about; between them, Mary and her mother drove several dress-makers almost distracted before they decided their new clothes would "do".

Elegantly dressed, the Endicotts proceeded one evening to dine with Sir Farrar Herschel, Solicitor General in Mr. Gladstone's Cabinet. Mary sat next to a brother of Lady Herschel, just back from India. "He was very nice and very good-looking, and we were getting on beautifully when a girl on the other side put her oar in, to my great indignation."[6] Large dinner-parties were still a fairly new experience to Mary, and she was piqued by competition. The other young lady had every right to address the handsome brother back from India; after all, she was sitting next to him, too; but in this situation, Mary was annoyed, and somewhat unsure of herself.

She was able to listen intelligently to legal and political talk at the Herschels' though, and enjoyed touring the Law Courts with Sir Farrar several days after the dinner-party. Were she a man, she gravely confided to her diary, she was almost sure she should choose the law for her profession. Most of the time she was less serious; she specially liked driving through the Park, and peering at the costumes of other ladies there. Having struggled over her own wardrobe, she was hyper-critical, and decided she had never seen such "dowds" as English women.

Mary's outstanding impression of Parliament was a social one. Sitting for the first time in the Ladies' Gallery of the House of Commons she marvelled at the unceremonious way in which the Members treated one another. Surely, she thought, men must have a lot of sang-froid to stand it. Their manners interested her far more than the history they were making.

At an evening reception given by the Lord Chancellor, Lord Selborne, Mary wore, not without qualms, her first dress with a train. Many people were introduced to her, and she enjoyed the evening she had been nervous about. But she felt greatly bolstered by the arrival of her brother, who had just graduated from Harvard. He accompanied her to Lord's for the Eton-Harrow cricket match, where they lunched with the Herschels. "The sun shone brightly . . . and a bright gay scene it was. Prettier in its way I thought than Ascot. As for the Cricket I understood little about it, and was rather ashamed of myself for they were all so well posted . . . In the middle of the afternoon, we had a sharp shower . . . In a moment all the carriages were closed, and waterproofs appeared, while the gayly colored parasols changed into umbrellas, and it was like a grand transformation scene at the theatre."[7]

Used by now to the English climate, Mary had also adjusted swiftly to the worldly level of party conversation. She and William dined at a Mr. Webster's, after which Mary remarked with pleasurable malice that "William had rather a heavy damsel, who is worth £20,000 a year, and had her hair wound with pearls. Mr. Webster asked me if I thought it would be worth while to take her for that. On the whole I enjoyed the evening very much."[8]

Mary's most interesting encounter came at a poetry recital she and her mother went to on July 20th. They found quite a company present, among them Matthew Arnold and Robert Browning, and presently their hostess asked if she might introduce Oscar Wilde. Mary found "He is much finer looking than I expected, and really has a good deal of beauty. He has cut his hair and wears it in close curls, which shows his head, which is very round and well formed. His conversation amused me rather, especially when he said, 'How do you *live* in Salem? I cannot live unless surrounded by the beautiful. The *world* is our home. I am more at home in Italy than anywhere. Fancy going back to *Salem* to live!' . . . By far the most extraordinary person there was Lady Wilde, Oscar's mother. She was a perfect horror, rigged in a flowing black silk covered with red ruffles, with an erection on her head just like the Duchess in Alice in Wonderland—and a long tulle veil flying in all directions. I should think her apparel would kill the delicate senses of her aesthetic offspring."

Soon after this occasion Mary, William, and their cousin Cotty (the Reverend Endicott Peabody, founder of Groton School), who was over for the summer, attended an English wedding, and were quite critical of the arrangements. There being no ushers, the guests fended for themselves in the church. After the bridal party had signed the Register in the vestry they shocked Mary by walking down the aisle in the most informal way. Then, too, at the wedding breakfast the bride was so busy greeting her special friends that no one bothered to receive the guests formally.

With the opera she went to the same evening, Mary had no fault to find. Patti was singing in *The Barber of Seville*, and as it was the last night of the season, the curtain came up at the end, "the whole opera house rose, utter silence prevailed, and then came this single beautiful voice singing the first verse of 'God Save the Queen'—she sang it *superbly*! . . . Ah, how I have enjoyed the Opera here. I wonder if I shall ever hear it again in Covent Garden."[9]

In September it was time to say good-bye to London. Walking for the last time down Piccadilly with William she felt just as if she were in Boston. She brooded sadly, "This is the last night I shall pass in this beloved London, and for how long? that is the question."[10] The rest of Europe she recalled perfectly, but it was in England Mary had found friends and scenes to love and remember, and to England that she longed to return. She was as wistful about leaving the city as she had been to leave home a year and a half before.

The voyage home was uneventful. Mary was thankful that her father's health had gradually been restored. But the trip abroad had made her restless; all sorts of new curiosities were alive in her. At New York she came rudely back to earth; the customs officers appeared "with their hats on, and acting like boors! The very idea, when we were all at dinner. They made themselves tremendously obnoxious, and I felt like flinging my plate at them. A typical American was our officer, and brought me to a realization of where I was, when on seeing one of my dresses he exclaimed, 'Well, ain't that really pretty now? I guess my hands are most too dirty to touch it'. I quite agreed with him."[11]

CHAPTER IV

At Home in Washington

ON her return from Europe Mary re-joined the phalanx of her cousins; she visited back and forth, sending notes home chiefly describing dresses, party favours, and misplaced dancing slippers. "Miserable" when she went abroad, Mary was now an accomplished young lady, "out" in the world. But to William, now a bluff young fellow with a black beard and chaffing ways, she was always "little sister". Anxious lest she should not receive her proper share of debutante flowers, William arranged for months that a large and exotic bouquet be delivered to Mary before any large party she was to attend, with the card signed, "From an unknown admirer". The deception succeeded entirely.

Meanwhile Judge Endicott, as an old-line Democrat, untouched by machine politics, had been approached and persuaded to run for Governor of Massachusetts in the election of 1884. Endicott's party allegiance (which is surprising, considering that most gentlemen of family and fortune of his time styled themselves Republicans or Independents) went back to the tradition of his grandfather, Jacob Crowninshield. He was in the Massachusetts Senate from 1800 to 1802, and a Member of Congress from 1802 to 1808; when offered the position of Secretary of the Navy by Jefferson, he declined it only for personal reasons. It took exceptional courage to be a Jeffersonian in the shipping town of Salem, whose livelihood was almost demolished by the Embargo. Crowninshield, with a few others in Salem, stood firm against the prevailing Federalism. His grandson continued the Democratic tradition so tactfully that when he was appointed to the Massachusetts Supreme Court it had been by a Republican governor to an all-Republican court. Now, in his second foray into public life, he would accept the nomination only on condition that he should do no campaigning!

This was agreeable to party leaders, who did not seriously expect to win the election, but wished to aid Grover Cleveland's campaign through their honorific choice of candidate. Endicott was, of course, defeated; but Cleveland was not. Immediately after the election he summoned Endicott to Albany, where for several days the two men discussed a matter of the highest importance.

In defeating James G. Blaine, a politician of highly questionable reputation, Cleveland was much indebted to the Massachusetts Mugwumps. These were prominent professional men who revolted at the corruption they felt Blaine represented, and shifted their allegiance to the Democrats. They were a well-born, dignified, and prosperous group, whose outlook was sympathetic with Judge Endicott's. While Democratic machine politics might dictate that the Cabinet post slated for the Northeast part of the country go to an Irish-American, this move would affront the Mugwumps. They might, on the other hand, be gratified and cooperative if it went to "one of themselves". Accordingly the President-elect shrewdly offered, and Judge Endicott accepted, the office of Secretary of War in the new Cabinet.

After a preliminary trip to Washington, and a careful study of their needs, the Endicotts presently leased the Pendleton mansion, a large Gothic house at 1313 Sixteenth Street, set in the fashionable country-like part of town, nearby the house of Navy Secretary William C. Whitney and his family. As it was rented furnished, Mary's family brought only china, silver, and pictures to their new house. In no time at all Mary's bedroom, at least, looked as if she had lived there always. Photographs, letters, dance cards, ribbons, and paperweights crowded every flat surface.

Mary could never get away from her feeling that things might come in handy sometime; and if they had sentimental connections at all, that was reason enough for her to keep and classify them.

Her possessions might get cluttered, but Mary was scrupulous about her dress. It was usually simple, and always becoming. Of her father's sartorial style the press took rather an arch view: "Mr. Endicott adheres to a large brimmed silk hat, which he wears slightly upon the back of his head, emphatically a Boston hat and may have been worn for a season or so back. It is conservative in style, aggressive in its eminent respectability. Beacon Street has a hundred such, Fifth Avenue or Regent Street never a one."[1] For Mary there was nothing but praise; of the President's first reception, on April 23, 1885, it was reported, "Miss Endicott, in flowing draperies of white tulle over white satin was quite the belle of the Blue Parlor. She has a fresh pink and white complexion and adds to her unlimited personal beauty and sweet unconsciousness more than the usual intellectual strength, so that men of distinction seek her side and are fascinated by her conversation."

Mary served as her mother's social secretary, and together they got through an enormous amount of calling, and leaving of cards. Society decreed that cards must be left with one's host after an entertainment of any size at all, so during a crowded Washington season social calls were quite mechanical. Ladies rolled round to each others' houses in carriages, and, finding no one home, would leave their cards and drive on. If one called on a lady having her regular afternoon "at home", one's progress was greatly delayed, especially if one had to linger over tea.

During Lent there were no official functions, and in the muggy summers everyone who could manage it fled the Capital; but for the rest of the year the series of teas, small dinners, and evening receptions was relentless. Mary found the only time she had to herself for writing letters came at the end of an evening party. She slept late in the mornings, then dressed, and perhaps did some shopping or small errands before lunch. Then more dressing in the afternoon, and out to call. In the evening one changed clothes again, and perhaps called in the hairdresser. The practice of being brushed, combed, unhooked, and laced in and out of one tiny-waisted and full-skirted dress after another made for a busy, if not profound, existence.

Mrs. Endicott's standards of entertainment were uncompromising. Crystal, china, and linens must be immaculate, menus perfect, guest lists thoughtfully arranged. Austere in appearance, of ramrod carriage and noble expression, Mrs. Endicott had the devotion of all her servants; they sprang to her bidding. Her family found her crotchets, and exhausting zeal, rather an amusement; Secretary Endicott wrote to Mary: "You know so well what your mother does, and how she does it, when she is in a hurry and means business . . . a summer tornado, blowing laterally in every direction, and up and down at the same time, and before you realize that it is fairly begun, it is all over."[2]

From this remarkable mother Mary, though not consciously much interested in the subject, gathered perfectionist standards in household management. In all her undertakings she was plagued by her inability to keep up with all she wished to accomplish. She would stay up till three in the morning, writing a ten-page letter, then apologize to her friend for being a neglectful correspondent.

That spring of 1885 Mary joined her parents on a tour of Western military outposts and Indian reservations. Mary vastly enjoyed their private railway car; and the military escorts accompanying their tours of inspection. She was practiced now in saying the diplomatic thing, and murmuring pleasantries to total strangers, so the military balls and receptions were no strain. Except for her father's position she might never have gone West; and though her impressions were not always profound they were far more extensive than those of most young ladies, who seldom swerved from the New York, Washington, and Newport circle, except for occasional European orbits.

It appeared that Mary could do no wrong. The press declared she was an "English" beauty; her devoutness in church, the charm of her costume, and the ease of her conversation were equally admired. Yet Mary's head was not turned. She was amused and often annoyed by the inaccuracies of journalism; but as she went through her day she was unselfconscious to a point which aroused the exasperation of other girls. *They* might fret and fuss over their curls, or a wrinkle in their dresses. On their sleeves might appear unsightly spots, or in their hemlines unfortunate rips; but Mary would sweep into the cloak-room at a party, give scarcely a glance in the glass, then sweep on to new conquests with no thought of shyness. She *knew* she looked well, and that no buttons were out of place, because she had done them properly before she came. She was much too busy thinking of those she met to be shy about herself.

The announcement of a British-American Fisheries Conference arranged for the autumn of 1887 caused quite a stir in Washington.

For generations Canadian and American fishermen had quarrelled about boundaries. Technically, Americans were only meant to put into foreign shores for fuel, water, and necessary repairs; but in fact they were forever poaching in forbidden preserves, openly drying their fish, or even catching them, where they had by a treaty of 1818 no business to be. It was hoped that the Fisheries Conference would do much to strengthen Anglo-American amity. When Her Britannic Majesty's choice of Joseph Chamberlain as Chief Plenipotentiary was announced, the newspapers searched their files, and at once a buzz of discussion began about the statesman and the mission which brought him to our shores.

Though Chamberlain had never been to America the papers found a good deal to inform the curious. His career and character were such as to inspire strong feelings: though he came of respectable middle-class stock, he could not be called fashionable. He was, however, a business success, and Americans generally were willing to forgo the one in favour of the other. He was known to have been a Radical, with ideas of workers' benefits which sounded dangerous and socialistic. On the other hand in his mayoral career he had again been successful, and that was what counted. Birmingham's death rate had been spectacularly reduced, she had a dependable water and gas supply, her slums were razed. The achievements wrought by this man in a sooty metropolis were surely worth notice in the sister nation whose industry now saddled her cities with similar problems.

It seemed that the English visitor had certain cultural interests which would also recommend him. He collected orchids, elaborate china, and water-colour paintings. The orchid collection was most famous; cartoons always showed "Orchid Joe" with an elaborate buttonhole. As some men read detective stories, Chamberlain found relaxation in French novels; he also enjoyed theatricals, and listening to his children play the piano.

He was fearless and outspoken, sometimes dubbed "Pushful Joe". For some years past it had been rumoured he meant one day to be Prime Minister. A man of undoubted energy and ambition, Joseph Chamberlain would soon be accorded a spectacular welcome.

CHAPTER V

The Lion Rampant

AFTER a stormy passage, Joseph Chamberlain debarked from the *Etruria* in New York on November 7, 1887. He brought with him Henry Bergne, an expert on the fisheries question, to serve as Conference Secretary, and Willoughby Maycock, Assistant Secretary. At their hotel, the party found reporters swarming; with all of them Chamberlain was firm but diplomatic. Pinkerton detectives were assigned to shadow him at all times, in case an attempt on his life should be made by hostile Irish-Americans; they soon found what strenuous work it was to keep up with him. For ten days Chamberlain and his companions dined out and went sight-seeing, as the Canadian contingent, headed by Sir Charles Tupper, Minister of Finance, was delayed by the elections in New Brunswick. The Canadians arrived on the 17th, and the augmented party set out by train for Washington.

Sir Lionel Sackville-West, British Minister at Washington, completed the British delegation at the Fisheries Conference. His personality can hardly be said to have dominated the group: Maycock later recorded, "so retiring was he that his only oral contribution to the thirty meetings of the Conference was the expression of a wish that a certain window might be closed."[1]

The American delegation consisted of: Chief Plenipotentiary, Secretary of State Thomas F. Bayard; Mr. William Putnam, a lawyer, thoroughly versed in the fisheries disputes; and Mr. James Angell, past Minister to China. As both Putnam and Angell were staying at the Arlington Hotel, where the British group was also lodged, there were frequent and friendly meetings outside the conference chamber.

On November 20th Sir Lionel Sackville-West gave a dinner where Chamberlain met informally with Secretary Bayard, Secretary of the Treasury Charles S. Fairchild, and Secretary Endicott. The next day the Conference held its first official meeting. On November 26th Sir Lionel launched Chamberlain officially on society at a Legation reception. The brave and fair of Washington thronged to meet him, but the elder Endicotts were not among them, having returned to Salem for the Thanksgiving holiday. William, who had accompanied them, returned in time to take his sister to the party. There Mary was presented by Miss West, Sir Lionel's oldest daughter, to the Right Honourable Joseph Chamberlain.

There have been many accounts of this occasion, but those who trace the romance as beginning then might be disappointed by the principals' reticent reactions. Mary noted in her pocket diary, "British Legation to meet Mr. Chamberlain," while he recorded, "Dined with Mr. Bayard . . . afterwards, a reception at the Legation." Chamberlain next day wrote his daughter Beatrice in amusement that one young lady had asked Mr. Bergne which was the Chief Commissioner. On that individual's being pointed out she said, "Wal, I think he's just lovely." He also told how an American gentleman had been disappointed in Chamberlain's almost-six-foot stature: "I thought your principal men in England were taller than that."[2]

If not tremendously tall, Joseph Chamberlain was certainly dynamic. His dark hair bore no evidence of grey, his skin was firm, and the expression in his eyes piercing. His tailoring passed muster in Washington, though some conservative Bostonians privately considered the checks in his trousers too loud. With a flamboyant buttonhole and a ringing laugh he was an attractive and compelling figure. Small wonder that a jealous buzz arose among the young ladies at the Legation soon after Mary met the guest of honour. One of them gloomily declared, "He froze to her an hour ago, and hasn't left her yet."[3]

Legend, elaborately built in England and America, insists romance was born that evening, and while we can admit the possibility, that is all. Certainly it is *not* true that Mary had met Joseph Chamberlain on her trip to England. Nor is it true that it was actually Austen Chamberlain who first captured Mary's heart, and was cut out by his father on the occasion of introducing his would-be bride at tea. In 1882, when Mary was in England, Austen Chamberlain had still been at Rugby; his father, though acquainted with the gentleman, was not at dinner with Sir Farrar Herschel in 1883, when Mary was. Nor had any of them met elsewhere in England.

"They met in a boat, my dear, they met in a boat!" is a favourite Boston legend which must be reluctantly discarded. Mary Endicott and Joseph Chamberlain did indeed take a boat trip together, but it was aboard a government cutter, the *Despatch*, with approximately one hundred government officials also present. The voyage was scarcely epic, being an excursion along the Potomac to Mount Vernon. This was a standard form of entertainment for visiting dignitaries; Henry Adams once growled to his great friend Elizabeth Cameron, "Tomorrow . . . I am going to Mt. Vernon with the Endicotts and Herschels. If this melancholy procession does not finish me, I shall try to survive until you come."[4] Mary and Mr. Chamberlain found the procession there far from melancholy; in a picture taken that day he looks jaunty in a light shooting-suit, and Mary is standing only three people away from him. Though their courtship was under way at this time, it definitely did *not* begin by moonlight at sea.

The second and third week of fisheries discussions passed off without crisis. The evenings were filled with new experiences for Chamberlain. At a dance given by the Whitneys he found that "The Americans dance with more vigor and noise than we do. The honours are performed much as I have seen them in a public outdoor ballroom, with stamping of feet and much waltzing around."[5] There were several large dinners, rather similar to those in England, though he noted: "At a gentlemen's party the host takes his principal guest out arm in arm. Many different wines are served generally in the following order: Hock, Sherry, Claret, Champagne and Burgundy . . . No wine is drunk after dinner. The great delicacies at this season are Bluepoint oysters, Terrapin . . . and Canvas-back Ducks and Red Head Ducks . . . As soon as dinner is finished if ladies are present they retire . . . and then the gentlemen go to a separate room to smoke, returning afterwards for a short time to the ladies."[6] Chamberlain enjoyed the company: at dinner with Professor Alexander Graham Bell, he met Senator Cabot Lodge; then he met a large group of Republican Senators, gathered by Colonel John Hay.[7]

On December 7th the Endicotts had a dinner of fourteen for Joseph Chamberlain, and asked a few people to come in afterwards. The guest of honour wrote home, "I have dined with Mr. Endicott, Secretary of War. He is of the bluest New England blood, descendant of the first Governor of Massachusetts . . . who must have been a pretty grim old Puritan since he is said to have hanged 20 Quakers in one day for Nonconformity. Mrs. Endicott is a very pleasant woman and their daughter one of the brightest and most intelligent girls I have yet met."[8]

Though he had enjoyed the hospitality of the Capital, Joseph Chamberlain was less attracted by Washington's marts of trade; after a stroll through the principal shopping streets he returned convinced "the shops are rather common, and with a poor display —not equal to a second class street in Birmingham."[9]

The Fisheries Conference recessed on December 10th until after the holidays. This freedom from care was pleasantly employed; Mary announced on December 13th she had had a "glorious "day, having received a superb basket of roses, and a poem, from Mr. Chamberlain. The poet took tea that afternoon at the White House with Mrs. Cleveland. Clearly his mind was already turning over the notion of middle-aged husbands with young wives. President Cleveland was then fifty, his bride of eighteen months, the former Frances Folsom, was only twenty-four. Charming as she was, there seems no special evidence to support Chamberlain's contention that "She has made her mark in American history and will be the first notable President's lady."[10]

About the public's free access to the White House he was less enthusiastic. He hoped in time Americans might see "that their Chief Officer should be necessarily raised above them for at least the term of his office, and that he represents the dignity and the strength of the whole country. But at present he is almost at the call of every loafer and impudent fellow in the States, and if he resented the intrusions upon him he would be thought stuck up and aristocratic."

On December 17th Chamberlain called on Miss Endicott at her

home. Mary's mother may already have started to worry about her seeing too much of the visiting statesman; for that evening Mary dined quietly with a Mr. and Mrs. Chew, though she had been asked by Henry Edwardes (Secretary at the British Legation) and his wife "to meet Mr. Chamberlain". Her place at dinner was taken by a Miss Grant; also at the Edwardes' was a friend of Mary's, Miss Gwynne, whom Chamberlain, never averse to pretty women, noted as "a very bright talker."

Two days later Chamberlain left with his party for New York. Interviewed by the press, he naturally avoided any discussion of the fisheries; and spoke largely of his reactions to the United States: "I have been made to feel at home, quite as much so as in England. I brought with me strong feelings of sympathy and goodwill for the American people. They have been made stronger by personal acquaintance with them. But what has struck me most . . . is the resemblance between us and the Americans. I don't feel like a stranger here; I feel at home."[11]

Mary spent the holidays quietly, sorting newspaper clippings about Mr. Chamberlain, and catching up on her letters. Settling down for a lengthy bulletin to her cousin Fanny Mason on December 27th, she asked: "Have I [written] since the Chamberlain episode? If not, Clara probably told you I had seen a good deal of the great man, had superb flowers and a *poem* from him, visits, he 'did not want to come on Sunday, for there were too many people,' etc., and on Christmas I received a book from him. He is coming back on the 4th, and I am looking forward to his return. Really, he is *charming*, very attractive and agreeable . . . I wish you could see him, for he is such an interesting person to meet—and strikes one as extremely upright and sincere. What I want to do is to hear him speak, Spring-Rice[12] says he is wonderful—simply carries everything before him. Of the latter gentleman I have also seen a good deal and we are splendid friends. I do like him so much, and am delighted that he is to remain through the winter . . .

"I feel like a safety match warranted not to go off—till struck on the right box. In fact I am in a very cool frame of mind—it must be confessed that I enjoy my diversions like the one I have been telling you about. Don't think I am becoming conceited. It is such a joke, and I have only spoken to you and Clara. The family don't know quite what to make of it. They look on it as a joke—but very unexpected. I neatly arranged it so that when Mr. C. came to say good-bye before going to Canada, they were all out of the way. The book came with no name, but as he had told me about it, and I had never spoken of it to anyone else there was no mistaking it. It is a life of Burke by Morley, in the English Men of Letters [series]. It begins delightfully—Mr. C. says it is one of the best written as well as most interesting short lives he has ever read."

Mary enjoyed reading what the columnists had to say about Mr. Chamberlain. There being no official transactions to report, most accounts were of the banquets given for or by the Fisheries Commission. The Americans had got together an orchid dinner for the British, with flowers gathered from all over the country. Chamberlain returned the courtesy with a dinner on December 10th. For this he designed the floral arrangements, of American Beauty roses and maidenhair fern, himself; and commissioned Tiffany to render a menu honoring Anglo-American friendship. The card, with American and British flags crossed, bore the motto, "Blood is thicker than water", together with a portrait of a famous American, such as Lincoln, Clay, and Adams. The bill of fare, ranging from turtle soup and canvas-back duck, through to Chamberlain's favorite black cigars, was sumptuous. The expense of this entertainment, and others, would later be questioned in Parliament. But heavy hospitality was part of diplomacy; and had helped assure the harmony of the Fisheries Conference in their official meetings.

Mary had many adventures to catch up with when the holidays were over. Chamberlain and his party spent Christmas week with the Canadian Governor-General, Lord Lansdowne, in Ottawa. It was a highly athletic holiday. Coached by his host, Chamberlain, though not much given to outdoor exercise, tried out the Canadian version of curling. His first manful thrust at the curling stone brought him down hard on the ice. Maycock, meanwhile, who was never slender, rubbed his aching ankles, and tried to keep up with the Canadians in skating. Dinners and discussions with Government officials were far less strenuous.

Leaving Ottawa on December 29th, Chamberlain went on to To-

ronto, where the high point of his tour was a speech to the Board of
Trade. Talk was rife about a possible lowering of tariffs between the
United States and Canada, and even commercial union. Joseph
Chamberlain scouted this notion: "It is a very restricted reciprocity, indeed, which would make you dependent for your financial
freedom upon the government of another State, and, perhaps, pave
the way for the surrender of . . . your political freedom . . . I have
not discovered in the course of my stay in the United States any
general desire on the part of the American people, who have a good
stock of territory of their own, to increase it and increase their responsibilities at the same time—" on the other hand, "if you desire
to remain an integral part of the vast Empire of the Queen, your
interests will be maintained, your rights will be respected with all
the influence which that Empire can wield." It was only twenty
years since the creation of a federal government in Canada; Chamberlain prophesied "the federation of Canada may be the lamp
lighting our path to the federation of the British Empire." Cheers
and shouting greeted this speech of December 30, 1887; it was the
end of Queen Victoria's Golden Jubilee year, and vivid oratory was
right in style.

The balance of the holiday season, insignificant politically,
brought Chamberlain and his companions in some peril. The Prospect House, on the American side of Niagara Falls, was specially
opened to accommodate their party; the visitors were determined to
"do" the Falls thoroughly. Bergne, Maycock, Chamberlain, and the
inevitable detective went touring by sleigh; they crept down icy
paths, in oilskins, to peer at the Horseshoe Falls; they next hired a
four-wheeled carriage to take them up a nearby hill on the Canadian
side, for a panoramic view of Niagara. It came close to being their
last adventure. At every moment the outer wheels seemed about to
leave the road, and plunge the carriage into the whirling river below. The danger pointed out, Chamberlain remarked, "Humph!
I suppose if I'm killed someone will catch it. It isn't my business!"
The detective, whose business it was, was chagrined to find when
they at last reached the summit in safety, that the driver's route had
been along an icy cattle track, up which no vehicle had previously
travelled. With nothing worse than ruffled nerves, the group now

set off for Washington. En route, a miscalculation in the height of a bridge knocked the top off their special railway car, to the distress of Bergne and Maycock. Chamberlain, who went right on putting his safety in other people's hands, had confidently retired to bed, where he slept through the commotion. Without further event the train limped on to Washington, arriving there on January 3rd.

The following night there was a ball at the British Legation. Family legend maintains that it was here that Mrs. Endicott stepped in to rebuke her daughter for talking too long in public to Joseph Chamberlain. Recalling the occasion a year after, Mary declared dramatically her "fate was sealed" that evening. At any rate, there were over four hundred people swirling about, the dancing went on till three a.m. and the singing of "God Save the Queen"; after which Joseph Chamberlain went home to smoke a cigar, and brood about his future.

All the following week he and Mary were at the same dances. By this time the Endicotts realized the attachment between their daughter and the British Plenipotentiary. There was little they could do but wait upon events, and chaperone her rather more than usual.

Mary had much to consider in the small hours of the morning, when she returned from her parties. Mr. Chamberlain had singled her out, but his campaign must at times have seemed upsetting and unfair. He drew her out intellectually, then spoke of his own aims and ambitions; he made her life in Washington seem trivial and worldly.

He spoke of his family, and she knew how deeply he felt towards his children; but she also realized that both they, and any future mistress of his household, must always follow second to his career. The woman who married Mr. Chamberlain must listen to his opinions, comfort him when he failed, manage domestic problems, and stand always to one side: tactful, charming, intelligent, but unobtrusive. Joseph Chamberlain, a man of action, and restless dreamer, had brilliant ideas about his country's future. He meant to carry on himself, but Mary could not let him go alone.

For his part, Chamberlain had thought it almost impossible to marry again. He had adored, and lost, two wives, both of them in

childbirth. How could he now consider taking yet a third young
and pretty bride? Twice he had been tragically hurt, and twice had
come to terms with life, throwing himself into public work, hiding
from all his pain.

He had been a widower now for thirteen years, but at fifty-one
Joseph Chamberlain was young in energy and outlook. He must
have been thankful now the romance with Beatrice Potter had gone
no further. For though her intellect was keen, her spirit was com-
petitive; she must have her own career in order to be happy. This
he found intolerable. The wife he chose would be responsible: she
would be chatelaine, hostess, and companion; confidante, and
sharer of hard times. She might, as Mary Endicott did, gently prod
him, and laugh at his pomposities. She might be bright and light
and youthful, and demand that he be also; but she must respect his
judgement utterly, never criticize.

Brooding away their sleepless nights, a thoroughly bemused couple saw each other nearly every day. They seemed cheerful to the
world at large. Chamberlain wrote home, "I have taken to dancing
and have revived my waltzing and polkaing . . . The liveliness of the
proceeding delights the politicians here who are white-headed at 40
and who are all anxious they say to have my secret of perpetual
youth. I give them my receipt freely 'no exercise and smoke all day,'
but they think I am joking. One man said yesterday, 'We all like
you, Mr. Chamberlain, but we don't believe you.' 'What do you
mean?' 'Well, we think you are carrying on a little too much when
you tell us that you have a son ready to enter Parliament.' "[13] He
reported proudly of one week, "My record shows 6 dinner parties,
3 evening receptions, 3 balls, 1 supper, 1 theatre, 1 luncheon party
and various afternoon receptions—just enough to keep one from
resting."[14]

Meanwhile the work of the Fisheries Commission lay in troublous
waters. Chamberlain felt Secretary Bayard was not considering the
British position fairly. He wrote his daughter Beatrice he had had
to use "very plain language" with him, and for a time it even seemed
the whole Conference might break up. Then matters were smoothed
over; both sides turned to writing up a workable treaty. It seemed
to Chamberlain "It has been a very difficult business from the first,

and if I do succeed I shall deserve a peerage and the Garter!'"[15]

The strain of courtship in the public eye was hard on Mary; she told Fanny Mason on February 3rd: "I have seen him twice and had two nice chats, quite free from the theme uppermost in our minds. Last night at the Grants' someone interrupted, so the talk was a short one—he was just verging on to *me*, for he told me that as far as he could see my present life was utterly frivolous, and I was worthy of something better. I tried feebly to remonstrate, and he said, 'Well, what do you *do*—make calls?' and bore down on me with that eye till I felt 'What *do* I do?'

"I was to have gone to Baltimore tomorrow, but this morning Ma changed her mind, owing to these horrid papers. Unfortunately Mr. C. sent over and ordered lunch etc. so they knew he was coming, therefore we thought reporters would be on hand and the thing would get into the Sunday papers . . . Tonight, too, I am not going to the Whitneys', but I shall continue to go out and talk to him, too . . . There is an end to everything and this can't last forever . . ."

At first it had been amusing to have a man almost her father's age come courting. Then Chamberlain declared that Mary was wasting her life, that she was made for better things, and implied that he could show them to her. His single-mindedness, and his constant appeal to her intellect won her round, and put her in the mood for flowers and poetry. Now Mary chatted and danced away her evenings, charming as ever, but her gestures were mechanical. She was anxious and worried, not only for herself, but for her family.

Mary's father was impressed with Chamberlain's intellectual powers, and enjoyed talking politics with him. Together they explored the relation of the United States to its member states; Chamberlain drew parallels with England and her Empire. Secretary Endicott acknowledged Chamberlain's honesty, and admired his far-ranging ambitions, but he feared his daughter might be lost among them.

Brother William was in evidence as little as possible. He was frankly dismayed by Chamberlain as Mary's suitor. He liked and respected the man well enough as a politician. It was also true that he had a taste for fine food, wine, china, and flowers. Yet, fortune and political future set aside, Joseph Chamberlain was an aggressive, hard-hitting businessman, from a middle-class background. William, ever ancestor-conscious, could not consider him as a brother-in-law. He sulked and glowered; all the Endicotts were tense, and seemed to hold their breath.

Saturday, February 11th, was snowy. Using the code indicating a call from Chamberlain, Mary marked the day with an "X" in her diary, followed it with three exclamation points, and then wrote down "5 p.m.!!!!!" She then received, and accepted, a proposal of marriage from Joseph Chamberlain. Sunday he had his photograph taken for her, and that afternoon, nervous but determined, Chamberlain walked from his hotel to the Endicotts' house. He was bent on the hardest mission of his career: the formal request for Mary Endicott's hand in marriage.

There was an epic storm. So far from wanting an engagement, Secretary Endicott did not even wish any communication between the couple once Chamberlain had left America. He felt, with three thousand miles between them, they would come to their senses. Let Chamberlain get back to England, and not try to influence Mary by writing letters to her. Mary insisted her feelings would not change, that she knew what she wanted, and was going to marry Joseph Chamberlain. Separation would do nothing but make her feelings stronger. She struggled, but it was Chamberlain who finally carried the point that they should be allowed to write.

Assuming the remaining details of the treaty were settled then, Chamberlain was scheduled to leave for England early in March. He wanted to return for his bride in June, but Secretary Endicott would not hear of this. The whole question of the couple's engagement was further complicated by 1888 being an American election year.

Even when the Fisheries Treaty was finished, it would still need official acceptance. It might be devastating if it were learned too soon there was a romance between a Cabinet Minister's daughter and the Chief British Commissioner. Certainly, the Irish-American vote would swing away from Cleveland in the fall, should Chamberlain's engagement to Miss Endicott become known. The whole En-

dicott family was drawn into the fray; young William, turning that
night to his diary, recorded only that "the question was finally settled at six p.m."

The engagement, now acknowledged in the family, became no
joyful state, but a source of aggravation and upset. Mary did wring
the important concession that Chamberlain be allowed to call on
her both mornings and afternoons, until he left, but with that she
had to be content. Though dismayed, the Endicotts seemed to come
round gradually to this new idea of Mary's marriage. Five days after
their engagement Joseph Chamberlain came to dine alone with the
family. Mary was on pins and needles about the whole thing, but
her father was "affable, and Mama remarked after he left that she
thought him 'perfectly charming' which pleased me." He came
alone again a week later; but William meanwhile was anything but
affable; he wrote so cheerlessly to Fanny Mason she gave him strong
advice. He must not come to Boston in this bellicose mood, "for if
you show that you are going to be on the defensive, they will try to
tease you."

On February 15th the Second Treaty of Washington was formally signed; after that Chamberlain was busy only with last details, and could devote himself to his farewells. He called on Mary
every morning, a pleasant but risky occupation. Fortunately an understanding Endicott servant took charge in the house, and blandly
told all would-be callers that everyone was out. Mary was given a
pretty sapphire ring set with diamonds, which her mother said she
might wear, as it was so much like one she had no one would notice
it. But the ring turned Mary's thoughts to the future in a disturbing
way.

Soon the man she loved would be leaving, perhaps not to return
until November. And all that weary time she would have to pursue
the social life which now she saw as "this eternal round". She knew
that her engagement was right, but would Chamberlain's children
agree? Might they not even hate her? And what about the houses in
Birmingham and London where she would one day live? What
would they be like? Her friends were inquisitive, one even came out
and asked, "Are you going to England?" Somehow she fended off
the questions, but she could not put to rest the doubts in her own
mind.

On February 28th Chamberlain came for his last morning call, and returned for a family dinner. He gave Mary another ring, a canary diamond, surrounded by brilliants; she longed to wear it, but knew that she could not. The good-byes she dreaded came at last, and he was gone. She went off to her room, and got out writing-paper; went through the motions of a cheerful letter to Fanny Mason. She tried to concentrate: marriage would bring her closer to, not take her away from, her family; old ties would be strengthened. Nothing helped; the thought of all the empty months ahead came crowding in. How could she keep up her spirits? This seemed impossibly hard, "though I know it is foolish, I can't help it!"

So ended Joseph Chamberlain's first journey to America. It had been a curious, kaleidoscopic time: hours of demanding, black-and-white conference-table work, mixed with gaily coloured evenings, bright companions, good dinners, theatre parties. There were comic flashes: Willoughby Maycock, introduced at the White House as "Mr. Haycock", Senator Evarts being asked by a lady "if drinking so many different wines did not make him feel seedy the next day. 'No, madam,' he replied, 'it's the indifferent wines that produce that result.' "[16] Maycock again, strumming on his banjo at the hotel, rendering "He Did, and He Didn't Know Why."

And then the flash of light that was to change his life: his love for Mary Endicott. Chamberlain's work seemed full of purpose now, and his diversions secondary. It had been novel to be a social lion; Washington had been most kind. But now he could return to his real work—go forward, encouraged, a whole man again—unafraid of the past and happy with his future.

On the long voyage home Chamberlain pondered how his children would receive Mary, and how he himself would be received. Though the coming months would be difficult for him, his path was certainly easier than Mary's. For she had to hold her spirits up, be bright and cheerful, and never mind the world's murmurs. She had no career to turn to, only a society which seemed empty and pointless. She was separated from the man she loved, but when she saw him next must face another separation: this one from her family and her whole way of life.

CHAPTER VI

"And Leave Thee for Awhile"

SINCE his American trip Joseph Chamberlain was more and more empire-minded: in his speeches he constantly stressed the need for closer union of Great Britain with her colonies. Mary's politicking, though domestic, was no less intense. Through the spring of 1888 her great project was to try to shorten her engagement. With his daughter's suitor safely across the Atlantic, Secretary Endicott may have hoped she would turn the clock back, and look elsewhere for a husband. He under-estimated Mary. Every day she had to go on driving, calling, changing for dinner, and making conversation, she felt more desperate. She begged her mother to stir up her father; surely the separation could end in June. She even went to Secretary Whitney to plead her case: he took her driving, and Mary told her troubles. But the Secretary of the Navy, though sympathetic, was non-committal.

When her father's sister came for a visit, Mary could not even talk freely at home, "Mama is *sweet*, and has done her utmost; and for the next few days I shall keep quiet, then I think I shall take the bull by the horns and speak seriously to Papa—I have spoken casually many times. Of course he does not realize the state I am kept in, for to all outward appearance our life goes on the same as ever, the more so that the subject must be tabooed in Aunty's presence.

"Do what I will, as time goes on, it grows worse and worse, and at times I feel as if I *must* see him. His letters are the only things which keep me in any sort of resignation . . . Am I unreasonable, I wonder? When one is fairly consumed with longing for a person it is difficult to restrain oneself. Before, I had no idea how bad it could be."[1]

Beatrice Chamberlain wrote sympathetically, but she, too, deplored the secrecy and delay of the wedding plans. She had been in charge of her father's household for four years now; Mary had worried how she might react to the news of his engagement. From the first Beatrice assured Mary of a warm welcome, "I cannot bring myself to think that the woman who is to be my father's wife can be otherwise regarded than as greatly to be envied . . . I believe that his children would be considered by many as a heavy drawback. I venture to promise that you will not find us so . . . Papa promises that we shall be great friends; I believe and hope very much that you will let this be so, and that I shall gain in this a sister for myself."[2]

Austen Chamberlain was as generous: "I am so glad and so thankful that you have promised to be his wife. You will be to him all that we could not be, and make him far happier than we have been able to . . . I hope it won't be long before we have you here."[3]

The three younger Chamberlain daughters, and their nineteen-year-old brother Neville, also reacted encouragingly. All of them were shy, and found it hard to put their feelings into words; acutely aware of their father's loneliness, they had been unable to penetrate it. So Neville spoke for them all in writing, "We agree in looking forward to this great change not only for Father's sake, but also for our own. With such good feeling on both sides how can we help being friends?"[4]

This was encouraging, but Mary had to resign herself to an autumn wedding. From his letters, and others that Beatrice wrote, she knew how hard Joseph Chamberlain was working, and how the strain was telling on him. He was prone to fierce headaches, and was having more than his share now. And Mary's aunt, though she had not been told of the engagement, had some shrewd suspicions about it, and remarked during her visit how thin her niece was growing, and cold her hands were. Mary, restless and anxious, realized she must work harder than ever at seeming cheerful and light-hearted.

At last it was summer, and Mary set off for Massachusetts and a round of family visits. William was going abroad, and so would have the chance to meet the Chamberlains at home. Mary waited anxiously for his reactions: on meeting Austen in London, William declared him "a fine fellow". When he went to Birmingham (though he told her hardly anything about Highbury, her future home), William reassured his sister that the rest of the family were "agreeable". It was not much to go on, but Mary was relieved that her gruff elder brother had apparently been tactful.

Mary's mother, herself strong-minded, acknowledged the same quality in her daughter. Once convinced how strongly Mary felt about Mr. Chamberlain, she was on her side. Just the same, she was pleased when her brother, George Augustus Peabody, to whom she had made discreet murmurings, wrote: "Feeling such great interest in Mary, and being untrammelled by confidences, I have persistently taken every opportunity that offered to find out what I could about Mr. Chamberlain, and I can frankly say I have heard nothing but good."[5]

Secretary Endicott only wanted to be sure his daughter would be happy. Being assured she was not merely infatuated, but deeply in love with, and bound to marry, this man so close to himself in years, yet so different in experience, he did the generous thing. He told Mary she should have the prettiest trousseau she could assemble; and the half-dozen dinner and ball dresses she needed were to come from Paris, from the House of Worth.

Ruefully, the Secretary saw that he had set a storm in motion. The Endicott house filled up with samples of material and sketches of dresses. Whenever there were no outside guests his family's conversation seemed all to be of petticoats and slippers. Mary's father grew restless. The annoying publicity linking Mary and Mr. Chamberlain last spring had now completely died down. Mary had been her usual charming self wherever she went; while Chamberlain had been so tactful to Washington belles that the rumour of an engagement had been quelled almost before his departure. Now, the Endicotts gloomily reflected, the fanfare would begin again.

The time could not go too quickly for Mary. She was never too busy with dress-making to sit down and despatch a long letter to England; now, on October 22nd, she had sent her last. Joseph Chamberlain would be here himself in less than three weeks; every day it grew harder to keep her secret. Mary had to go back to New York for a final fitting of her wedding dress; she passed the night at the Fifth Avenue Hotel, "where as luck would have it I met Cousins

Endicott and Kitty. They looked a little surprised at seeing me a lone female, and Cousin Endicott remarked: 'There is nothing like being independent and a "*spinster*" ', with a twinkle in his eye. Well, in another fortnight they will all know my fate . . . The 7th of November is the day of the announcement. Then I hope everyone will speak of it, so that it may get noised about as quickly as possible, since the wedding is to take place so quickly."[6]

The Endicotts had been entirely discreet about the engagement. The Senate had on August 21st rejected the Fisheries Treaty, thirty Republicans out-voting twenty-seven Democrats, but this was an expression of party jealousies in an election year. No real damage was done, as Chamberlain, anticipating this possibility, had drafted a workable modus vivendi. On payment of a licensing fee American fishermen could once more fish in Canadian waters; ancient quarrels were resolved, and people spoke of Chamberlain as a skillful diplomat. Irish-Americans would lose no chance to twist the British lion's tail, but so far as Chamberlain was concerned, there was no opportunity. He would not arrive in America until the election was over; playing his part as dutifully as Mary, he had secretly embarked.

On November 3rd the *Aurania* put out to sea with a passenger disguised under the name of Willoughby Maycock. Not till England was well astern did Joseph Chamberlain's real identity become known. He left behind him a statement for the press, explaining his second trip to America, and his reason for missing the autumn session of Parliament. Meanwhile, the Endicotts returned to Salem to vote; and on November 6th, after all this cloak-and-dagger work, President Cleveland was defeated. There was no time for wry speculation on the length of Mary's engagement. The separation had helped reconcile her family; it had also given her a chance to prepare for a new life abroad. She had followed Chamberlain's speeches carefully in the papers; through letters she had come to know his family; and she had amassed a wardrobe which should carry her through any occasion. The time, needlessly long, had been well-spent.

On the evening of November 12th, when the clans were already marshalling in Washington for the wedding, Joseph Chamberlain arrived from New York. All his athletic exploits in leaping from the

Aurania's deck, while the ship was still moving, down a swaying ladder to the pier, had been in vain. Sprinting across town without his baggage, he had just missed the early train; and was forced to retire, disgruntled, to await the next. Not until nine-thirty did the Endicotts' carriage draw up at their door, with Chamberlain inside; it was midnight before his reunion with Mary ended.

That evening the date of the wedding was set for Thursday, November 15th. Mary and her mother had quietly gone ahead with many of the arrangements, but the next two days went by in a haze of packing, present opening, and family greetings. Mary had very little time alone with her bridegroom.

In all the flurry Mary managed to keep accurate lists of both trousseau and wedding fashions. In good New England style, she wrote them up in a battered leather address-book she happened to have, with the used pages torn out.

Her luggage would have been formidable enough if it had only included dresses; even in Washington Mary changed clothes three and sometimes four times a day. But the underpinnings of the eighteen-eighties, elaborate and be-ruffled, took several trunks all to themselves.

Mary had by the dozen chemises, drawers, short white skirts, flannel petticoats, white skirts, corset waists, and corsets. Handkerchiefs she categorized as "plain", "fine", and some, presumably for colds in the head, merely "common". Besides beribboned lawn nightdresses, Mary was well equipped for damp English evenings: she had flannel nightgowns, "dressing sacks", woolly jackets and wraps, and, most luxurious, a cashmere dressing gown.

Shoes and stockings went from plain to glamorous: she had everything from Balbriggan stockings and thick boots, to fine silk stockings and bronze embroidered party slippers. There were a dozen pairs each of day-time eight-button and evening eighteen-button gloves; sundry laces, veils, ruffles, and parasols completed the accessories.

For "at home" wear, Mary had dresses of pink silk and blue cashmere, for the street and travelling green, brown, and white dresses. As the Endicotts were lately out of mourning for the Secretary's parents, the wedding would be small and simple; Mary had ordered for her wedding dress a grey camel's hair travelling dress. Then there were capes, shawls, and steamer rugs, and to surmount her evening dresses a "long blue plush sortie du bal".

The order to Worth was, as it deserved, listed separately. Here Mary's father had touched the pinnacle of generosity. There were to be two dinner dresses: white and silver satin, and green silk; and three ball dresses of lilac, pink, and white tulle. A light blue brocaded tea-gown and a high-necked "at home" silk dress, with matching slippers and stockings for all the outfits completed Mary's wardrobe magnificently.

Of course the trousseau took in linens: there were sheets, towels, and tea-cloths by the dozen. Then, as if none of these commodities would be available abroad, she was provided with brushes, combs, thread, mirrors, hairpins, powder. She had a brandy flask, medicine chest, and all the apparatus for making tea. Also, Mrs. Endicott, always anxious about health, extracted the promise from Mary that if ever she were ill she would cable America immediately. A few trinkets and pictures from Mary's bedroom were tucked into the trunks to make her room in England more familiar; only the wedding presents now awaited sorting.

Of nearly a hundred and fifty presents which came to Mary in America and England, the great majority were jewellery or silver objects. As she did not have to polish any of them herself, she was delighted with the hair-pin boxes, stamp boxes, and bon-bonnières which arrived. There were trays, vases and inkstands, paper knives and picture frames; even a silver-handled feather duster and silver-mounted mucilage bottle! From her father there came an enchanting diamond crescent, which could be worn in her hair or as a brooch. From cousin William Endicott in London there was a diamond, sapphire, and pearl necklace. Pierpont Morgan sent a diamond-and-sapphire pansy pin and a diamond bracelet; Dorothy Payne Whitney a sapphire-and-diamond horseshoe, and Henry Adams an opal ring.

Thursday, November 15th, dawned cold and drizzly. Crowds gathered outside St. John's Church on Sixteenth Street, across from the White House, in the morning. Some persons, asked to a one o'clock wedding there, stayed curiously in their seats to watch

the Endicott wedding, following at two. If they had hoped for fanfare and dazzling display, they were disappointed. President and
Mrs. Cleveland, the Cabinet and members of their families had been
asked; beyond that there were about fifty relatives of the Endicotts.
Four young ushers, friends of Mary and William, shepherded the
guests to pews marked off with satin ribbon; the rest of the church
was open to the public. There were no bridesmaids and no best
man. Mary and her father simply followed the ushers up the aisle.
Lohengrin was softly played, and Joseph Chamberlain smiled at his
approaching bride.

The gas-light flickered on crimson-covered pews and crimson altar cloth, contrasting Mary's small grey figure and her husband's
tall one, all in black. For his usual orchid, Chamberlain today wore
violets, a present from his bride. There were no flowers in the chan-
cel, nothing to detract from the ceremony itself.

Chamberlain, nervous and a little pale, spoke his lines forth-
rightly. Mary, graceful and unafraid, promised sweetly and clearly
to love, honour, and obey. They knelt for the blessing, and rose and
shook hands with the two ministers who had married them. Then
they walked slowly down the aisle, smiling at their friends. Pausing
in the vestibule for his bride to be wrapped in a white lambswool
boa, Chamberlain tucked it close to her throat, and with beaming
face escorted her to their carriage. There was a new spring in his
step; he shut the door with a bang, and the Right Honourable Joseph and Mrs. Chamberlain drove smartly away.

At the Endicotts' house the rooms were filled with roses. Mary
and her husband moved quickly about, being congratulated by the
servants; then her parents' carriage drew up, and they had a few
quiet moments before the wedding guests arrived. To her parents
the scene was dream-like: roses in November, and Mary, a bride,
pink-cheeked and sparkling, standing among them. Joseph Chamberlain stood closely by, tall and protective. For the hundredth
time, Mrs. Endicott hoped he would take care of Mary; while the
Secretary, gruff, but good-natured, looked longingly at his little
girl, so soon grown up.

The laughs and chatter of their guests broke quickly on the family scene. Then there was no time for thought: only smiles, hand-

shaking, kisses, and a few tears. When all had finished their congratulations, the bride and groom led the way to the dining room, President Cleveland escorting Mrs. Endicott, and Secretary Endicott following with Mrs. Cleveland. Glasses clinked as the President proposed Mary's health. Crystal and silver shimmered in the candlelight; everywhere were roses and ferns. An elaborate wedding breakfast finished with ice cream doves and two wedding cakes: pound cake for the bride, and fruitcake for the groom, delicately iced and topped with roses.

The Endicotts had taken measures against reporters; a carriage was ordered in time for the afternoon train to the North. There were hasty farewells and waves; then Mary, enchanting in her dark grey velvet bonnet, kissed her parents and took her husband's arm. Chamberlain, his eyeglass firmly in position, smiled broadly, and ducked a shower of rice and old slippers. They were off at last, and laughed as they thought how baffled the press would be. Instead of going to the station their carriage turned toward Chevy Chase, where a house had been lent them for their honeymoon, and fitted out in perfect secrecy. For three whole days the Chamberlains were undiscovered in this retreat.

Having spent a "cozy evening" in their domain, Mary was all practicality next day when she sent a note to her mother: "Send us some papers, and some wedding and bride cake, also some granulated sugar." On Saturday, even more the mistress of the house, she advised: "[The cook] needs lard, cooking butter and table butter, also some wine for cooking. We have not used the champagne, so the claret is nearly exhausted: could you send us some more? . . . The cook is very satisfactory, and all is going well. Keep some accounts of the wedding for us to see."[7]

Joseph Chamberlain, amused by his wife's bustling energy, wrote more romantically: "We are perfectly happy . . . Mary is looking prettier this morning than I ever saw her, which as you know is saying a good deal. How can I ever thank you enough for trusting me with such a treasure?"[8]

On Saturday the rain had cleared; the Chamberlains went for a drive in the country, then sat on the piazza laughing over the newspapers. Mary was depicted throughout their accounts as "the little

Puritan maid", flower of American aristocracy. Her husband was the vigorous statesman, and orchid grower par excellence, whose "fabulous" income was quoted at £150,000 a year. Chamberlain, whose capital was less than this, chuckled at the latest American exaggeration. There were thank-you notes to be sent; Mary wrote off to her mother for addresses. Then there was her laundry— would Mother make sure the ribbons were taken out of her under-clothes, and have them put back when they were done up? And the kitchen needed some more eggs and sweet oil—could they be sent out? Of course the last packing should be carefully supervised, "I want the pieces of all the dresses I take with me . . . The fans can also go into the big trunk.

"Joe sends much love with mine to all . . . You did not tell me how much you thought we ought to give the woman in the house. She is very attentive and obliging. We are enjoying every moment, sweet Mother, we are *very happy*."[9]

Next day Mary proudly entertained William and her cousin Clara Payson to lunch; then on Tuesday Mother and a favourite aunt, Fanny Mason's mother, came to call. Then it was time to re-turn to Washington. Rushed as she was with last-minute arrange-ments, Mary found time to smile over a letter to Mother from Grandma Peabody. The Peabodys had felt their years too much to journey to the wedding, but they listened eagerly to eyewitness ac-counts, were touched that Mary had written them herself the day after, and shocked at the newspapers' vulgar tone: "The public here have made up their minds that Mary and Mr. C. are to come to Salem, accordingly the Paul Pry's have been on the alert about it, and feel we are deceiving them when told they have nothing to ex-pect. Were it not that our venerable Mother England sets the ex-ample we might be still more ashamed at the vulgarity and con-trariness of the whole thing."[10]

Mary would have cause to smile again when, in 1895, she read *Punch*'s indignant view of the Marlborough-Vanderbilt wedding. Here the blame was neatly shifted: "The American public may de-clare that it was not excited, but, in that case, it is difficult to under-stand why . . . not even the bride's underclothing is spared from publicity . . .

"The whole business is . . . an illustration of that passion for taw-dry display and vulgar ostentation in which the great American Republic seems to have gone not one but about a million better (or worse) than the parent stock. I sincerely hope that the supply of marriageable peers and American heiresses is now exhausted, and that we may hear no more of these international engagements."[11]

The Chamberlains had hoped for a leisurely honeymoon in the West Indies; but when yellow fever broke out there, they decided to go to Paris, and thence to the Riviera for sunshine. On November 23rd, Secretary Endicott, mustering what cheer he could, put his daughter and son-in-law aboard a private car on the New York train. With them went Mrs. Endicott and William. They dined quietly at the Brevoort House, joking, and talking of inconsequential things. Mrs. Endicott promised to come to England in the spring; William, realizing the pangs Mary was feeling now it was actually time to leave, was determinedly cheery. She wrote some farewell notes, and he wrote to his grandmother, "We shall have time to think of ourselves after she has gone."[12]

Then the Endicotts set off for the midnight train, and the Chamberlains to their saloon-deck suite aboard *La Bourgogne*, a French mail packet. Their cabins were fresh and clean, and filled with flowers and wine sent by friends, but Mary could not settle down. To her dismay she found Sir Lionel Sackville-West and his daughters also on board. After seven years in Washington as Minister, Sir Lionel had undone his career at a stroke. He unwisely answered a letter inquiring about the British sympathies of the Democratic government. He went on record that Cleveland, if re-elected, would probably be conciliatory. Then the Republicans, who had forged the letter, used Sir Lionel's letter to stir up the Irish-American vote. It was the eve of the election and tremendous publicity fanned the issue into a flame. Rather summarily Sir Lionel was handed his passports. This was just the sort of indiscretion the Endicotts had feared, and had avoided. It was ironic that Sir Lionel, whose hospitality had helped along Mary's romance, should have committed it.

The voyage was a stormy one, and for the first few days Mary lay, feeling miserable, in her cabin; her husband admitted to seasickness for the first time in his life. Once recovered, they bundled up like polar bears and sat out on deck, reading aloud *The Count of Monte Cristo*, and talking over their wedding. There were letters to read over, too; Mary especially enjoyed John Hay's congratulations to her husband: "You certainly have everything your own way in this Republic. The first time you came you got the better of our elders; and this time you gloriously defeat our young men!"[13]

At Havre a courier and maid for Mary joined the Chamberlains; their week in Paris was largely spent in fittings at Worth's. They tried to avoid social calls, though they did have lunch with the British Ambassador. Evenings were spent at the theatre; in true honeymoon mood the Chamberlains laughed over "Les Surprises du Divorce" and "Il Ne Faut Jurer de Rien"; but were bored when they saw *Carmen* and left before the last act.

When they reached the Riviera the Chamberlains went out driving, had picnics, and shopped desultorily. At Vallauris, where they toured a small pottery, Mary was charmed by her husband's tactfulness. The proprietor, seeing the name of his smartly-got-up visitors, mistook them for the Lord Chamberlain and his wife. Beaming and rubbing his hands, he insisted on sending along an extra bit of pottery as a present for Madame; while Monsieur must sign his visitors' book. Joseph Chamberlain did so, with a flourish, and he and Mary went on their way.

The sunshine, and their time alone together, did wonders for Mary, who had been quite worn-out at the time of her wedding. She and her husband had no arguments more serious than the one about her letter-writing. All his life, Chamberlain would try without success to get his wife to bed early. On the bottom of one of her letters home he asked, "Will you not back me in insisting that she shall not write too many letters?", while Mary indignantly added, "Don't believe a word . . . I shall not sacrifice my life to it, and mean to write as many as I choose!!!!! Won't you sustain *me*? It is all nonsense!"[14]

Since her first trip to Monaco, Mary's attitude to gambling had changed. Now she saw it as something daring, to be indulged in briefly, for a sense of adventure. Since Mary's birthday was March 15th, Chamberlain put down a gold napoleon (about $4.00) on the number fifteen. While their courier stood by in alarm, and begged him to stop, he then stood firm till his original bet had won four times, and brought him thirty-six napoleons. After that, resolved to buy a souvenir with their ill-gotten gains, and not to tempt fate again, the Chamberlains swept happily away.

At San Remo the weather remained fine; the Chamberlains began to talk on their drives through the hills about what Mary's life would be like in England. Chamberlain told her the citizens of Birmingham were to stage a huge public welcome. Mary thought it was most kind of them, but what on earth was she to do on such an occasion? She felt rested and ready for new encounters now; and on December 22nd the Chamberlains set forth on the thirty-hour trip to England.

Austen Chamberlain met them at the end of their journey, and, tired as she was, Mary held up her end of the conversation, and studied her step-son carefully. Certainly, as William had said, he was tall and good-looking. He was on the surface a youthful reproduction of his father, even to the eyeglass. He talked well at dinner, and Mary went to sleep that night confident they would be friends.

Next day the Chamberlain carriage came to their hotel to take them to 40, Prince's Gardens, Mary's new town house. Though the day was foggy and the house filled with workmen, Mary was all enthusiasm: "The dining room, which is in the front downstairs . . . so far as I could judge promised extremely well . . . very bright and cheerful, as the window is extremely broad . . . Behind the dining room is a very nice room for Austen . . . and in the rear is a large library, which one enters through a smaller room, which is occupied by the secretary . . . Above, the drawing room extends the whole width of the house and . . . is as big as Austen's room and the dining room . . . Then behind is a little morning room . . . My room upstairs has been a spare room, and so something must be done to it . . . It is in the front of the house, and also very light . . . The rest of the house is given up to bedrooms, and when the family is at home, every inch will be occupied."[15]

Before going to the Birmingham train, Mary wanted to do some important shopping. She had a legacy of £140 from her Endicott grandparents, which she wished to spend on jewellery. She wavered over an opal-and-diamond bracelet: it was very tempting, but she balked at the price of £155. The shop's proprietors hurried off to consult with each other, then announced that for the sake of Mrs. Chamberlain's patronage, they would let her have it for £140. Cautiously, she agreed to take it on approval; when she got it together with her pearl necklace, and her father's diamond crescent, she was won over completely: not only did she have something she really liked, but she had struck a good Yankee bargain in buying it.

The Chamberlains journeyed quietly to Birmingham, arriving at four-thirty on Christmas eve, when it was almost dark. To Mary's relief, since it was not known they were returning, the station was nearly empty, and they escaped to their waiting carriage almost unnoticed. The evening shadows had drawn in completely when they reached Highbury: the house, lit up in welcome, looked enormous. Then the great door was flung open: there were Beatrice and "the children", looking just like their pictures. There was a babel of greeting, but Mary felt especially the warmth of Beatrice's greeting. It must be hard for her to hand over the household; marvelling at Beatrice's generosity, Mary forgot her own qualms. There was tea waiting, then wedding presents upstairs to be opened. Ida, Hilda, and Ethel clustered round to watch; they were very anxious to make Mary feel at home. Neville, too, was likable, though at nineteen he seemed very young, the oldest of "the children"; while Beatrice and Austen seemed like sister and brother to Mary. There was so much to think about it was hard for Mary to settle down that night; but she knew she must get some rest, for it would be a long day tomorrow.

Christmas was so crowded she could not chronicle it all. Dear Joe gave her a pendant of pearls and diamonds—"Did you ever know anything like my jewels!"; there were family presents from England and America; and though she missed the Endicotts, there were throngs of Chamberlains eager to welcome her. Late in the day Joe's brother Arthur with his wife and his sister Mrs. James came to call. Mother would want to know just what they had said: Arthur's wife, to Joe, "Now I *really do* congratulate you!", and Mrs. James, "She is as sweet and lovely as her picture looks!"[16]

The next day others of the clan arrived, and Mary liked them all. If she had not been trained in Salem genealogies she could never have kept these in-laws straight. Joseph Chamberlain's second wife, Florence Kenrick, was a first cousin of his first wife, Harriet Kenrick. Harriet's brother William married Joe's eldest sister Mary; Florence's sister Louisa married Joe's brother Arthur. Joe's middle sister, Lina, was Mrs. James. His youngest sister, Clara, was Mrs. Ryland. Each, before her marriage, had taken care of Joe's children. Mary had been schooled in all this sort of thing: Endicotts and Peabodys were much given to marrying their cousins; but she felt quite nervous when she thought of herself presiding over a New Year's Day family dinner. Still, there would be time enough to worry about that when she had found her way around the house.

The day after Christmas Beatrice took Mary on a complete tour of Highbury. Mary knew what to expect from the pictures she had been sent in America: the house was red brick, Gothic style. The rooms opened off a huge central hall, two stories high, and were decorated in the most extreme Ruskin-William Morris style. Everywhere there was pattern, colour, and elaboration: arches of polished wood, flowered wallpaper, inlaid ebony furniture, stained glass, ferns, and potted palms. Brought up among the graceful ship-like lines of Salem architecture, Mary might well have winced at Highbury. But her mother's parlours were Victorian and cluttered; and the Washington house was Gothic-style; so that Mary was neither surprised by, nor critical of, her new home. She was dying to do something about the drawing-room, but tactfully waited till Beatrice said the family thought it needed re-arranging. Then they had a grand set-to, trying this chair here, that table there, and hoping the master of the house would approve the changes.

The gardens were wonderful: there were so many evergreens and rhododendrons, and the grass was so green Mary could hardly realize it was almost January. If fogs and rain kept her from out-of-door strolling there were always the greenhouses to explore. Off the drawing-room was the conservatory; then a long corridor, festooned with flowering creepers, led away to the orchids. Joe had had a rose house built as a present for his bride; here Mary found three roses in bloom: they were her very own, and she felt for the first time she was mistress of Highbury.

Mary did nothing to disturb the master's sanctum, his library. Everywhere there were books and Parliamentary papers. Joe had a huge writing-table before the fire; here, puffing on his beloved black cigars, he would work over his speeches; Mary, curled up in a corner, would write her letters home. Joe liked having her there beside him, though they might not speak for hours; and Mary spent many contented evenings there. In the day-time she had her own small boudoir, overlooking the garden; her writing-table sat in a sunny south window, and there she went each morning to write notes, give orders, and do the accounts. A pretty red-embroidered screen in the doorway shielded her from family traffic; when Joe finished in the library he would take up his pipe and bowler hat, stride down the hall to her room and call out, "I'm going to the houses." Then Mary would finish up her letters, while Joe communed with the orchids. She would then put on her hat and set out after Joe, taking one or another of the girls with her. If it were fine they toured the gardens completely as well as the greenhouses, so that it was always twelve and often two before they were ready for lunch. To Mary, who breakfasted with Joe at ten, or even ten-thirty, the garden tour was a pleasant constitutional, none too long. Ida, Hilda, and Ethel had schoolgirl appetites, and breakfasted at eight; they got hungrier and hungrier while Papa and the gardener discussed the welfare of each plant, and the circuit seemed interminable!

Mary slipped gradually into the household, taking over the management so tactfully the change was hardly felt. At luncheon and dinner tables she was happy to sit back and listen to her husband talk. Meals were usually noisy, but at this exciting Christmas season they were even more so. The young Chamberlains were arranging parties with their cousins, also home from school; their elders were trying to arrange as many family reunions as possible to entertain Mary. She was glad she had taken such trouble over her clothes, for she could go anywhere and know that she looked well and that Joe was proud of her. Even before she spoke, Mary's smile won her friends; and Joseph Chamberlain, who had wondered if his bride would flourish so far from home, rejoiced. Remembering that Mrs. Endicott was wondering and worrying about Mary each day, he wrote early in the new year, "You may rest assured that your daughter is already as completely one of this family as she is of the other across the water."[17]

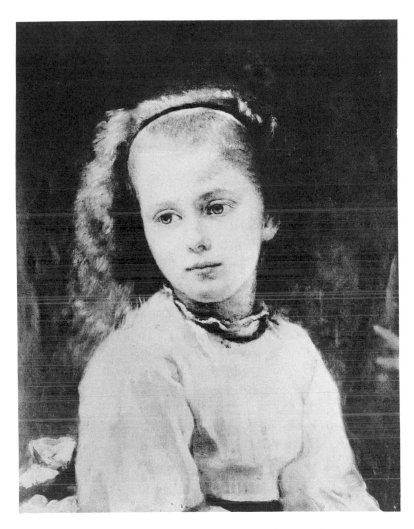

Mary Crowninshield Endicott, oil portrait
by William Morris Hunt, 1871

Mary Crowninshield Endicott, photograph
by John Lowell Gardner, 2nd, 1884

Mary Crowninshield Endicott at Nahant about 1885

Mrs. George Peabody and her granddaughter, Mary Crowninshield
Endicott, at Nahant, 1887, in a barouche bought in Paris in 1852

Mary Crowninshield Endicott
in Washington, 1887

Joseph Chamberlain in
Washington, February 12, 1888

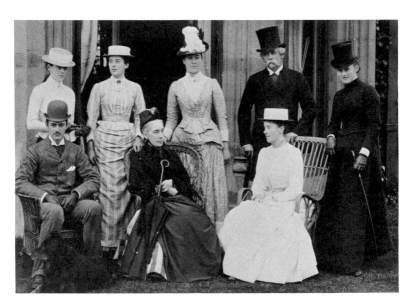

Family group at Highbury, Birmingham, September 10, 1889
Standing (left to right): Ethel Chamberlain, Hilda Chamberlain,
Beatrice Chamberlain, Hon. William Crowninshield Endicott,
Ida Chamberlain
Seated (left to right): Neville Chamberlain, Mrs. William
Crowninshield Endicott, Mrs. Joseph Chamberlain

Family group in the Highbury conservatory, September, 1897
Standing (left to right): William Powell Mason, Fanny Peabody
Mason, Ida Chamberlain, Hilda Chamberlain
Seated (left to right): Ethel Chamberlain, Beatrice Chamberlain,
Mr. and Mrs. Joseph Chamberlain, Mrs. William
Crowninshield Endicott, Jr.
Seated on floor: William Crowninshield Endicott, Jr.

Highbury, Birmingham, June, 1903

Mrs. Joseph Chamberlain in court dress, March 13, 1891, when she
presented her step-daughters, Ida and Hilda Chamberlain,
at the Court of Queen Victoria

Mrs. Joseph Chamberlain dressed for the Devonshire House Ball,
July 1, 1897

Mary and Joseph Chamberlain leaving for the polls in Birmingham,
January 17, 1906

Mrs. Joseph Chamberlain,
oil portrait by John Singer
Sargent, 1902

Joseph Chamberlain,
oil portrait by John Singer
Sargent, 1896

Mary and Joseph Chamberlain leaving the polls in Birmingham,
January 17, 1906

Birmingham motorcade celebrating Joseph Chamberlain's seventieth
birthday, July 7, 1906

Mary and Joseph Chamberlain, about 1911, accompanied by
Sidney Pink

Wedding group on the steps leading to the Jerusalem Chamber,
Westminster Abbey, after the marriage of Mary Endicott Chamberlain
to Rev. William Hartley Carnegie, August 3, 1916, photographed
by Alice Hughes

The five daughters of Rev.William Hartley Carnegie, photographed by
Alice Hughes, 1916, as a wedding present to their new step-mother

Rev. and Mrs. William Hartley Carnegie and Mrs. William
Crowninshield Endicott, about 1920

Mary Endicott Carnegie on her ninetieth birthday, March 15, 1954

Mary Endicott Carnegie in the drawing room at 41, Lennox
Gardens, London, painted by her step-daughter, Rachel Carnegie
Chaytor, May, 1953

CHAPTER VII

"Dear Lady, Welcome Home"

MARY was not shy, only wondering, as she dressed for the evening of welcome at Birmingham Town Hall. School children, working men, city fathers, and business people would all be there, all dressed up and anxious to please. Mary chose a pink silk dress and diamond ornaments, dressed her hair with special care. Her eyes sparkled, and her cheeks were pinker than usual; she hoped Joe would be proud of her tonight.

At quarter to nine the Chamberlains reached the Hall, and were ushered in by an organ pealing "Hail Columbia"! Mirrors, Oriental rugs, and potted palms had been set among thousands of people to turn the Hall into a drawing-room for this one night. And the flowers! There were orchids, of course, but poinsettias, cyclamen, and lilies of the valley, too. Mary's practiced eye noticed flowers as much as people. She walked slowly and surely through the cheering throng, accepted a bouquet, and settled down. Inquiring ladies lowered their lorgnettes, and the speeches began.

The addresses of welcome to Joe and Mary were read from illuminated books, like medieval manuscripts. They were the first of scores of such addresses Mary would see her husband receive. The citizens of Birmingham gave Mary a string of Oriental pearls, clasped with diamonds. From the Women's Liberal Unionist Association came a six-pointed diamond star; and from Joe's West Birmingham constituents a gold filigree necklace, brooch, and bracelets, made right in the city. Birmingham was famous for her jewellery and Mary noticed how carefully Joe remarked this in his speech of thanks. Mary blushed a little when the speaker referred to Joe's second, domestic, mission to America. How good-hearted these people were, and how well Joe answered them. He spoke of the need for harmony between England and America on the larger as

well as on the domestic scene, and when the crowd was at the height
of enthusiasm, rang out about his wife, "I know that she is prepared
to take up her life amongst us, in the country to which she has
come, in all its fulness and that she will say, with Ruth of old, 'Thy
people shall be my people!' "

They went round receiving congratulations afterward. Mary nod-
ded, smiled, and chatted; but what she liked best were the spontaneous cries that rose from the crowd: "Joe can make love even
more successfully than he makes laws!", and, in gruff tones from
the gallery, "Our Joey's a match for any Yankee!"

For all her adaptability, Mary was a little chilled at the thought of
her first winter country-house visit. She and Joe were asked to
Hardwick Hall by Lord Hartington, head of the Liberal Unionists.
The house had been built to honour a visit from Queen Elizabeth;
but that changeable lady had never come. Mary had heard the house
was hung with tapestries, and had stone floors. She supposed
gloomily it would be full of cold breezes, and preserve all the old
discomforts as well.[1] Once arrived there she succumbed to the
charm of the place, and discarded all her New England ideas of
convenience. It seemed that bells would not work, so, like the
others, Mary cheerfully shouted down the passage when she wanted
a maid. Though it was a very damp January, she loyally insisted
hot water pipes kept one perfectly comfortable. She wrote sagely to
her mother, "They have been so wise not to spoil it by trying to
modernize everything."[2]

Lord Hartington, whose manners she had heard were quite boor-
ish, was most polite to Mary, and told her all about the house. There
were so many portraited figures in ruffs and hoops it was startling to
find the dinner company entirely nineteenth-century. Mary went in
to dinner with Mr. Colcraft, President of the Board of Trade.
Among the guests was the Duchess of Manchester. (She was the
mother-in-law of Consuelo Yznaga, who had married Viscount
Mandeville in 1876. After Lord Hartington succeeded as Duke of
Devonshire, the Duchess of Manchester married him, and was
thereafter sometimes termed the "Double Duchess".) Mary held
her own: she was quite undismayed by titles, frank in her appraisal
of their owners: the Duchess of Manchester was most friendly and

pleasant to her, and, as Mary said, bore the marks of beauty which had faded!

Coming home from Hardwick, the Chamberlains' carriage was blocked at Birmingham station by Joe's admirers. The welcome at Town Hall had been arranged, but these were spontaneous cheers; and whenever Joe made any kind of a speech, he was cheered. Mary realized how much they lived in the public eye, and tried her best not to slip up about any engagement. The days were busy, though, and she presently committed what she thought a "really dreadful" social offense. She was tucked up comfortably in the library, writing her mother, when Austen hurried in with an ominous telephone message. One of Joe's cousins, a Mrs. Nettlefold, asked if any of the Chamberlains were ill? She wondered why they had not come to a dinner she had given in their honour that evening, and hoped that nothing was wrong. Mary was appalled; she had forgotten to look in her book, and could now only concoct a note of apology. But it was embarrassing, and she took care not to repeat the mistake.

She was gaining confidence in her own household. They had a good cook, and she had got through the first firing of a servant; "there was no reason except total incapacity."[3] Things ran smoothly when they held their first large political party at Highbury. There were dinners and a ball, to which came, among other young men, Cecil Spring-Rice. He was all gallantry about the latest news in the Endicott family. William had suddenly cabled of his engagement to Marie-Louise Thoron of New York. Louise was a gentle, thoughtful girl who would soften William's wrath when he blustered and blew. She had been a friend for some time, but Mary had not thought of William's getting married to her. It now seemed like the best thing that could have happened, for it would give the Endicotts another daughter. Spring-Rice told Mary "he didn't see what else William could have done after I departed, which was flattering to my vanity."[4]

The ball itself went off perfectly. All the furniture had been shifted upstairs. To Mary's surprise the two hundred and twenty guests turned up promptly. She soon found out that couples engaged each other for all the dances; if you were late, you got no partners. There were fireworks outside, the music was good, and the supper party held late in the evening went off well.

The Chamberlains then travelled to Scotland for a week of speeches to boost the Liberal Unionist cause. A disgruntled Gladstonian said of Joe's Dundee speech, "It was diabolically clever!", and Mary felt Joe was in top form throughout the tour. There were entertainments by day, dinners at night. At all of them he spoke forcefully, and was full of practical suggestions. Now it was time to go to London for the winter Parliamentary session. Mary would be under scrutiny when she reached London, but before she could "belong" to society, she must be presented to the Queen at a Court Drawing-Room.

Sketches and samples of silk went back and forth between M. Worth in Paris and Mrs. Chamberlain. In three weeks Mary's presentation dress was finished. Mary's dressmakers had to consider a birthmark which ran down her neck, shoulder, and left arm; with concealing layers of net and lace, and long gloves, they had always managed triumphantly. Mary was saved from any embarrassment by a change in Court regulations about décolletage that year. Usually ladies either came in low-cut dresses or in high-necked ones with long sleeves. Now, largely to benefit elderly ladies who wished to look their best, but found the corridors of Buckingham Palace draughty, a compromise between the two was effected. Mary applied for a special dispensation in dress from the Lord Chamberlain. Her receiving it, and the dress she wore, gave rise to a series of legends.

Some said young Mrs. Chamberlain was so modest she would *not* wear full décolletage. A rumour about the birthmark reached the papers, but was quashed: people must be confusing the Lord Chamberlain with *Mrs.* Chamberlain, and imputing some defect of his to her. In afteryears it was not remembered the dispensation was generally available, for sound reasons; and it suited people's fancy to think of "the little maid from Massachusetts", modestly dressed among the glittering London ladies.

Mary kept her own counsel, and continued to wear long gloves. She was in the habit of removing the right one, and leaving the left one on; some ladies of fashion, not knowing the reason, assumed she was exceptionally stylish and adopted the custom themselves. Mary's dress for the Drawing Room was far from Puritan in appearance; but as she wore over it her blue plush cloak, the papers started off another legend. A bride customarily wore white to be presented, but it was said Mrs. Chamberlain, in her forthright American way, wore blue. Seeing all the confusion, Mary cautioned her family not to believe *anything* personal the papers said about her and Joe. She took pains to describe M. Worth's creation: of white flowered brocade, lace, and silver-spangled tulle, it was topped with a silvered tulle veil, and ostrich feathers arranged according to Court custom. Mary had been practicing a curtsey nearly to the ground. She also had to kiss the Queen's hand, but she objected to the idea of taking lessons for this.

The Duchess of Bedford, who was one of the Queen's Ladies of the Bedchamber, and whose husband was a Liberal Unionist, was to present Mary. It was disconcerting to discover, though, that the Duchess would not accompany her down the long line of Royalties. Mary was vastly relieved to hear that Joe might accompany her.

Amid many groans Joe dressed himself up on the appointed day, February 26th. It was cold and dull out, with occasional spittings of snow. As he climbed into a lace-covered coat, cocked hat, sword, and knee breeches, he grumbled that he was nothing but a "glorified flunkey"; while Mary offered the soothing advice that he looked "very nice". Mary was pleased with her dress, but felt very foolish being done up in veil and ostrich tips in the middle of the day. She was ablaze with jewellery: Joe had given her two diamond stars to fasten the veil; she wore also two necklaces, two bracelets, the Birmingham diamond star, and her father's diamond crescent. When at last they were arrayed, Mary put on her cloak and took her bouquet, Joe settled himself and his sword beside her, the coachman and footman adjusted their bouquets (de rigueur on such an occasion), and their carriage swept away.

As Joe was an ex-Privy Councillor, the Chamberlains were able to enter the Palace earlier than most of the ladies. Mary was introduced to many people in the next fifteen minutes, among them Lady Salisbury and Mrs. Gladstone. Then the Duchess of Bedford moved on to the Throne Room, Mary's train was spread out properly for her, and Joe followed her into the royal presence, where "I made a very low curtsey and she held out her hand. I placed the

back of mine under it and kissed it (lightly). It seems I should have
taken off my glove to do it, but though I made careful enquiries of
Lady Abercromby and others (she was in waiting for a long time)
no one had informed me of the fact . . . Then came the Princess of
Wales and the Princess Christian (third daughter of the Queen) to
both of whom I made deep curtseys. I took the three daughters of
the Prince of Wales, and also Prince Christian and son in one . . .

"When I had passed Lady Salisbury very kindly took me back
among the Ambassadresses so that I could catch all the proceedings for some little time . . . In spite of my misdemeanor [a qualifica-
tion Mary crossed out before sending her letter] the Queen was
very gracious and said to Joe who followed me immediately: 'I am
very glad to see Mrs. Chamberlain *here*, Mr. Chamberlain.' "5

With the Drawing Room safely over, Mary supposed she was
now a proper British subject. She had no intention of forgetting the
Stars and Stripes, however. The Chamberlains, amused by her defense of the American point of view, saw that Mary's patriotism
seemed to give her extra confidence in London. This was all to the
good. Washington and her experiences in Cabinet entertaining
were helpful now; Lady Abercromby also offered details of etiquette.
Mary was unselfconscious and charming with those she met, and
the lions of politics and society began to notice her. But London
drawing rooms were rather formidably anti-American in the eighteen-eighties. American girls were regarded as brassy and pushing;
their loud voices and bright plumage were notorious. Mary, quiet
and graceful, provided an unexpected contrast.

At dinner one evening Mary was introduced to Lady Dorothy
Nevill, a niece of Horace Walpole, celebrated for her wit, who
commanded a wide circle in London. She had once declared there
were two things about America she could not stand: its girls and
its tinned lobsters. Joe had written Lady Dorothy on his marriage
that he hoped she would change her mind about the girls, and
when she met Mary, she promptly did. She began to arrange parties
for her. Mary wrote that she was "bewildered" by those first weeks
in London, but she certainly did not show it. Joe had made no special effort in London drawing-rooms, and realizing what a maze of
ritual Mary had entered on, he was surprised by her assurance.

They were asked to meet the Prince and Princess of Wales. The Princess remembered Mary from the Drawing-Room, and said she hoped she liked England. Mary was a little embarrassed, for the room was silent, and she had to shout back her replies as the Princess was very deaf. After dinner no one of the ladies could sit down, but stood around in stiff groups, waiting for the Princess to talk to them. When the Royalties had gone there was a clamour of conversation; Mary was "very glad when they left, for the unfortunate women had not been able to sit down once since dinner . . ."[6]

The Prince of Wales had noticed Mary with approval that evening, and hearing she was to lunch with Lady Dorothy Nevill the next day, insisted on joining the party. Mary was distinctly piqued, "The little party to which I was quite looking forward will be spoiled. Lady Dorothy is so amusing left to herself that I am convinced it would be more entertaining with no royalty present."[7] At the luncheon for eight she was seated next to the Prince; she dismissed him as "chatty and pleasant, not a 'fazzinator.' "[8] These tidbits of social life in high places tantalized all Mary's American cousins; Mrs. Endicott would only read scraps of her letters aloud, and it sounded to them as if Mary were making a thoroughgoing conquest of worldly London. Look how well she managed a standoffish attitude, for instance. Who but Mary would have managed so gracefully, but firmly, when introduced to the Marchioness of Bute, and her step-mother, Lady Howard of Glossop.

"This last lady requested me to call upon her—which brought forth a stiff 'thank you' from Mrs. Chamberlain, who had no intention of doing so first, and intended to convey the intelligence. Result—Lady Howard of Glossop left her cards here yesterday—and I come off with flying colours and triumph over Joe, who thought my 'thank you' might have led her ladyship to suppose I was pleased at her invitation, and that perhaps I might have made my meaning clearer. After the dénouement he said he thought my 'thank you' could be trusted."[9]

Joe stood by proudly, watching his wife sweep down obstacles, and wrote his mother-in-law that Mary was "a 'charmeuse', as I discovered more than a year ago, and she continues without effort to please all who come near her . . . she has quite as much to do as

I like, but I am watching her with a cat-like jealousy, and I hope you will not find her worn when you come."[10]

Mary did not feel worn at all, only exhilarated by her new experiences. Beatrice took care of many dull chores in household management, and with Austen helped chaperone the girls when they were home on school vacations. She also helped Mary get through the long list of calls she always had to carry out. In the first month after arriving in London the Chamberlains received nearly fifty invitations to dinner. Some of these were no doubt sent out of curiosity to meet the American bride, but the pace continued in succeeding months. As the House did not sit on Wednesday and Saturday evenings, many invitations were scheduled for these nights, so Mary and Joe were left with a few evenings free to dine at home.

Mary was very conscientious about describing these meals all over town; and Salem marvelled at the way she grew so familiar with the drawing-rooms of the great. Mary's grandmother was particularly amazed: "My dear, how strange it seems that you should be sharer in all this. You have always had a good deal of equanimity and self-possession, it is evident you will need it all, to acquit yourself of your part of the duties involved. Happily you are exempt from the family infirmity of shyness, which would be an exceedingly inconvenient trait under the circumstances."[11]

In due course, too, the good impression Mary made on every hostess was to help Joe's daughters, as well as herself. It was not long before Mr. and Mrs. Chamberlain began to go about with the Misses Chamberlain; and Mary, by then, was so familiar with the intricacies of London, that she smoothed the way for the girls, who were shy. Her days took on what she found a pleasant routine; Mary made it all sound simpler than it was. To begin with "we are very late in the morning: breakfast at 10 means often a later hour. Then Joe disappears with his letters, and I resort to the morning room . . . and then perhaps go for a walk or shopping . . .

"After lunch Joe goes to the House, and I start out, sometimes with Beatrice, sometimes alone, and leave cards in every direction, very often bringing up somewhere for a quiet cup of tea with someone . . .

"People are certainly more than kind, and I have no reason to believe in the frigidity of the British race. Wherever I have been and gone they have been cordiality itself . . .

"I have not yet been to the House of Commons—to my infinite disgust I could not go when Joe spoke . . . He is very hard at work, and I see comparatively little of him. But that I knew I had to expect: we make the most of the odd minutes we do get, and I invade his library when I get a chance."[12]

That winter was particularly raw and disagreeable, and Mary wrote many of her letters tucked up in bed. For her Highbury room Mother had sent her a polar-bear rug. In London she was provided with a small fur bag to keep her toes warm in bed. She used the full complement of shawls and flannel nightgowns, and even then her husband fretted over her. Hard-pressed himself, Joe was always urging Mary not to overwork. Never having survived a New England winter, he feared his bride might languish in an English one. City dirt and fog did discourage Mary; but at last the parks turned green, and spring came. At Highbury they could once more have the long garden walks they loved.

Shortly before Mary's parents were to visit, the Chamberlains were summoned to dine and spend the night at Windsor Castle. They had had one invitation when they had just reached London, and all their clothes were packed away in tissue paper still. This they had had to refuse, but a second promptly arrived, and they journeyed to Windsor by train, arriving just at sunset. After a day of storm the rain-washed castle loomed huge and grey against a rosy sky. A royal carriage met them at the station, and at the Castle two secretaries conducted the Chamberlains to a luxurious room in the visitors' apartments.

Though she delighted in sitting at the bedroom desk, and filling pages of the royal stationery with a letter to her parents, Mary was anxious to tell them about Windsor in person. She was sketchy in her impressions: the Long Gallery was filled with "beautiful things and interesting pictures;" their dinner was "on the whole, pleasant." In her mind she stored away all the colour and movement she would later recall so clearly of the visit. She looked out the window at trees coming into leaf; green buds and birds singing spoke of new, fresh life; while all about her great stone walls enclosed ritual, and timeless tradition. At exactly quarter to nine she and Joe were summoned to join the other guests, and lords and ladies of waiting. In fifteen minutes the Queen and her daughter Princess Beatrice appeared, spoke briefly to the company, then led the way to dinner. Here the conversation was somewhat subdued. Mary could respond to the stateliness of the sovereign without being overawed; this did not escape the newspapers.

When the Endicotts reached Liverpool they found a news item which declared that Mrs. Chamberlain had created "a very favourable impression . . . [the Queen] engaging in conversation with her for some time. Mrs. Chamberlain was very charmingly dressed in a costume of great richness, but which was characterized by conspicuous neatness and elegant taste." Of course this was despatched to Grandma Peabody who wrote, "This sounds very fine to us, but I suppose it must be nice. Another tribute of appreciation to Mr. Chamberlain that must be gratifying to Mary."[13]

The Endicotts were full of nervous excitement. Leaving William to settle the Washington house they had retired to Salem after the inauguration of President Harrison. All winter they had written anxiously to know if they should really come to England; would they be in the way? They worried that Mary, with all the new things she had to do, and the new friends she had made, might grudge time spent entertaining her parents. But eventually, in late April, they set sail, laden with things Mary had left behind. They also brought something she had especially asked for: a copy of the family portrait of Governor Endecott.

When they reached Birmingham all Mrs. Endicott's fears were swept away. There was Mary on the platform, with her husband beside her. She looked just the same, and she ran into her parents' arms. At Highbury Beatrice, Ida, Austen, and Neville were there to add their welcome, and the Endicotts were delighted with them. Mr. Endicott, whose correspondence was rather juridical, wrote William that Austen was very intelligent and of much promise. He also observed that the English summer was at its best, and Highbury more attractive than he anticipated. Happily he pottered round the gardens, and talked to the young Chamberlains. His wife meanwhile took to her bed with a tooth-ache. Mr. Endicott was "much impressed and delighted with the harmony and happiness of this household. The relations of one and all with Mary are most affectionate and tender, really there seems to be no jar or coolness, she has won them all, their respect and their love. There are some peculiarities of manner, and some ways that you might criticize, but in the essentials there seems to be no thing wanting. Miss Chamberlain is a *trifle* English in her ways, and has a tendency to chaff which more town and less country, more strangers and less family, will probably cut away; but she has the makings of a fine and robust character, and warm womanly instincts and feelings. The younger that are at school I have yet to see."[14]

When Mrs. Endicott recovered, the ménage moved to London. There the Endicotts stayed at the Berkeley Hotel. Mary called on them daily, and they ate most of their meals at Prince's Gardens. Always her mother found Mary's visits too short: "It was hard to think she was to leave us to go home, so completely is she as she was, and so naturally did she buzz round to make us comfortable. But the hour came, and so it does come each day, and we would not have it otherwise, when the radiance of happiness marks every line, and gives new meaning to all she says, and all she does."[15]

What the Endicotts noticed most in Mary's London house was that "the atmosphere is hers, and with all the life that has existed there, one feels it is her home."[16]

The Endicotts gathered reports of Mary's success in London from all over the city. Lady Camperdown called expressly to say how natural and lovely Mrs. Chamberlain was. Her daughter, Lady Abercromby, spoke of her "delightfully"; and Mrs. White, wife of the American Minister, said she had never known anything like the interest Mary had excited. This was all pleasing to Mrs. Endicott's heart. She had been a bit dismayed to think of Mary constantly on display—how good it was to hear that she had made a success simply by being herself. And she was pleased with her son-in-law as well. He encouraged Mary in what she did, and gave her great independence; which was surely why Mary managed everything so calmly and well. She coped with husband, family, household, and social obligations; and he knew when to give her a change of scene. In June the Endicotts went for a bracing week at Ramsgate; the Chamberlain clan trooped off to Paris.

En masse excursions there seemed a poor idea; so Mary and Joe went one way, and the children another. It was wonderful to have Joe to herself again; Mary made him come with her to her fittings at Worth's. They laughed together at the theatre over "Belle Maman" (mother-in-law); and after a week of relaxation Mary returned ready to take up where she had left off. She promptly put on two large formal dinners.

Mary's mother was much impressed with the arrangements for these parties. Ordinarily butter and cream came up daily from the Highbury farm, along with two orchids for Mr. Chamberlain, and, twice a week, flowers for the house. For parties, though, the quantity of orchids that turned up was spectacular. They were not overwhelming; Mary's silver blended in beautifully; she had given time and thought to the menu and the seating arrangements. Both food and conversation were good at the dinners; it was clear her mother's coaching had paid off.

Even in Salem, word of the magnificence of the Rothschilds and their estates had got around; Mrs. Endicott wrote home in detail about a weekend the Chamberlains had spent at the Rothschilds' country place, styled after the Chateau of Blois. They had strolled among huge and magnificent trees. Luxuriance was all about—in the house, the landscape, and the delicious menus. Reaching the dairy they found that unseen hands had laid out bowls of strawberries and cream. Wandering on, refreshed, they found a tea tent, all floored and furnished. The glories of the garden were assisted by a good cup of tea.

Then there was the State Visit of the Shah of Persia. The Chamberlains had taken the Endicotts down to the Foreign Office to watch the state coaches roll by. There were a series of luncheons in the Shah's honour, and Lord Salisbury had him to stay at Hatfield House. This was not without its headaches: the Shah's retinue was numerous, quarrelsome, also light-fingered. Lord Hartington, who was staying in the house, left his room for five minutes and returned to find his watch gone. The Chamberlains were glad they were only asked to lunch.

Presently Joe and Mary spent the weekend at Hatfield House, in a party honouring the German Emperor. Queen Victoria's grandson, William II, had succeeded his father the previous summer. At Hatfield Mary only spoke briefly with the Emperor. Both Endicotts and Chamberlains, however, were asked to the Aldershot Military Review honouring the Emperor.

Mary would think bitterly about the Kaiser's war-like nature in later years; but in that summer of 1889 she saw the war games planned as just another pageant her parents would enjoy. As a past Minister of War, Mr. Endicott was offered "a steady charger", with accompanying orderly, from which to watch the day's maneuvers. Mary stressed that this would be quite in order; but her father, whether nervous of horses, or fearing to presume, stayed with his womenfolk and son-in-law. Sightseers gathered in a gravel pit, intended to shield them from combat. Ten miles of the surrounding countryside were devoted to maneuvers. The Chamberlains and their party spent hours with Lady Salisbury and her family, following the troops.

"The Emperor with his staff was galloping from place to place, and at last we found ourselves close behind him in his gold and silver helmet. This was on a high bluff, and suddenly we were hemmed in by troops, rushing up the hillside preparing for another attack. [We had] six lancers as our body guard . . . we started for our gravel pit, but they hemmed us in at a meeting of roads, where carts and carriages had fancied themselves in safety, and our carriages had come to meet us. Such confusion, such noise, such terror-struck horses, you cannot imagine; but we came out of it, as did everybody, safely."

The climax of the day was the review parade; when the Emperor had taken his place, and "God Save the Queen" had been played, "All the crack regiments, and the artillery, which is the finest in the world, went trotting by with a precision wonderful, the horses almost in step with the music."[17]

With red eyes and streaming noses, the Chamberlain party re-

turned from battle to London that night, where they fell into exhausted sleep. Mr. Endicott reflected he had had at least as much
exercise dodging the cavalry, and swirling through dust clouds, as
he would have done on his steady charger.

The rest of the summer was spent peacefully at Highbury. There
the Endicotts lingered happily over coffee in the conservatory,
wandered through the fragrant gardens, or chatted, in wicker chairs,
upon the lawn. Mary had done everything for the "first" time; and
she took pleasure in having her parents share her new experiences.
They heard the thunderous welcome accorded Chamberlain in Birmingham Town Hall, saw Mary seated by his side, and when they
left heard voices shout for "Joey!", while one man shrieked, "Three
cheers for our American cousin!" Mary told her mother about a
cornerstone-laying she had been to with Joe after this speech. She
had been asked to lay the stone; Joe had refused, as he refused all
public acts for his wife; but agreed to do the job himself. He spoke
as earnestly of the Methodist Sunday School a-building as he did
about the future of empire.

In these early months evolved the lasting pattern of Mary's life
with Joseph Chamberlain. She was always with him, but never
spoke on her own. She made no speeches, asked for no votes; when
he worked on his speeches, she sat quietly by. She listened when he
talked, and listened well, without unnecessary questions or comments. When she could she joined the group of what Lady Randolph Churchill called the "ultra-political" ladies who gathered in
the Ladies' and Speakers' Galleries in the House of Commons.[18]
There, crowded in hard chairs, peering through a grillwork which
hid them from the lawmakers' gaze, a few devoted ladies followed
the debates. Later it was fashionable to "drop in" at the House, to
gather a veneer of political awareness. Mary's absorption in her
husband's career was genuine.

She always sat up late awaiting the weary warrior's return from
the House. She would read aloud with the girls, then when they
went off to bed, start on her letters. A photographic memory allowed her to unreel the scenes of her day almost automatically; she
meanwhile wondered what state Joe would come home in. Had he
had a chance to say his say, or would he be gloomy, and head-

achey, suffering from a "speech rentré"? At midnight or later, when Joe came in, they would go over his day. He knew he could speak freely, for Mary's tongue never wagged. While not appearing to with-hold information, she never gave away secrets. In Washington she had learned diplomacy; in London she perfected it. If she disapproved personally of a man's politics or actions, it was hard to discover this from what she said. She needed all her discretion, for the bitterest political enemies would often be together socially. Randolph Churchill and Joe, united though they were in opposing Gladstonians and Irish Home Rule, quarrelled and made up constantly. Randolph wanted to be candidate for Central Birmingham; Joe wanted the seat for the Liberal Unionists. Lady Randolph was furious when her husband gave in; and Mary had her own views about ladies who canvassed votes for their husbands. One had to remember that you could carry on a cordial friendship, and maintain political enmity with the same person. Joe was constantly under attack, yet Mary never displayed hostility to his opponents. She was above controversy; her silence in strife was from choice, not ignorance.

When it was time for Mary to send her parents back to America, in September, 1889, Mary lost for awhile her calmness and cheerful competence. She knew the path which lay ahead for her in London and Birmingham; she was eager for new adventures; but still it was hard to send the Endicotts to America without her. They were growing old; it comforted her to think that William and Louise could help so much. And now her parents had seen so much of her new life, they would not seem so far away. It had been a strenuous year of trial for "the little Puritan maid", but most of Mary's doubts and qualms about England were laid to rest. She had arrived in pioneer spirit; she had made her way through unfamiliar ground; she now moved forward with assurance.

CHAPTER VIII

The Road to Office

MARY smiled over a letter from her brother William. He never would get used to her living in England; now he was inquiring "how the roses have turned out. I hope well, for I should like to have you show those Britishers how much finer our roses are than theirs." He was convinced that American sunshine made the difference; he shivered a little as he recalled that "in London when the lackey used to come to my room . . . if it did not actually pour with rain, he always *insisted* upon its being pleasant."[1]

The roses were wonderful; they thrived in the house Joe had had built as a present for his bride, so she would feel at home at Highbury. There were in all thirty-three greenhouses on the place; it might be pouring with rain, but the Chamberlains were always close to summer. Joe called it "the Italian climate of Birmingham", and Mary, dreaming over a fragrant bouquet, forgot the mists and smoke and bitter winds that swirled around their Eden. She quite agreed with Joe, and was enchanted when he planned a tea-house à la Rothschild. Their little farm was doing well; he had to build a dairy, but the pretty hexagonal room attached, with glassed-in piazza, was pure frivolity. There was a thatched roof, and the little dairy was set in shrubbery. Mary installed a special set of blue-and-white china for tea; and loved to preside there over peaches and cream à la bergère.

Such distractions were welcome for Joe, who was having a hard time in Parliament getting the Tories to put through some of the reforms he had urged since 1885. The Unionists must not only oppose Gladstone and Irish Home Rule; but must force their Conservative allies to democratic action. Chamberlain stood for free primary education, graduated real estate and death taxes, local government and land reforms. He was concerned, as ever, with the small farmer, poor laborer, and hard-pressed factory worker.

The Conservatives agreed to extend free education from Scotland to England and Wales if denominational schools remained. Joe was of solid Unitarian background; his daughters had been to a progressive non-denominational high school, yet he saw the wisdom of compromise. Denominational schools were firmly entrenched; let them stay, and be free like the board schools. In local government, too, he saw progress, for the County Councils Act had passed in 1888, allowing centrally appointed justices of the peace to keep judicial functions, but granting their administrative ones to locally elected bodies.

Away from these ponderous considerations, Joe was lively and light-hearted. Mary was now at home in London, and he wanted her portrait done, as a lady of fashion, by Millais. She sat several times; Joe hovered round the result, and found it fine, except for the mouth. That he said was too much of a rosebud; he demanded that the artist "put a little more vice into it"![2]

Certainly Mary had had enough adventures recently to make her sparkle as she sat for her portrait. Their steamer trip along the Nile, though supervised by Thomas Cook, had had its wilder moments. Would she ever forget Neville, jogging along on a donkey, his long legs dangling to the ground! And then, in Nubia, she had had a try at dromedary-riding. The colonel of the garrison, who had been engaged in driving off dervishes from invading Egypt for years, found Mrs. Chamberlain an enchanting diversion. He offered her his mount, complete with padded sheepskin saddle; the others pitched about on less upholstered camels, and Mary stayed the course the longest. But it was diverting to see the soldiers, solemn-faced in Army uniform, pass by for review atop these sullen beasts.

Egypt, with the sunshine and sparkle of desert air, had been just the tonic to brace Mary for a second year in England. She was a diligent sight-seer, but had been glad of the English overtones to their visit. There was plum-pudding for Christmas dinner; and at Cairo, when the Khedive gave them dinner there was English food, English music, and their host conversed in English, too. What a contrast to the sheik's harem Mary had visited. The ladies were slovenly, dowdy, and distressingly affectionate. They had crowded round her; she had been afraid they were going to kiss her. She amazed the ladies when she told them her grey camel's hair dress had been her wedding gown. They marvelled she could get into it, being themselves arrayed in dark dressing gowns, grown sadly stouter on a diet of boredom and sweetmeats.

Mary had not been bored yet. She had, in fact, to hide her horror when, as a special privilege, she was taken to see a mummy unrolled. And then there was the native dinner, served so proudly to the Chamberlains by their host, Achmet Effendi, British Consul at Cairo. She was still aggrieved, and amused, months later, as she recalled the fifteen courses she had survived, eating with thumb, forefinger, and a bit of bread. She was guest of honor, so the communal spoon went first to her; she dipped from a huge central dish bits of sausage, rice, fruit, and spinach; even, with Neville twinkling at her across the way, and trying to make her laugh, tore away at a turkey to get a manageable bit of meat. Then, when they were finally through, what a relief to join in ceremonial hand-washing. And what ear-splitting squeaky sounds the native musicians made, as they played love songs to the Chamberlains. Thank goodness for brandy and biscuits, which revived them all when they returned to their own quarters!

Joe, whose gout persisted despite Egyptian sunshine, had stumped around, and brooded about the military future. The British could not think of getting out of Egypt for another generation; and he was inclined to agree with Kitchener that one day too the Sudan must be re-conquered. The Mahdi (or "guide"), preaching death to foreigners, had led his followers to overthrow Egyptian rulers; in 1885 he had also murdered General Gordon, former Governor of Sudan, at Khartoum. His successor had tried to carry on with invading Egypt, but was halted at the battle of Toski. In 1889 the Egyptians could not afford to battle the Sudanese, and the British did not want to. When Joe got back to England his speech on Egypt marked him as leader of the new Imperialism;[3] he had sifted out impressions as he strolled the sands, and heard about the howling of the dervishes.

What a far cry from desert sunshine, and herself decked out in camel-riding costume, to the exigencies of Mary's Court life. Joe thought she should go to another Drawing-Room, as the Queen had been so kind to them her first year. So Mary wrote back and forth to Worth about her dress: a confection of creamy satin brocade, with little vines of pink flowers and green leaves. It was an extravagance, but last year Worth had overcharged her for something, and this year, in settlement, Mary got him to reduce her dress's price from 2500 to 2100 francs.

Her dress-maker's bill was formidable; and Mary was trying to help the Chamberlain girls arrange their wardrobes, too. Beatrice had taught them to budget from their earliest years. She had taken to heart a maxim of her grandfather's, delivered after she once borrowed money from her nursemaid to buy candy. He paid her debt, but gravely informed her and Austen, "You never buy what you can't pay for." So there was Ida, finished school, and ready for parties, trying to figure how her new green ball-dress with pink hyacinths would fit into the budget, along with gifts to charity, and plans for a winter coat. Mary was glad she had never had to struggle with allowances.

And as for Joe—when it came to presents for his wife, he refused to budget at all. He had bought a satin bedspread in Egypt, and back at Highbury installed new bedroom light fittings, shaped like pink and blue lilies. Their bedroom was so light and flowery now; and then he would keep adding to her jewels. Mary now had a diamond spray which came apart to form a group of brooches, and even a diadem! He liked her to look pretty, and Mary, though worried about Joe's extravagance, flourished and enjoyed his presents thoroughly!

The best present of all was a family trip to America, for three whole months in the summer of 1890. The Chamberlains were delighted with Mary's house in Salem, so different from an English one: yellow clapboards and green shutters, set back only a few feet from the street, with a hall running from front door straight through to the garden. Visitors came each day, or they drove out to see Mary's friends and family. And there was the inevitable reporter, come to look closely at this international marriage. Mary smiled at him, and passed him along to her father, who was in a cheerful mood: "Yes, nobody knows a thing about these marriages except parents. It's the fathers that have to suffer! Yet, after all, our daughters leave us and it is not so far to England nowadays as it used to be to the Western Reserve. People felt that the young folks who went out there completely expatriated themselves. They said good-bye to them for life, and never expected to see them again this side of the grave. Ohio is next door, and England is not much farther now."[4]

For all this fine talk, Mary's father was enchanted to have her with him all those weeks; and Mary's mother was in the seventh heaven. She had been nervously polite about her son-in-law's coming: "Tell Mr. Chamberlain how great is our happiness that we are to have him under our roof."[5] When he arrived, he was so genial she forgot formality. And Beatrice was a real sister for Mary; the boys, though shy, were eager and intelligent. It was a wonderful reunion.

Joe, always full of restless energy, had made a trip to Montreal; when he returned, he had a new, exciting plan. Sir Ambrose Shea, Governor of the Bahamas, said there was a fortune to be made in sisal fibres. And so the boys were sent to the wilderness to investigate while Mary, Joe, and Beatrice went back to England. The Bahamas did seem wild, for Austen and Neville could only write fortnightly, and there was no cable laid, which seemed benighted for a British colony!

From dreams of sisal fortunes Joe was swept, on his return, away into the latest Irish crisis. Charles Stewart Parnell, the celebrated Irish nationalist, had since his election to Parliament in 1875 been fighting for Home Rule. The Irish had been making themselves a nuisance in the Commons ever since, "so that their British colleagues would be glad to get rid of them by granting them their demand."[6] In Ireland Parnell associated with a peasant agitator, Michael Davitt, who organized the "Land League" to fight for agrarian reforms. Gladstone's Land Acts did not satisfy the peasants, who turned violently on their landlords until martial law was declared in Ireland. Parnell was jailed at Kilmainham under the new coercion policy. And Joseph Chamberlain, then head of the Board of Trade, had been appointed by Gladstone chief negotiator with the Irish party. Acting as go-between, Captain O'Shea, a moderate Home Ruler, had negotiated Parnell's release in 1882.

Ironically, Mrs. O'Shea was well known as Parnell's mistress. The Captain was a man of vast ambition, who envisioned high office for himself, so he ignored the usual conventions in espousing Parnell's cause. The Captain depended on his wife's money; not until 1886, when Gladstone's Home Rule Bill failed, did he repudiate her lover. Then he clung to Chamberlain with the avowed intention to destroy Parnell. *The Times* published a letter purportedly by Parnell, condoning the Phoenix Park murders of 1882 (in which Lord Frederick Cavendish, newly appointed Irish Chief Secretary, and Mr. Burke, the Under-Secretary, were fatally stabbed). O'Shea thought Parnell was done for. The letter proved to be a forgery, and a Parliamentary Commission cleared Parnell. O'Shea, disappointed, then sued for divorce. His wife's rich aunt had died, leaving her sole heiress. The thought of continuing as her hanger-on he could not bear. It was an untidy business. The divorce had been granted only two days before the Chamberlains returned from America in 1890, and Parliament was in a furor.

At first, despite the scandal, it seemed the Irish Nationalists would retain Parnell as their leader. Then they fell into dispute and in the midst of it Parnell himself died. Home Rule had been dealt a severe blow—so much the better; but O'Shea's office-seeking and hope for influence had not yet ended. Mary had followed these affairs by letter during her engagement; she now watched admiringly while Joe dealt with O'Shea. Critics alleged he had paid off the Captain to bring the divorce suit, and destroy Parnell. There were always those who would shout Joe down, and the Irish would for several years to come break out with the cry of "Judas Chamberlain!" These things were the politician's lot, Mary discovered. Criticism must be ignored, or cleverly turned at the critic. Hangers-on must be discouraged, but diplomatically. Joe seemed unperturbed by all the complications, and returned to Highbury for Christmas full of confidence and energy.

Mary didn't think he ever took a real holiday; over that Christmas Joe made eleven speeches, a typical one to the Women's Liberal Unionist Institute. Here the ladies were packed in, some with squalling babies. Mary admired and approved of their interest, as long as they got no ideas of suffrage. She took up Joe's view here, as in most causes; he once declared he preferred Parnellites to Petti-coats!

Both the Chamberlains entered 1891 optimistically. Neville was despatched to Andros Island, and first reports of his sisal plantation were encouraging. Mary presented Ida and Hilda at Court in good style, and she and Joe went again to Windsor for a visit. They also visited Knole, home of the Sackville-Wests. Just before he left Washington Sir Lionel had succeeded as Lord Sackville; his estate was ample consolation for the loss of his career. There were 365 rooms in the house; Mary was most impressed by the Silver Room, furnished for James I with everything from fire irons to bed coverings made of the precious metal!

At Christmas-time Lord Hartington succeeded as Duke of Devonshire, and when he went to the House of Lords Joe became Liberal Unionist leader in the Commons. Though his selection was unanimous, there was unrest among many Conservatives. Joe's views were too radical for them: he favored old-age pensions, and accident compensation in industry. He had already insisted on free education. What next? Lord Hartington had drowsed away thirty-five years in the House of Commons. Joe, ever alert and aggressive, was an all-too-lively replacement.

In April, 1892, Austen joined his father in the House as Member for East Worcestershire, and the Chamberlain dinner-table became noisier than ever. Austen had discussed dogs, horses, and gardens eagerly enough with the girls before. Now he and Joe argued their common political cause in all its ups and downs; the girls listened raptly and broke in with ideas of their own, and questions. Mary, the arbiter and peace-maker, smiled as she sat among these earnest Chamberlains. It was not hard to see why Ethel, when smaller, used to bang her knife in frustration on the table until noticed: "Hush! little Ethel wants to speak!"

The Endicotts, arriving for a visit, thought Mary needed refreshment from the sound and fury of electioneering. So they swept her off to Paris with them, and she returned to the political battleground refreshed. Joe, though, would not let her go to all his meetings; for it was a furiously fought campaign. He tore into Home Rule, insisting that Ulster would rise to arms rather than submit to a Parliament at Dublin. There was a brief breathing-space when they went to Windsor. There was the great, grey castle, and the Queen within, gracious and welcoming. Her courtiers the Chamberlains found rather melancholy. Night after night found them sitting around the drawing-room. Mary and Joe, busy as they were, felt sorry for these ladies and gentlemen of the household, prisoners of etiquette, who longed each evening for the time when they could decently retire.

At the end of the election the Gladstonians and Irish Nationalists had a majority of forty over the Conservatives. And at eighty-three Gladstone became Prime Minister for the fourth time. He was burdened not only with age but the conflict of his colleagues. His Foreign Secretary, Lord Rosebery, was a convinced imperialist, far more in line with Salisbury's and Chamberlain's ideas than Gladstone's. Worse than this, in electioneering the Liberal Party had committed itself to a hopeless program of reforms. Though diehard Conservatives might distrust Joseph Chamberlain, he had at least brought many rich and powerful followers to their ranks when he broke with the Liberals in 1886. Gladstone was left with a fractious group of radicals whom he could ill direct.

Pledged to Home Rule, Gladstone summoned all his remaining rhetoric and entered in debate. Implacable as ever, his opponents returned his cannonades. In April, 1893, the Second Home Rule Bill was in its Second Reading, and there was a great row in the House. Joe said the Grand Old Man had accused him of inaccurate quotation; so next day he got up with the words he had quoted to prove their accuracy, whereupon Gladstone became enormously excited and could hardly restrain himself. "That is the chief indication of his age; he interrupts frequently and often to no purpose, and his irritation is intense if thwarted in any way."[7]

But Gladstone could also do his opponents honour. He recalled Austen Chamberlain's recently delivered maiden speech, turned towards Joe saying, " 'I will not enter into any elaborate eulogy . . . I will endeavour to sum up my opinion of it by simply saying that it was a speech which must have been dear and refreshing to a father's heart.' The words, the tone and the manner were all perfect . . . Joe is delighted, and when he tells me what people have said I see his eye glisten."[8]

After forty-seven evenings of debate, Mary went down to the House, feeling there was trouble brewing. She was not disappointed.

"About twenty minutes to ten Joe got up and from the moment he rose the Irish showed signs of excitement. From time to time he was interrupted; and then at the close he began 'Never since the days of Herod,' meaning to go on to say 'had men followed so blindly' but his voice was drowned by cries of 'Judas!' This continued for some minutes amid a perfect hubbub!"

There followed a thunderstorm of shouting; the Conservatives protesting the language, Radicals shouting back, then one Radical plumped himself down on the Front Opposition Bench, where he had no business to be, a Conservative member gave him a shove, and the fight was on. There was a shout from the Irish and soon there were "blows given in all directions, and faces livid with anger and passion . . . At once many peacemakers mingled with the throng, and soon succeeded in parting the combatants. Fortunately no one was seriously injured; but one's feeling of indignation and humiliation was great that the English House of Commons should sink to such a level.

"While it was going on Mr. Gladstone sat on the Treasury Bench, very pale and grave. I wondered what his sensations were, for one felt that the first responsibility rested with him. He has censured and repressed debate, and this was the outcome of the pent up passion of the Ulstermen and Irish . . .

"The Speaker's Gallery was filled with ladies, several of whose husbands were in the thick of the fray, but the wives behaved very well on the whole. I found a quiet word to one of my neighbours was necessary, but fortunately it was all over so quickly that they were soon re-assured. Beatrice said in the Ladies' Gallery where she was, some of the ladies screamed."[9]

Early that autumn Gladstone did get his bill through the Commons, but the House of Lords swiftly rejected it. He tried to ignore the defeat, but his control as Prime Minister was gone. A few months later, after disapproving an increase in naval spending, Gladstone resigned, giving as reasons his eighty-five years and failing senses. The appointment of Lord Rosebery as his successor was a decision for imperialism; but the Liberals were so divided on domestic issues that Rosebery's ministry was a troubled one.

A Royal wedding formed a pleasant contrast to political strife. Mary was delighted with the marriage of Princess May of Teck to George, Duke of York. The princess had been engaged to the Duke of Clarence; and his death a month before their wedding had shocked the Empire. Now she was marrying his younger brother, the heir apparent to the throne, and London was in a "happy ever after" mood. There were banners and flowers everywhere; flags waved, and thousands cheered. In the Chapel Royal at St. James Palace Mary, Joe, and the other guests had to wait an hour and a half before the Queen arrived, and eventually also the bride, followed by ten Princesses, her bridesmaids. Afterwards the Chamberlains went to Buckingham Palace; after another long wait they finally had lunch, and then the Lord Chamberlain said, rather unceremoniously, that it was all over, and they had better go home. To Mary's great indignation the Queen appeared after they had gone, and received the few remaining guests. She had been in England long enough now to take a proprietary view of Royalty. All ceremonial occasions, she felt, ought to be free from mistake.

In the autumn of 1893 Mary and Joe went to America, and spent happy days with the Endicotts at "the Farm" in Danvers, which Mrs. Endicott had inherited from her parents. Purchased by Joseph Peabody as a refuge for his family and possessions should they have to flee Salem in the War of 1812, the Farm was now in need of considerable renovation. Mary, who had always loved it, watched the re-modelling with enthusiasm, and Joe laid out two new gardens before setting out for the Bahamas to see Neville.

The Andros Fibre Company he found well established. Half of Neville's 7000 acres were under cultivation. With only one white foreman for company, he supervised hundreds of Negro workers. He had a profitable shop running to sell food, clothing, and trinkets. He was setting up a school and a bank, and was busy discouraging the liquor traffic. As the workers were in hand, and the plants growing well, Neville's father authorized new expenditures for a plantation railway and machinery to make the sisal fibre. Joe thought his prospects bright for recovering heavy losses he had suffered in South American stocks. He returned to America pleased with the venture, and with Neville's self-reliance.

Their stay at Danvers was cut short out of consideration for Mary's parents. Since the Phoenix Park murders Joe had been shadowed by detectives, protecting him from Irish assassins. He accepted these precautions as a necessary nuisance. For years the man who passed as Joe's valet was a private detective. So discreet was he that he invented stories of his time in Chamberlain's service to still suspicions in the servants' halls he visited. And he was so conscientious that, on duty in the shrubbery during Joe's infrequent games of tennis, he would scout for stray balls as well as assassins. Now upon the autumn peace of the Farm broke word of a plot against Chamberlain's life. Where was the victim? He could not be found. To the chagrin of several detectives he had slipped off to Boston by an early train, and came back quite happily when his work was done.

Joe and Mary strolled through the gardens and went to sit on a little bench, side by side. There they chatted and admired the sunset, at last wandered slowly home. Agitation again on the part of the detectives, who were searching the underbrush, and speaking of barbed wire barricades. All night they camped outside the house, a bonfire roaring to keep them warm and discourage intruders. Next day they found their man. He confessed he had been hiding in the bushes, waiting to shoot Mr. Chamberlain, but Mrs. Chamberlain had sat so closely beside his target that he dared not fire, fearing to hit her. Obviously they could not alarm the Endicotts further. Joe had a great contempt for plots against his life, but he would not endanger Mary, so they returned at once to England.[10]

When Gladstone's era quavered to a close, and Rosebery succeeded him, it was Joe's voice, as the leading Unionist, which dominated politics. Yet the alliance between Unionists and Conservatives was still uneasy. In the election of 1892 Lord Salisbury had counselled Joe to tread lightly on the subject of social legislation, so he had campaigned against Home Rule. In the next General Election the Liberals were bound to lose; a strong Coalition Government would be vital. Joe now called himself a Unionist, without Radical, Liberal, or Conservative prefix. He took as text for his speeches,

"Empire and social progress, and more national unity for the sake of both." Yet Salisbury, when Prime Minister, might slight the social progress. Joe wondered whether, in that case, he would want to be a Minister himself.

Mary was an ever-patient sounding-board for all that worried him. When they were at Highbury there were many pleasant things to distract Joe. They admired orchids, counted baby lambs, had tea at the dairy, and admired their little herd of cows. Pastoral pleasures had a rude setback when Austen had an encounter with a young Jersey bull. He took it out, and finding it hard to manage, tried to pen it up; it jerked away, Austen fell, and the bull rushed in and gored him in the thigh. Austen yelled for help, tried to grab the bull, and flailed around looking for his eyeglass. Without it he could hardly see. Finally he grabbed the ring in the bull's nose, and held him, angry and pawing, at bay. The gardener arrived, and the Member for East Worcestershire was borne away, fortunately not seriously wounded. They were all more wary of bulls in the future!

Both Mary and Joe begrudged the time they had to spend away from Highbury. One of the many political dinners they went to was given by the Duke and Duchess of York. Mary thought the Duke did his job well, but what a pity that the Duchess was so shy. Then they came to Birmingham for him to lay a cornerstone; and the Duke was miserable about the speech he had to make. He insisted on reading it, though Mary thought he ought to be able to manage with short notes. Though they hated to be away from home, Mary and Joe did enjoy these views of Royalty; on a visit to Windsor they met the Czarevitch, soon to become Nicholas II of Russia, and his fiancée, Princess Alix of Hesse.

There were gratifying tours through Durham, Leeds, and Liverpool; Mary blushed when an earnest man in the gallery at Liverpool shouted out, "It's all very well, I want three cheers for Mrs. Chamberlain! I *will* have three cheers for Mrs. Chamberlain—everyone else has their cheers!"[11]

In late autumn of 1894 the Endicotts came to England. There was a snowy Christmas at Highbury with blazing fires and a huge Christmas tree. But in the midst of these festivities Mary realized how much older her father had grown. She and Joe had to visit the

Duke of Devonshire and Lord Salisbury. There were conferences all round as Rosebery's government grew shakier, and they wondered what they would do if a new government were formed. As soon as they could manage it Mary and Joe took the Endicotts off to the Riviera. Joe soon had to get back to Parliament, but Mary stayed, daughter and nurse, for six weeks.

It was difficult all around. Mrs. Endicott had colds, aches, and pains. Distressingly, Mr. Endicott showed signs of the nervous depression he had suffered years before. One or the other of them was "poorly" or "wretched" nearly every day, and Mary felt they were gaining little from their holiday.

Back in Birmingham Joe had bleak intelligence from the Bahamas: Neville feared the sisal crop was failing. The winter's fogs and cold were the worst in living memory. Also a horrid housing development was to encroach upon Highbury. As for politics there were times when Joe thought seriously of abandoning them altogether. He was not at all sure he wanted to play second fiddle to Salisbury; and money worries were pressing hard: "If we were in ordinary circumstances it would not be difficult to cut down expenses, but I do not know how to retrench without giving up London altogether . . . I have largely assisted to make Home Rule impossible, and now there is nothing but personal ambition to keep me in harness . . . Should I not be acting rightly if I were to close my political life at this stage, and make room for Austen who has a future before him?"[12]

These were black reflections, but Mary was at least thankful Joe could indulge in them by letter. Before his marriage he had been subject to fits of gloom. Since then, he had always been able to talk out his troubles. It seemed now this crisis might engulf him entirely. She was relieved to be back by his side in March, for a pending by-election, in nearby Warwick and Leamington, threatened the whole Unionist alliance. The Tories wanted one of their own in the seat, to keep Chamberlain's influence from growing any stronger. Joe wrote to the Duke of Devonshire, threatening to leave public life, "If any considerable number of Conservatives believe that they are strong enough to stand alone . . . I am ready to be thrown aside."[13] His strategic sense told him the Gladstonians would delight in this rift, and might entrench themselves in the Midlands if he were not very careful. In this case care meant determination, sticking to his guns, and following the Chamberlain motto, "Je tiens ferme."

It worked. The Duke, Lord Salisbury, and Arthur Balfour came to Joe's defense, decried the Tory criticism, and saw that Warwick and Leamington stayed Unionist. Joe's dark mood altered. He had won his point and could afford to be generous. Now it only remained for Rosebery to fall.

Rather unexpectedly the crisis came on the 21st of June. The vote was to reduce the Secretary of War's, Mr. Campbell-Bannerman's, salary, as censure for maintaining low stocks of cordite. The reproach was petty, for this able man had just eased out the old Duke of Cambridge, Commander-in-Chief of the Army for almost forty years, with the least possible upset. Still, there it was, a seven-vote majority against the Government. Would this be the end? Mary wondered, when Joe brought the news home from the House. The Government had scraped by so often Mary had rather thought it would last out the year.

Still pondering, she and Joe went to spend Sunday with Lord and Lady Rayleigh at Terling Place. Balfour was there, too. It was hard to chat and be sociable with so much at stake. In the middle of the house-party arrived a messenger. Lord Rosebery had resigned, and Lord Salisbury was summoned as Prime Minister.

All was turmoil in Mary's mind that night. Joe would surely take office. Ahead of her lay many unknown duties. And for him the wheel had turned full circle. He had been Gladstone's heir until the split, and years of opposition came. Gladstone, in old age and defeat, had been more than kind. Mary and Joe had been at an al fresco luncheon with the Gladstones; they had walked and talked most pleasantly, with no sense of strain. And Gladstone had labelled Joe the most remarkable man of his generation.[14] Now his hour had come, and Joe's prediction of years before was coming true. There was work to be done in the colonies, and as Colonial Secretary he would do it.

CHAPTER IX

"To Visit the Queen"

EARLY in the morning of June 24, 1895, Joseph Chamberlain and Arthur Balfour went up to London, where they conferred all day with Lord Salisbury and the Duke of Devonshire. Salisbury planned to combine the office of Foreign Secretary with Prime Minister, as he had before. The Duke would be President of the Council and President of the Council of Defence; Mr. Balfour First Lord of the Treasury and Leader of the House of Commons; and Joseph Chamberlain Secretary of State for the Colonies. Things were settled in such friendly fashion that it was hard for Mary to realize how recently Joe had been cast in depression, ready to forswear politics forever. Outsiders wondered why he had not chosen the War Office, or the Exchequer, which at that time carried more prestige. Mary and his children, knowing Joe's dream of a federated empire, understood. As theirs was a minority ministry Salisbury pressed for immediate dissolution of Parliament and a General Election.

The whole Chamberlain family was wildly excited. Mary realized at once she had entered on a new life in England. Their first public appearance, at a Dominion Day reception, gave her some idea of what things would be like. Joe was immediately mobbed, and would stand talking in the only passage between the rooms. Mary tried to extract him, and get him where the admiring crowds could have some room, but he didn't understand what she was trying to do, and stuck steadily where he was.

With no promptings on Joe's part, but to his great delight, Austen had been appointed Civil Lord of the Admiralty. This made two statesmen anxious about their constituencies to stride among the shrubs at Highbury. Neville, back on holiday from the Bahamas, provided badly needed comic relief with his tales of plantation life.

Hearty laughs were in short supply just then, for a rebellious Conservative group tried to place its own candidate in Central Birmingham. Joe held firm: the seat was Unionist and must remain so. The quarrel might spread to East Birmingham, where the Conservative candidate depended entirely on Unionist support. Once divided, the Liberals would rush in and triumph. Fortunately, the unwanted candidate withdrew, and Joe turned back to notes and speeches.

Mary somehow managed to run the household, give the girls her apparently unhurried attention, and yet be always waiting by the garden door for her menfolk. Joe strode out, then Austen; and Mary was always there to waylay them, walk them round and round, and hear their troubles out. Neville was ready to make speeches for them, and Mary hoped they would use him; she had a shrewd idea Neville would finish as a politician, and not a planter. Since his speeches would not be reported, why shouldn't he get started in this campaign?

Neville did just that at Newcastle-under-Lyme, addressing a restless crowd of eight hundred, who were feeling the heat and had been shouting "Time!" at the previous speaker. In the middle of Neville's speech he said, "If you will bear with me a little longer," and a voice cried out, "Go on, go on, we'll stay with you all night if you like."[1] A few days later the seat in question went to the Unionists.

The Unionist triumph everywhere was staggering. Sir William Harcourt, Gladstone's devoted colleague (and Joe's, too, before the split) was turned out of a seat in Derby he had held for fifteen years; the Unionists had not dreamed of winning there. Knowing what the defeat meant to Sir William, Joe was sympathetic, and sat down at once to write him about it. As for his own progress, it was triumphant. His opponent, a Dr. O'Connor, was greeted at a meeting by crowds singing "Go Back to Erin, Mavourneen, my darling"; they refused to listen to his speech.

When the returns were in Joe had a majority of 4278, and Austen was unopposed. Joe's brother-in-law, William Kenrick, and his other Birmingham colleagues, Jesse Collings and Powell Williams, had large majorities also. Elsewhere in the Midlands the Unionists won seats at Coventry, Stoke, and Newcastle-under-Lyme.

Though Joe had all sorts of papers and accounts left in arrears because of the Election, he and Mary had a few pleasant dallying days. They slept late, walked round the gardens, and sat over coffee in the conservatory. Just before Parliament was to open the Queen summoned Joe to Osborne. It was a long, hot journey, and Mary grumbled a bit that he had to go; but when he returned she was glad to hear about his meeting with the Kaiser. That personage displayed the Royal memory; recalling their luncheon in 1889, he said when introduced, "Oh, I know Mr. Chamberlain, I was introduced to him at Hatfield. Why, where is your orchid?"[2]

The Colonial Office, which had hitherto been rather obsolete and muddled, found itself swept by a vigorous new broom. All maps and reports were to be up-to-date; decades of dusty records disappeared. Joe was responsible for about fifty million people, occupying one-fifth of the globe. There were the Crown colonies and dependencies, and then eleven self-governing colonies to administer (the Dominion of Canada, Newfoundland, six Australian colonies, New Zealand, the Cape, and Natal; India came under a separate ministry). Joe was alert to all their problems. From his years in business he had learned how to delegate; yet he never lost touch, and was always inquiring. His staff dubbed him "the Chief" and set to work energetically. Mary felt they had never had such a hard worker. Joe had four secretaries, and as far as Mary could see they were all of them always busy.

In hopes of a short summer session, the House of Commons suspended its twelve o'clock rule. Now Joe and Austen might leave Prince's Gardens about noon and not return until two in the morning. When the session was done Mary insisted on a proper holiday, taking no heed of Joe's objections. He could call her all the names he liked, he could tell her it was wicked to go when he had so much work; but Mary only smiled and went on with her plans. Joe grumbled and gave in. He wrote to the Queen, asking approval to spend six or seven weeks abroad for his health. The Queen cabled back that of course he must go, and the Chamberlains set off for the Pyrenees, pursued to the last by messengers with despatch boxes. They would never be more than three days from England in their travels, but would get a rest and change of scene impossible at home.

Austen and Neville were full of high spirits, and the family went about sight-seeing, sketching, and eating prodigiously. The only trouble was the flies: Neville, with a fine attention to detail, sat opposite Mary one afternoon while she wrote and counted fourteen of them on her!

In October the Chamberlains went to Spain, where the English Ambassador arranged to present them at Court. Maria Christina, the Queen Regent, was having her troubles with Cuba just then; and was interested to learn how Crown Ministers, and especially, the Colonial Secretary, worked in England.

On the appointed day the Chamberlains were driven to a large house, set rather like one in Newport on a lawn sloping down to cliffs, with a fine sea view. Settled in the reception hall, they soon heard children's laughter, and a scuffling of feet. Presently, bobbing curiously over the banister, appeared the fair head of the nine-year-old Alphonso XIII. His two older sisters, pigtails flying, rushed off upstairs with him. Soon others arrived for the audience, and Mary and Joe had their talk with the Queen Regent.

Maria Christina was astonished how seldom English ministers saw their Queen. She herself had to see one of her Ministers every day: they went over their work in detail, and told her what was to be done. Then once a week she had to meet with all the Ministers together. This sounded complex and tedious, but the Chamberlains were much impressed with the Queen Regent. Everyone they spoke to mentioned her strength of character and good sense.

From San Sebastian the Chamberlains went to Burgos to see the Cathedral, then on to Madrid, when after a trip to the Prado to see the pictures, they decided on a bullfight. To Mary's surprise her maid, Curtis, and Joe's valet, Seaton, both very prim and proper, asked if they might go, too. After the first bull had been despatched Joe and Austen had had quite enough. It was a disgusting sight, and their curiosity was more than satisfied. The maid and valet were made of stouter stuff, and lasted through the second bull. He was even more ferocious; after he was killed, the slaughter and the shouting overcame them. Curtis shuddered to Mary, "Oh, I can't think or speak of it, ma'am," while Seaton assured his master, "It was the most 'orrible sight I ever see in my life, sir."

Once on the Baedeker circuit again, the party's spirits lifted.

Mary was enthralled by the vast and sombre Escorial. Toledo, seen on a sunny day, was brilliant and beautiful. They went through a great many picture galleries; but when they got to Granada planned a social call on the English Vice-Consul. This was ill-advised; to their dismay, the Chamberlains found a party full of Spaniards there before them, conversing in their native tongue! Mary found this exhausting. It was much more to her taste when they boarded a British torpedo boat at Algeciras and were whisked to Gibraltar in twelve minutes flat. Their reception there by the Governor and his lady was entirely predictable. They toured a cork factory and the cathedral, rode donkeys to the top of the Rock, and went through a hospital. Then, regretfully, they turned to home.

Mary had enjoyed this first tour as a Minister's wife. It was pleasant also to find at home that people thought Joe was the right man for his job. Official entertaining soon came her way. Joe had been conferring with the Bechuana Chiefs about their territorial rights. South Africa seemed to Mary a sort of hornet's nest, filled with different claims and interests, and very hard to deal with. Joe was to have a gentlemen's dinner, after which Mary would have a reception for them in the drawing-room. There were three chiefs, with attendant minor chiefs, and some missionary-interpreters. As they couldn't speak English, Mary decided to have a conjuror to entertain them.

Both conferences and conjuror were a success. "The Chiefs have given Joe a name, 'Moatlodi', the man who rights things. He has had a great success and (between ourselves) is the one person in the Cabinet of whom the papers are full . . . it is quite a new sensation for him. He is very well, busy as the day is long, and in excellent spirits—many fewer headaches than before."[3]

In taking office Joe meant to try to draw Great Britain closer to her self-governing colonies, and to develop the resources of the Crown Colonies. Though mainly concerned with trade and government, another of his strong interests was in tropical medicine. Mary soon got involved in this field. She had always fretted that Neville might fall ill in Andros, without proper medical care. So when Lady Piggott, wife of a colonial official in Mauritius, came calling with a scheme of sending nurses to the colonies, Mary was most receptive.

Joe agreed to Mary's joining the executive committee of the Colonial Nursing Association, and over the next three years, though she
loathed begging for money, Mary helped collect most of the £5000
needed to get the group organized.

A pleasant diversion was a weekend with the Prince and Princess
of Wales at Sandringham. They walked over to York Cottage to see
the baby Prince Edward. He grasped his grandmother's hand, and
toddled round, curtseying to the company. Mary was delighted
with his sociability, for she still found his mother, Princess May, so
shy it was hard to get a word out of her. As for York Cottage (so
overcrowded in later years with Royal children and their attendants
that George V remarked he supposed the servants must sleep in the
trees) Mary thought it "all very small and unpretending".[4]

Princess Alexandra, having shown off her grandson, then gave
her guests the traditional tour of her kennels. Here the dogs jumped
up and down for crusts of bread she had brought them; at the stables the Royal horses were given carrots. After all this hiking about
the guests returned to the house and ate heartily themselves, only
to find on departure they must list not only names but weights in
the guest book. Mary was glad she and Joe had been travelling, for
they always lost weight then. They solemnly took their turns on the
scales: Joe emerged at 156, Mary at 123½ pounds!

Several weeks later they were bidden to Windsor, where Mary
talked with Leopold, King of the Belgians. She did not inquire
about that monarch's exploitation of the Congo, nor about the talks
he must have had with Joe. What mattered to her was one powerful man's judgement of another. "Your husband," said Leopold,
"is a great man."[5]

Mary never doubted this, but seldom had Joe to herself to tell
him so. One winter evening they did have a quiet tête-à-tête dinner
at Prince's Gardens. Afterwards Mary sat while Joe puffed on his
cigar, and they discussed all the changes of the past year. Had she
not been right, asked Mary, not to go along with his gloomy views
last spring? Now look at him, handling the job he had spoken of so
long, and performing it so well. They smiled at an admiring letter
from a converted Tory, who had heard Joe speak on Empire: "One
had almost begun to despair of ever getting a real leader again.

They only run about one to a century. I suppose Pitt was our last and I think on the whole you are greater than Pitt . . . your ideas practically govern England, and as England still comes first among the nations it seems as if that rate you must be almost the most important human being present in our globe." What, Mary wondered, would Mrs. Gladstone say if she could read that!⁶

Such a pleasant domestic scene was not soon to recur, for in a few days Joe was deep in the Venezuela crisis. There had been boundary disputes for years between British Guiana and neighboring Venezuela. Now the United States was sabre-rattling, and Cleveland's Secretary of State, Richard Olney, had declared that the United States was "practically sovereign" upon the American continent. Any attempt by the British to enforce their territorial claims, except by arbitration, might justify the United States in going to war. As an extension of the Monroe Doctrine, Olney's statement was peremptory, and threatened to stir up anti-British feeling to fever pitch. In taking up Venezuela's cause against "foreign colonization" President Cleveland loosed a storm of criticism.

Mary was furious. "What has come to the President? It seems to me almost inconceivable that he should have been in his right mind when he sent that message to Congress about the Venezuela dispute [on December 18, 1895] . . . While the Monroe Doctrine is a policy so important to American interests that all other Powers would agree in her right to maintain it . . . this dispute does not come within its limits . . . This is . . . over a boundary and land which has been in actual occupation by the English for years . . . There is absolutely no question of acquiring new territory . . . Think of how terrible it would be for America and England to go to war about a boundary line in Venezuela!!! And yet how can England be dictated to . . . the position has been made almost intolerable for her . . . I feel that if [my own and my adopted country] were to come into conflict it would be a crime against the civilized world."⁷

Fanny Mason wrote in similar vein. "Has Mr. Cleveland taken leave of his senses? I think the childishness, discourtesy, and sinfulness of his action is inconceivable."⁸ Mary was so aroused she could hardly speak to Joe about the crisis. He, having been in America, and keeping in such close touch by letter, realized the subject must be handled with great care. There must be arbitration, but in calming American passions he must not, as Colonial Secretary, betray the interests of British settlers in Guiana.

Joe recalled a pleasant meeting he had had two years earlier in America with Mr. Olney. In Cabinet meetings he urged moderation. Though the British press was not so agitated as the American, it would be all too easy to drift into war. Presently Lord Salisbury authorized him to negotiate with the American Ambassador, Mr. Bayard, using Lord Playfair (an eminent scientist, whose American wife was a friend of Mary's) as intermediary. Letters went back and forth, achieving little, but in the meantime tempers had cooled.

In the summer of 1896 Joe resolved to try some personal diplomacy. When he and Mary visited the Farm he brought authority to meet with Olney in Boston. Their first meeting was a draw: Olney was aggressive, and not disposed to compromise. After a week he had thawed somewhat. Joe had been reasonable and polite, but firm. His persuasions had good effect. All Guiana territory continuously occupied by the British for a long time was to be exempt from arbitration. When Joe reported this decision to Lord Salisbury, the British Minister at Washington was authorized to continue discussions.

Though final settlement was not reached until 1899, as far as Joe was concerned it was his chats in Boston with Olney that had turned the trick. All through the crisis Mary was impressed with Joe's coolness and thoroughness. She had seen his diplomacy in Washington, but since then Joe had learned a great deal more about America. Mary's own feelings about the need for Anglo-American harmony could not help rubbing off on Joe. Here for the first time Mary could see the undoubted political result of her marriage with him.[9]

Affairs in South Africa were not so readily settled. Cecil Rhodes, Prime Minister of the Cape Colony, was also head of the Chartered Company, and as such held sway over vast portions of South Africa. He wanted to develop a railway from the Cape to Cairo. Though Joe's imagination was fired by this, he would not be hurried into making the arrangements. It meant ceding a portion of Bechuanaland, adjacent to the Transvaal frontier. The Bechuana Chiefs were

most urgent in their anxiety to be independent of the Chartered
Company's influence. They conferred nervously while Joe was in
Spain. On his return he gave Rhodes 100,000 square miles of terri-
tory, the balance remaining as the Protectorate of Bechuanaland.
Thus Joe became the "Man who Rights Things" to the Chiefs, but
Rhodes was by no means satisfied.

Rhodes was free to develop the railway north from Mafeking, on
the Transvaal border, to Bulawayo, in Matabeleland (part of Southern Rhodesia). Yet with a fascinated colleague, Dr. Leander Starr
Jameson, administrator of Rhodesia, he dreamed now of far more
than railway-building. The Boers, Dutch farmers, had trekked away
from the British Cape Colony in the 1830's, and set up the Republic of Natal. When this, too, came under British influence, they
moved on to set up the South African Republic, or Transvaal. Other
Boer trekkers had settled the neighbouring Orange Free State, which
was established as independent of the British in 1854. Things were
less simple in the Transvaal. It was placed under the Crown in
1877, after which followed five years of warfare between British and
Boer. After the defeat of the British at Majuba in 1881, the Gladstone government rather ignominiously faced facts and ceded the
Transvaal once more to the Boers. Paul Kruger became President
of the new Republic, whose boundaries and obligations to the British were fixed at the London Convention of 1884. A staunch old
patriarch, Kruger wanted to build a homeland completely Dutch in
spirit and completely free from British influence.

Kruger's problems began with the discovery of gold in the Witwatersrand, a section of the Transvaal. Thousands of Europeans,
Americans, and South Africans from the Cape, Natal, and Orange
Free State, poured in to prospect. Land values rose, and from the
new prosperity grew, in 1886, the city of Johannesburg. To all the
"uitlanders" Kruger, ever fearful of British supremacy, refused
the vote. They were, although they owned much of the land, and
paid most of the taxes, in no better position than the natives. Kruger, ever wily, devised a series of franchise qualifications which his
Raad (parliament) passed into law. Each was more complex than
the last. Piet Joubert, a Reform candidate who would have extended the franchise, was narrowly defeated in 1893. Kruger hung

grimly onto office, ignoring demands for reform, and making friendly noises to Germany, whose colonial interests in Africa he supported over England's. The time was ripe when Rhodes and Dr. Jameson made their master plan.

A last attempt would be made to wring concessions from Kruger peaceably. Then Jameson with a band of eight hundred (hopefully: even including the disbanded Bechuanaland Border Police in their numbers, the Chartered Company's forces never passed five hundred) would march upon the Transvaal. Simultaneously Johannesburg would rise in revolt. The weeks went by, and the plan was whittled down. It was hard to distribute smuggled arms among the insurgents. Also reform leaders in Johannesburg suspected (with justice) that Rhodes would conduct the whole show flying the imperial flag, while they sought independence for their country. There were quarrels, delays, and changes of plan.

The Colonial Office was alive to the possibility of civil war in the Transvaal. Chamberlain expected an uprising in Johannesburg. When trouble came, the High Commissioner would go to Pretoria, and with the aid of Jameson's police and British troops, if needed, would maintain order while Boers and Uitlanders together elected a Constituent Assembly, and set up a new government. Chamberlain did not bargain on two things: the quixotic nature of Dr. Jameson, and the ineffectiveness of his aged High Commissioner, Sir Hercules Robinson.

By Christmas so much disagreement had arisen in Johannesburg that a postponement of the uprising seemed advisable. Chamberlain had word that the revolt was fizzling out, and on December 29th so advised Lord Salisbury. The same day came word that Jameson might march in with Company forces, and start the revolution. It seemed improbable, but an admonitory telegram went from Highbury to Sir Hercules. Rhodes must be warned against any such raid. Before the telegram arrived, Dr. Jameson, tired of waiting about, started the raid on his own accord. He had a wild confidence in his mission. Messengers from the Reform Committee in Johannesburg could not stop him. Jameson had obtained a letter, signed by the five chief reform leaders, pleading for the relief of unarmed British men, women, and children at the mercy of the Boers. This was his

justification. He did not care that with the revolt called off, his letter was spurious; he charged ahead anyway.

  First word of the raid reached Highbury on December 30th. Sir
Hercules had despatched a rider to try to stop Jameson, but it was
too late. Joe at once determined to go up to town; he declared, "If
this thing succeeds, it will ruin me."[10] He insisted that dinner, and
the Highbury Servants' Ball go on as scheduled; somehow he got
through the evening and then went to the train. Mary stayed behind, anxious and troubled. She telegraphed ahead to Prince's Gardens, so fires would be lit, and Joe's room made ready; for Joe's
journey did not end till four a.m. and she worried that he might
take cold.

  Mary, so close to the trouble, could not at once grasp its signifi-
cance. She just supposed that a whirlwind in any one of the colonies
would snatch Joe away from whatever he was doing, and that she
must get used to it. By New Year's Day her indignation against
Rhodes had mounted. She wrote that he was "a very headstrong
person, and I doubt whether he has yet grasped that there is some
one now at the head of the Colonial Office whose will is as strong as
his own, and who is not to be trifled with. But he will find out if the
disturbance his people are making continues."

  As soon as she could Mary joined Joe in town. Clearly this was
no tempest in a teapot. Jameson by his filibustering expedition had
seriously hurt the chances of winning reforms from the Transvaal
Government. His forces were surrounded and captured on January
2, 1896. Joe had at once telegraphed repudiating the raid, both to
Kruger and to Rhodes, via Sir Hercules. Before the news came of
Jameson's defeat, his "women and children" letter had been cabled
to *The Times* in London, with the date December 28th added, and
for the next day and a half Jameson was a national hero, Joe a vil-
lain. Then came the dénouement, and the scales tipped in the other
direction.

  Mary, camping out in Prince's Gardens with Joe, rather thrived
on the air of siege and excitement. Messengers came and went
around the clock. Joe, confident he was doing the right thing, was
equal to everything. The German Emperor congratulated Kruger
by telegram on Jameson's defeat; this made the third major crisis in

a month. First Venezuela, and the Olney ultimatum; then trouble in the Transvaal; now thinly veiled threats from Germany. The three together might cripple British prestige. Mary marvelled at her husband's firm handling of each: "It is more certain than ever that Joe's prompt action in trying to stop the expedition was the only course for the government and his public repudiation of Jameson made at once has rendered it impossible for other nations seriously to bring the charge of complicity against the Imperial Government. They would have been all ready to do this, as one can see by the insinuations in some of the continental papers. The German Emperor has been putting his finger in the pie . . . and England is ringing with indignation. Six warships have been put into commission at once, so perhaps he will see that his telegram to Kruger has stirred up a hornet's nest, and if he does not take care he will be stung. This nation is in no temper to sit down under . . . interference with her suzerain rights.

". . . The Jingo papers (*The Times* among them) are all prepared to support Jameson in his filibustering raid, and almost denounced Joe for condemning his infringement of the law before particulars were to be had. Now that Jameson has been defeated they are supporting Joe's policy, but if he had won I really think they would have turned on Joe altogether . . .

"Now Joe is receiving the support of all parties, and I heard in London that there is but one voice, that of approval. My own opinion is that had it turned out to be a successful expedition many would have been found to dissent. Still, the absolute ignorance of the expedition on the part of the Government, and its disapproval of it were so promptly expressed that no member of it could have been accused of aiding and abetting such an affair—even though it was done by Englishmen."[11]

Mary was more of a prophet than she realized. For the moment Joe was the man of the hour, but in the tense days while the world waited to hear of Jameson's fate, his feeling that he had done right to denounce the raid was pretty cold comfort. Joe went down with a fierce headache, which lasted until a new call to action came.

After the Kruger telegram, it was agreed there must be an inquiry into the raid. The conspirators must be promptly dealt with.

Joe felt that such action would take care of not only the German menace, but President Kruger. Sir Hercules Robinson went to Pretoria. There, age and ill health, plus a stubborn determination to paddle his own canoe (he had been appointed in the Liberal administration, and had little use for the new Colonial Secretary) made him yield to Kruger's demands, and hurry nervously back to Cape Town. He did not even look in on Jameson and his men, now in Pretoria Jail, and soon to be shipped home for questioning. And he agreed, in the face of what Kruger assured him was the mounting ire of the Boers, that Johannesburg should be disarmed before any discussion of reforms even began. Meanwhile Kruger cleverly rounded up the Johannesburg Reform Committee, sixty-four strong, and consigned these wealthy and voluble citizens to the filth and squalor of jail.

Great was the wrath and confusion then. Mary naturally preferred to write home about the scenes which favoured Joe. He had simply been himself in this crisis, strong and masterful. Ugly talk about the Colonial Office being party to the raid ahead of time distressed Mary; but Joe's firm, business-like manner in the Transvaal debate quelled even the jeers of the Irish. He spoke for an hour and a half; Mary was there, listening as raptly as anyone in the House.

Early in February Rhodes arrived in England. Joe interviewed him at length, and declared he thought him ignorant of Jameson's precipitate flight. He urged his colleagues to remember the real services he had performed for South Africa. Rhodes was no longer Prime Minister, and the British South Africa Company, though keeping its Charter, would be disarmed. Joe's speech was generous to Rhodes; so Mary was all the more indignant at rumour-mongers who raised the spectre of complicity. She felt the inquiry would be a relief. Refusing to brood on Joe's enemies, Mary smiled at his friends, and proceeded calmly in her role of Minister's wife.

She had to ask all the Agents General of the colonies to separate dinner parties that spring; and Mary was especially glad to escape to Highbury, where with Hilda she succumbed to a new and popular enthusiasm—bicycling. Joe had no such relaxation. He had finally agreed, as a birthday present for Mary, to let Sargent paint his portrait. The only time he could sit was on Sunday mornings.

Weeks went by and still it was not done. What to do? Mr. Sargent wanted to exhibit the portrait at the Academy. The Chamberlains were just leaving for Highbury. Joe would not and could not manage another sitting in town. Mary could not and would not let the picture go as it was. Mr. Sargent was almost distracted. Then Mary had a happy thought. Why shouldn't the artist come to Highbury, too? So presently he appeared with the huge canvas, a studio was improvised in the drawing-room, and all the Chamberlains passed an agitating day.

Mary fussed over the orchid to be painted in Joe's buttonhole; then she wondered if Mr. Sargent could manage his mouth properly. Poor Joe was like a lamb led to the slaughter. The whole thing was a "confounded nuisance", but it was for Mary, and it had to be right. Mary thought a portrait was almost as bad as a lottery. Still, the pose Sargent had was excellent. Joe stood by a mahogany writing table, his right hand resting on a pile of papers (the latest bulletins about the Jameson Raid, actually) while a Colonial Office box was in the shadows behind. His left hand was at his side, half-closed. His head was three-quarters facing, the eyeglass in place, of course. When the mouth was done Mary thought Joe looked just ready to speak or smile; her fond eye discerned "a happy combination of strength and tenderness . . . altogether it is the portrait of a gentleman."[12] Joe was scornful, and heaped disparagement upon the result. Mr. Sargent packed up with sighs of relief, and took the finished work back to town.

Sometimes life went along pretty soberly when Parliament was in session. But there was one entertaining evening when Mary came in the house with a new footman, and he closed the door after her. She did not wait up for Joe and Austen; when she was half-asleep at two-thirty she heard a great shaking and banging and what sounded like a bell. She tried to doze off, but then realized the footman must have bolted the door. There were her lord and his son on the wrong side of it. Snatching up a dressing gown, she hurried down two flights of stairs, with her hair streaming round her shoulders. The doorbell rang and rang, the pounding continued. In vain she shouted, "I'm coming!" The door was firmly bolted, and just as she got it open, and her aggrieved menfolk burst into the hall, spluttering and exclaiming, Joe's valet arrived, in nightshirt and over-coat, looking scared to death. Giggling at him, and at the expression on Joe's and Austen's faces, Mary suddenly realized how she must look, and dashed away upstairs. The gentlemen followed. Now they were safely in, they granted the humour of the scene, and the Chamberlains went to bed in higher spirits than usual.

Joe was honorary President of the Chambers of Commerce of the Empire; and on June 13th, 1896, he and Mary gave an enormous reception welcoming their London Congress. Some 2800 delegates, with wives, sisters, cousins, and aunts, turned up for the party at the Imperial Institute. Mary, radiant in apricot satin, stood with Joe by the staircase shaking hands. She did wish her mouth would not get so stuck. It was frozen in a smile, and she had to keep turning to chat with one of the office secretaries to keep it working for the crowds. After an hour the Prince of Wales appeared, and the Chamberlains led him to a room where the Duke and Duchess of York, and the Duke and Duchess of Teck (Princess May's parents) were waiting. Then they emerged in full procession into the Hall, to curtseys, bows, and clapping. They strolled out to an enclosure in the garden, Japanese lanterns flickered, the Monte Carlo Orchestra played, and a pleasant supper was served to the Royalties. For this there was a certain amount of jostling.

"Mrs. Bayard was the only ambassadress there, and the Duke of Teck was enchanted when he thought he was going to take her to supper, for then he could go in before the Ambassadors, which is the end and object of his life. Great therefore was the blow when the Duke of Cambridge arrived [the ex-Commander-in-Chief was older brother to the Duchess of Teck, and the Queen's first cousin] and he had to give her up—and put up with a plain Countess *behind* the Ambassadors. Then there was a time because no ladies could be found of high enough rank for the Ambassadors (American and Turkish) and Beatrice and Ida were sent for in hot haste—for as hostesses they outranked everybody, and a war with Turkey could thereby be averted . . .

"Some funny scenes took place outside the [supper-room] door, where the secretaries had to be posted in force . . . One gentleman *insisted* on going in, he said he had arrived in England three days before, and he and the ladies had travelled 3000 miles (from Canada) to see the Prince of Wales. They and he had as good a right as anybody else to sit next the Prince of Wales, and what was more they were going to do it."[13]

Mary was thankful when this elaborate and tiring occasion was over. Soon after Joe received a great honor, when Oxford granted him an honorary degree. When his mood grew dark, Mary would remind her husband of bright occasions like that one. He had now realized the bitter truth about the Bahamas plantation. The crop was stunted, and sisal buyers would not accept Neville's crop. £50,000 had been invested in the enterprise; it was time now to acknowledge its loss and carry on. Neville came home, understandably discouraged, but Joe was a wonder. He made the best of things, and settled promptly with the Andros Fibre Company's creditors. Mary, knowing how miserable he was, took Neville firmly in tow, and made him take his sisters to dances and receptions. Though he protested, he was glad of the diversion. The rest of the family took the financial reverse very well. The girls stretched their dress allowances, and asked for no extravagances. Some charitable requests had to be turned down, and the maintaining of two houses became a steady drain on capital. At least, reflected Mary, they were all in health.

Their visit to America that autumn was a needed refreshment for both Mary and Joe. Though her parents seemed much older, Mary was thrilled to be with them quietly at the Farm. And Joe had the satisfaction of talking with Mr. Olney, getting through more than they had managed in months of correspondence. Both embarked for England with the sense of a job well done. Mary agreed with her mother that they should winter in Boston, as so many of their friends did. They rented a handsome and comfortable house at 163 Marlborough Street with ample room for William and Louise, back from four years in Washington. There Mother could have friends in for meals, tea, or to spend the night, and Papa could join them or not, as he chose. It was hard to leave, but Mary resolved to write as cheerfully and often as she could. Though her father's memory was nearly gone, he still liked to hear about his little girl, grown up and going out to parties.

The biggest party of Queen Victoria's sixty-year reign was about to begin. In afteryears the enquiries of the South African Committee, and mounting unrest in the Transvaal were matters of scholarly concern. What the world recalled of 1897 was a mighty Empire's display: the Diamond Jubilee.

CHAPTER X

"To Thy Jubilee Throng"

EVEN when Joe did manage to get home for dinner, messengers from the office generally pursued him with despatch boxes. Besides the time he spent in the House, he also had to give six hours a week to the hearings of the South African Committee. Mary tried to get him to relax, but in the winter of 1897 Joe had one attack of gout after another.

One of his most pressing problems was to replace old Sir Hercules Robinson. The post of High Commissioner and Governor of the Cape Colony was a thankless one. For it Joe finally chose Alfred Milner, head of the Inland Revenue Board, forty-three years old, and a highly sensitive and intellectual man. The uitlanders, still without the franchise, considered that the Colonial Office had abandoned them. The rest of the world suspected Great Britain of wanting to annex the Transvaal outright. Joe said optimistically that Milner must reconcile "to live together in peace and goodwill two races whose common interests are immeasurably greater than any differences which may unfortunately exist."[1] The differences were there, all right, and it was plain that no matter how much the British hoped to live amicably with the Dutch, the Dutch wished to be free of all British influence. Mary tried to take as much of the burden off Joe as she could by helping him with other Colonial Office affairs.

Joe and Lord Salisbury together had dreamed up the idea of a conference of Colonial Premiers held in Jubilee surroundings. Ceremonies and festivals should put the Premiers in a good mood for talking business. Each Premier was to bring troops to march in honour of the Queen. Each Premier would be sworn in as a Privy Councillor (happy and flattering notion!) and sumptuously entertained. Then they might all sit down and work over the idea of commercial union. Joe would also broach the idea of imperial defence, and the colonies' contribution to it. He would test their views on a federated empire. When all eleven Premiers had accepted, Mary had to plan parties for them.

Poor Joe! He did dislike large parties, and Mary tried to mention this one as little as possible, coming as it did only a year after their huge Chambers of Commerce reception. With the Colonial Office secretaries in tow she struggled round to find a house for the party. Scandalous rents were being asked. It seemed that anyone whose house lay along the route of the Jubilee Procession was out to make a fortune. At last, for 150 guineas, she settled on an empty and discouragingly dirty house in Piccadilly. With furniture, tapestries, and lots of flowers it should just do. But the guest list was formidable, and Royalty added the usual complications. The Duke and Duchess of York would dine with the Premiers before the Reception, but the Prince and Princess of Wales would not come till later, so a midnight supper must also be planned. Appalling thought!

A trip to Paris was pleasant relaxation from these concerns, and gave M. Worth a chance to support Mary in the Jubilee festivities. The most elaborate party she would go to besides their own was the Duchess of Devonshire's fancy dress ball. For this ladies all over London were poring over old books, ransacking their closets, and trying to out-do each other. Mrs. Endicott, worrying that Mary would be ruined by her dressmaker's bill that season wrote and offered to buy her a Puritan costume, so she and Joe could go as Governor and Mrs. Endecott. Mary regretfully refused the offer, for "you know how Joe likes me in fine feathers and he might think I looked like a Cinderella in the quiet dress of the Puritan . . . You will know that I am as appreciative and grateful as if I were wearing the quiet garb of my ancestresses instead of masquerading in powder as a great dame of a later age."[2] Mary would go à la bergère, in pink silk and satin, with powdered hair, a velvet hat with feathers, and shepherdess's crook—there was no danger of her being confused with Cinderella in this romantic get-up!

The first functions for the Colonial Premiers went off well, and they were pleased with the Royal carriages and liveried servants that had been provided. Mary was glad to have them come to Birmingham for a luncheon; the visitors saw the wild acclaim which always greeted Joe, and were plainly impressed. Then at an evening reception in London the Queen received representatives from all over her Empire. Joe stood beside the Queen and presented the Colonial Premiers and their wives. She was charming, and smiled at them all; and though her guests were rather in a flurry, they managed this ordeal well. To Mary's relief "most of them had got some fine clothes since their arrival, and were therefore more of a credit than I expected."[3]

On Jubilee Day itself the Chamberlains were up very early. Though the skies were grey and cloudy, it was impossible to think of rain; Mary would not even take an umbrella with her. Joe was muttering about being a sight in his cocked hat, but Mary would not be cooped up in the brougham. They were to ride to St. Paul's Cathedral in an open carriage, and she insisted no one would notice him, as so many people were in uniform.

At St. Paul's the entire churchyard was filled with stands. When they found their places there was a long wait, but three bands played, and a series of brightly bedecked officers passed by, arranging the last details of the Royal procession. Presently the Lord Mayor of London, in velvet robes, and on a black charger, advanced in good medieval fashion with his aldermen and sheriffs to greet the Queen at Temple Bar.

Then came the Life Guards, all shining, on prancing horses; and a detachment of bluejackets, swaggering along, and dragging great guns. Then the Royal escort, and finally the Queen's landau, drawn by cream-coloured horses in gorgeous trappings.

Mary was tremendously moved by the tiny figure of the Queen, head bowed reverently through the short outdoor service. All this pageantry and splendour had been devised to honour her. And now there was silence, while the Empire offered prayers of thanksgiving for their Queen. It seemed too soon when all the bells began to peal, carriages rolled away, and all the noise and colour of procession commenced again.

Waiting near the Colonial Office, the Chamberlains watched anxiously for the Colonial procession. Finally, after minutes of delay it turned up. The heat of London in June had been too much for those from Borneo and Ceylon, and the parade had had to halt its pace to keep the marchers going at all.

All London was garlanded in greens and flowers, and at night the illuminations were splendid. Mary was determined to go walking over the city and see them properly. Austen was dubious about this project, but she had asked two young men to dinner to escort her. Then to her surprise Joe turned out to be eager for the fray. He began to plot out a tremendous route for the family to pursue.

After dinner they split up. Mary and Joe went by brougham to Ludgate Hill, then got out and walked, admiring the lights on St. Paul's, the Mansion House, and Bank of England. Mary had prudently dressed in a bicycling skirt, so there was no problem about pushing among the crowds. They walked along the Embankment, looking at the lights reflected in the water, then reached Pall Mall, St. James Street, and Piccadilly, where all the houses glowed with coloured lights. Horns tooted, and there was a carnival air in the streets. The crowds were good-natured, and they met none of the rowdies Austen worried about. Mary and Joe returned home, tired but triumphant, after a five-mile walking tour of London!

The next day came the State Performance of the Opera. The entire house was festooned with yellow, pink, red, and white roses. Two boxes had been put together for the Royalties, and another big box made ready for the Chamberlains and their brood of Premiers and their families.

Mary was quite amused by the group. Poor old Lady Sprigg from the Cape went because she thought she ought to, and against her religious principles. She had never been to an opera before, and could not enjoy herself at all. And several of the other guests seemed to think this spectacular show was just an ordinary night at the opera. As for Lady Turner, who quite bore out in Mary's view the statement that Victoria was the most bumptious of the colonies, she remarked to someone, "You know, in Melbourne we should not call *this* opera!"

At the State Reception at Buckingham Palace, which really was a ball in all but name, Mary had another encounter with Lady Turner. She went up to say how do you do, turned, looked round at the room and said, "It's a pretty sight, isn't it?"

"Yes," she replied, "but the ball-room is very small."

"Oh," said Mary, "is it?" (It was an enormous room.)

"Well," replied Lady Turner, "it isn't half as big as the Ball-room at Government House [Melbourne again]."[4]

Two days later the good lady managed still another bon mot. Riding with the Chamberlains and the other Premiers and families on the yacht *Wildfire* Lady Turner turned to Mary at lunch-time to ask,

"What boat is this, Mrs. Chamberlain?"

"This is one of the Admiralty yachts."

"Oh indeed," said Lady Turner, "in the colonies we should call this a launch!"

The rest of the Colonial party was suitably impressed, as the *Wildfire* steamed along through miles of Her Majesty's fleet. The lines of ships stretched as far as the eye could see.

There was quite a procession of yachts, and of course they got mixed up to begin with. The yacht with the Royal Suite passed the *Enchantress*, which carried Austen and his sisters and others from the Admiralty, in order to follow the Prince of Wales in his yacht. Then the *Danube* carrying the House of Lords tried to get in front of the *Enchantress*, to the fury of the Admirals on board, and it was some time before they were all in order again. The fleet saluted the Prince of Wales; some of the guns were fired with gunpowder, and in the haze the ships disappeared, and then gradually re-appeared. There were flags all over the ships, and the sailors stood along the sides cheering as the Prince went by.

That night at nine-fifteen two signal-rockets went up, and every ship in the fleet was a blaze of electricity. It was a dazzling sight; and Mary and Joe felt their Premiers had been suitably impressed. Mr. Reid, Premier of New South Wales, was the only one of the group who had not wanted to come, and had been rather "sniffy" about the invitation. He was a big, rough man; during the evening he came on deck during the illuminations, and found Mary in a huddle of premiers.

" 'Now then,' he exclaimed at once, 'you colonial gentlemen are not to say another word to Mrs. Chamberlain. I won't have you talking to her any more. I've been watching her all day, and she's been talking, talking, and talked at, talked at, talked at, the whole time. I won't have you with your great colonial voices in her English ears any longer.'

"Of course Mary protested that she liked it, and then he went on to say, 'You know, I didn't want to come at all, not at all, but all my people were at me, and insisted I should come, and now I'm so glad I did. I wouldn't have missed this for anything. It's perfectly grand! I've been thinking all this afternoon that we colonials blow a good deal, and how fortunate it is that you English people don't blow as much. Why, if with that fleet you were to blow as much as we do, the whole world wouldn't be big enough to hold you!' "[5]

Indeed in that summer of 1897 it did seem there was scarcely room for all the Empire's splendours. London was a riot of colour and excitement: turbans and cloth of gold mingled with silk hats and frock coats; strange customs became familiar, and several new words entered the vocabulary. Before the celebrations all London was "jubilious"; when they were over, "jubilitated". Mary played her part throughout to perfection. Though she felt flustered on June 30th, the night of their big party, she did not show it at all.

The upholsterer and florist had transformed the house. There were tapestries and French chairs everywhere, the balustrade was wound with roses, and crimson carpets were laid down. With candles, potted palms, and a band playing in one corner of the drawing room the effect was dazzling. The Premiers and their wives arrived so promptly the workmen were barely out of the hall. As soon as the Duke and Duchess of York arrived, they went in to dinner. Mary didn't think much of the food, but the occasion went off well. They went upstairs afterwards, and Mary presented the ladies to the Duchess. Then the after-dinner guests began to stream in.

A crisis came at eleven o'clock. The Prince and Princess of Wales, with their daughter Princess Victoria, and Prince Charles of Denmark were to arrive then, but there was no sign of them. Mary shook hands anxiously with the throngs until eleven-twenty, then made her way to the door, for the crowd was so great she was afraid she would miss them. Finally, at eleven-thirty their carriage drove up; there was another long wait, and then in came General Stanley Clarke to say the crowd was so great the Royal guests could not possibly get out of their carriages, that they sent their regrets and had gone.

Mary was profoundly annoyed, for she had been herself to the Inspector of Police, and warned him of the crowds, and told him to have as many policemen as needed to keep the way clear. After all the trouble she had taken over the party, it was disheartening to have it end this way. Still, it was no use brooding about it. Mary hoped they would not have to launch such a huge affair for a long time, and if they did, she vowed that the defecting Royal guests would certainly have no part in her plans.

The mishap to her party was more of a blow than Mary cared to admit. From it the affair got some unfavorable publicity, and Joe's humiliation did not go unnoticed. Though this was galling to pride and pocketbook, Mary tried not to dwell on it. After all, London was in Jubilee mood, and the throngs were not her fault.

As far as the party publicity went, it had the good effect of drawing away attention from the South African Committee. After all these weary months of inquiry, Joe was cleared of any complicity in Jameson's Raid, and the Colonial Office staff with him. Mary had been convinced that this must happen, but the innuendoes of the press still had annoyed her.

The day after their party came the Devonshire House ball. To Mary's regret Joe was hardly in the spirit of it. He "was so driven with work and the annoyance of the previous night had prevented the full relief which he otherwise would have felt at having our own entertainment over".[6] Still, he struggled into his costume as a courtier of Louis XVI. He had a corded silk coat of rose colour, with breeches and waist coat of a pink matching Mary's dress. A wig, buckled shoes, tricorn, and sword completed the elegant picture.

Despite Joe's disgruntlement Mary enjoyed herself at the party. Maria Theresa, Marie Antoinette, Queen Elizabeth, the Doge of Venice, and King Arthur and his Table Round were all represented. Mary had many compliments on her hat; she saw two others like it, but under question would not admit that hers was Birmingham-made, and that she had adjusted its feather trimming herself.

After the grand procession there was supper, then the Chamberlains strolled round the gardens in their finery, and returned home.

The Prince of Wales was to give medals to the officers and men of the Colonial and Indian forces at Buckingham Palace next day. Joe had to be there in uniform, and Mary was planning to see the show; but, as it was not a Command performance, Joe would not let her come. He was still resentful: why should Mary go to watch the Prince, when he hadn't made the effort to come to their party?

A few days later Joe's pique had subsided. Both he and Mary enjoyed the trip to Windsor for the swearing in of the Premiers as Privy Councillors. Mary was to name the ladies to the Queen, so she came in at the head of the group. There were the Queen, her daughter Princess Beatrice, and her son the Duke of Connaught, a gentleman-in-waiting, and Joe. After Mary made her curtsey she stood next to the Queen's chair, and as each lady came up gave her name and colony. She was terribly afraid she would muddle the colonies, but managed to get through it all right; and the Queen, though surely wearied by all these ceremonies, smiled delightfully through the reception.

Mary herself made an especially good impression; for when the Jubilee was over the Queen sent her a gold commemorative medal, like those given the Royal family, rather than the usual silver one. The press praised her for her dignity, charm, and savoir-faire, and the disappointment of her overcrowded party was quite forgotten.

Though it brought grave professional anxieties for Joe, the year 1897 had for Mary probably more colour, gaiety, and glamour than any other in her life. Hard as it was to be under scrutiny as a Cabinet wife, it was rewarding when her efforts were appreciated. Queen Victoria's Diamond Jubilee was a wonderful pause in the world's occupation: a year of congratulation and self-esteem, when international rivalries and tensions could be forgotten or ignored.

Routine soon returned to the Chamberlains. At the Colonial Conference first steps were taken to establish preferential tariffs between colonies and mother country. Thus Lord Salisbury soon renounced old treaties with Germany and Belgium which had given them the same treatment as England in the colonies. Germany was in a sour mood when it came to discussions with the Colonial Office, and there were long arguments about the partitioning of West Africa. At the same time the French were squabbling for predominance with the British in Nigeria. In the same village the two flags might be hoisted in sight of each other.

No sooner were West African affairs simmering with France and Germany than the French renewed their struggle for the upper Nile territory, by which they hoped to connect their Congo lands with Abyssinia. The crisis came to a boil at Fashoda in 1898. Kitchener had just defeated the last of the Mahdi's followers, and the conquered land was to become the Anglo-Egyptian Sudan. Then a small group of French troops marched in and raised their flag at Fashoda. They were soon withdrawn, but the threat of a war with France remained.

Then there was the quarrel with Germany over Samoa; not to mention the encroachments of Russia, Germany, and France in China. Joseph Chamberlain and Lord Salisbury were in conference constantly, so much so that the Kaiser called them the "Two-Headed Government". Of the two the Colonial Secretary's views were the more aggressive. Yet the Prime Minister, together with most thoughtful people, could see that England's "splendid isolation" which had prevailed since the Crimean War, belonged in the past. Europe was divided in a formidable series of alliances; England could no longer stand aloof.

Joe was always at his best when too busy: dictating, asking questions, conferring, deciding. He was a confident and determined fighter: "Pushful Joe" would let no threats of war stampede him. If a boundary were British, and somebody else claimed it, the Colonial Office, confident of Salisbury's support, cracked down hard.

The contrast between Joe in the political arena and on an academic rostrum was great. In the autumn of 1897 he was elected Lord Rector of Glasgow University. To the preparation of his speech he gave long unaccustomed hours. Years before he used to brood for days over his speeches, being withdrawn and moody until they were done. With practice he had cut down. He had notebooks full of quotations, and a full record of what he had said where and when. A few concentrated hours, usually a day and night, would see him through most speeches. Now, though, he was acutely anxious, and consulted with Mary over his speech on this important academic occasion. Though his only university had been life, Joe was determined to follow his distinguished predecessors properly. And he did. He spoke on "Patriotism", declaimed on the manifest destiny of Empire, to a cheering audience of five thousand. Of course the foreign press lampooned him, and called him "jingo"; Mary expected and ignored that, and had "Patriotism" done up in white and gold vellum to send to brother William.

Mary had always assiduously forwarded Joe's speeches to her family. This Christmas she was on the receiving end. She was deluged with greetings from the Colonies. All those she had charmed in June now wanted her to read their works. The Premier of West Australia barraged her with speeches; even forwarded a copy of a financial statement he had prepared. Mary, who had tried hard to be agreeable to the gentleman, laughed when she thought how little he realized her "total incapacity to understand anything to do with finance."[7]

Though she left the accounts to Joe, Mary was an accomplished drawing-room diplomat. With two large houses to manage, and so many parties to supervise, she had also grown knowledgeable about house decoration. The Colonial Office was now under her sway—Beatrice reported that for her father's office Mary had "chosen a crimson paper and white paint, and today she had letters from two of the officials, each setting forth his own view and asking her to decide whether there was, or was not, to be a dado. She has decided in the affirmative, and does not know how to make her reply palatable to the anti-dado man! So you see the office has now discovered who really holds the reins!"[8]

When the Spanish-American War broke out in 1898, the yellow press in the U. S. played on the public imagination with tales of Spanish atrocities in Cuba. President McKinley bowed to the view that the Cubans must be freed from their oppressors. Mary and Joe, who had talked at length with the Queen Regent on their Spanish visit, were keenly interested in her problem. If she gave in and allowed the Cubans independence (for they were no longer satisfied with reforms) there would almost certainly be a revolution, and her son Alphonso would never come to power. On the other hand, if she did not give in she must fight America as well as the rebels. On April 20, 1898, came the United States Joint Resolution for War. Mary's family were horrified that American men were fighting: "In England all this would seem so natural, because there is always fighting of some sort to be met with among their colonies, but here we never dreamed another war would come, and everyone I know is outraged at it. The people do not want it. It is Congress that has *insisted* on it!"[9]

Joe felt strongly that England must stand aside from any European threat of interference in the war, even from a moral protest, which was all that was being considered. Anglo-American friendship was vital, and a letter and telegram of Joe's from Highbury to the Foreign Office ended England's part in the protest. America was grateful for this. A few weeks later the Colonial Office had an opportunity to help out America again. The Governor of the Straits Settlement had the very first word of Dewey's victory in Manila Bay, and sent it on to London. Joe had the message sent over to John Hay at the American Embassy, whence it went to President McKinley. Joe took the opportunity of the victory to speak on a favourite theme, "Terrible as war may be, even war itself would be cheaply purchased if in a great and noble cause the Stars and Stripes and the Union Jack should wave together over an Anglo-Saxon alliance."[10]

By the time Mary and Joe went to America in late summer, the war was over. Cuba was free, Puerto Rico ceded, and only the fate of the Philippines lay in doubt. In the old days Joe would have discussed all this with Mr. Endicott. There was strong imperialist sentiment for annexing the Philippines, but also a strenuous faction against it. America was emerging as a world power, but she was having growing pains. Now Mary's father was sadly changed. He smiled when his daughter came into the room, but did not really know she had been away. Mary was glad that William and Louise were there to help her mother. As they could not talk about anything serious with Papa, they spent much of their time enjoying the Farm gardens; ambling about, Joe would admire and make suggestions; William and Louise meanwhile asking about their progress at Highbury.

Mary was glad also to see the Marlborough Street house which her parents had bought for a permanent home. It was a comfort to think of them settling in there after she and Joe returned to England.

On his return from America, Joe found that South African affairs were in turmoil. Milner, home on leave, was impatient and frustrated. He was bitter that the Cape Dutch would not press Kruger for reforms in the Transvaal. He had become convinced that only war would give the uitlanders their reforms, but Joe counselled patience. If Kruger violated the London Convention he was ready to challenge him, but the British Government wanted to avert an all-out race war. Government policy was "to keep the peace with Kruger unless he were very outrageous."[11]

Meanwhile in Johannesburg a British subject, Tom Edgar, was shot dead by a Boer policeman who broke into his house after Edgar's retreat there following a street fight. Four thousand British subjects signed a petition protesting the policeman's release, without so much as a cash bail payment. The petition was to have gone to the Queen, but the Acting High Commissioner would have none of it, and the Boers arrested the two men who had led the petitioners to the British Vice Consul, charging them with an illegal open-air meeting. After Milner returned, the uitlanders tried again. This time the petition went to England, and Johannesburg was committed to seeking Imperial intervention for the redress of grievances.

Just after the Edgar incident Mary was asked to go with Joe to visit the Queen at Osborne. It was unusual for a Minister's wife to be asked, and Mary was all excited; but dismayed when they reached Southampton and none of their luggage could be found. Impossible situation—imagine spending two days with only one's travelling costume. At the last moment the missing trunks turned up, and the day was saved.

When Mary went to talk with the Queen on their second night she found her in a talkative mood; they began to discuss Thanksgiving in New England. From there they went on to the observance of Sunday. The lady whose name still connotes a Sabbath dreary and virtuous, expressed approval of "the less strict observances" of her day. "In former times little children were not allowed even to play. That was cruel, and only made them hate the day."[12] When Joe came up to talk, and Mary said good-night, the Queen interrupted her in the middle of her curtsey by leaning forward and kissing her.

This pleasing interlude helped Mary's morale when things grew difficult for Joe in succeeding months. Milner reported that "South Africa can prosper under two, three, or six Governments, but not under two absolutely conflicting social and political systems, perfect equality for Dutch and British in the British colonies side by side with permanent subjection of British to Dutch in one of the Republics. It is idle to talk of peace and unity under such a state of affairs."[13]

There were many in England to agree with Milner. The vote and the "reforms" sought by the uitlanders were not the real issue. It seemed now that Kruger, and his fervour for a Dutch homeland, might spread his ideas throughout South Africa, undoing all the harmony and efforts at unity the British had been striving for so long. Joe suggested that Milner meet with Kruger at Pretoria. The Cape Dutch had been hoping for a conference among the four South African states, but as Kruger would not discuss the internal affairs of the Transvaal that idea had been scrapped. It was hoped, though, that any conference held would be South African, rather than British. Presently the proposal was made that Milner meet Kruger at Bloemfontein, in the Orange Free State, using the Free State's President as intermediary, if he desired. Milner had not yet received Joe's suggestion about a conference at Pretoria, and he wanted to have a last try at franchise reform. So he cabled for approval, and Joe agreed to the Bloemfontein Conference, hoping that political equality might be reached through "Home Rule in the Rand."

Kruger went grumpily to the Conference; he thought he could do worse than bargain. Possibly by making a few nominal reforms in the franchise law he could get Swaziland ceded to the Transvaal. Milner was not in a bargaining mood: he had come solely to discuss the franchise law. As things were, the uitlanders were not represented in the Volksraad, and had no incentive to become naturalized citizens of the South African Republic. Kruger said he was not ready to give over his country to strangers. Throughout the Conference he argued against Milner's proposal that every foreigner of good character, with a certain amount of property or income, and five years' residence, should, on taking an oath of allegiance, be granted voting citizenship.

After five days they were at a stalemate, and the Bloemfontein Conference had failed. Throughout the summer there was some hope Kruger might undertake reforms on his own account. The British Government continued a policy of watchful waiting. To some observers the scene was reminiscent of the American Civil War: the Transvaal, and the fervour of the Boers for an all-Dutch nation, recalled the Southern Confederacy, whose members chose secession, as the price of preserving its institutions. And England stood in the position of the North: worlds apart in many ways of thinking, but hoping to preserve the Union.

It was a hot and anxious time. Mary spent most of the summer at Highbury, as they could not possibly go abroad in this state of affairs. But Joe had to keep going to London to keep abreast of the latest Transvaal developments. Mary was filled with the most profound resentment at the Old Man of Pretoria. She had seen the patience of the Government tried repeatedly; if Kruger had only given a fair share in the government to the uitlanders from the first, no one would be hectoring him now. As it was, the future lay "in Kruger's hands. It cannot be indefinitely delayed, for the situation is too critical, and the patience of the Government will one day be strained too far, if Oom Paul does not soon make up his mind to be less obdurate.

". . . People begin to see that the question is not one of detail. The franchise is a symbol only. The real question is the supremacy of Great Britain in South Africa, and throughout her dominions as a sequel to that."[14]

Late in August Joe told his constituents that the sands of time were running out: once and for all Great Britain must establish her paramountcy in South Africa. On September 8th the Cabinet decided to send out 10,000 troops to South Africa, raising total forces in the Cape and Natal to 22,000. Once again Kruger was offered the chance to reconsider the Bloemfontein franchise terms and refused. Mary was glad Joe performed so well under tension, for his position was "one of the gravest responsibility, and he has no one to share it with him, in one sense, for his colleagues cannot know the intricacies and details of the question, and it devolves on him to carry out all the negotiations and decisions of the Government."[15]

Mary was wryly amused to see the French papers decrying the actions of "ce malfaiseur, Chamberlain" and commending for his example the statesmanlike despatch sent to President Kruger. They assumed this had been written by Salisbury; actually, it was the work of the "malfaiseur" himself. It was hard to read all the accusations that Joe was working for war, the more so when Mary knew how desperately he had struggled to prevent an armed struggle. He firmly believed British and Dutch could live side by side amicably; but the Boers did not share this viewpoint.

A final British despatch on September 22nd heralded the end of friendly negotiation. There were rumours that the Boers might take the offensive, which Mary could not quite believe; but in the Transvaal and Free State British subjects had begun a mass exodus. The Transvaal commandos mobilized on September 27th, and those in the Free State were quick to follow. The Boers were eager for the fray, but as yet they had no proper system of supply. After a week the commandos had begun to gather stores and ammunition; meanwhile British reinforcements had arrived from India.

There was no time to be lost. The Biblical fervour of the commandos would no longer be held back. They believed they were engaging in a holy war to protect their homeland. On October 9th the Transvaal ultimatum was presented to the British Agent at Pretoria. Two days later the Free State cast its lot against "the high-handed and unjustifiable policy and conduct of Her Majesty's Government."[16] They felt the war should be blamed on British statesmen: "On their heads be the liability for bloodshed, and may a righteous Providence bring retribution on such as deserve it."[17]

CHAPTER XI

"We Are Marching to Pretoria"

WELL, they have done it!" Mary exclaimed. At six o'clock in the morning of October 10, 1899, Joseph Chamberlain was awakened to read the Transvaal ultimatum, "requiring in the most high and mighty language the immediate withdrawal of all troops on the British frontiers, the order that the re-inforcements now on their way should not be landed at any port in South Africa (not even in our own Colonies) etc. etc.— and if their terms are not accepted by 5 p.m. today that they should consider it as a declaration of war. If Mr. Kruger were the Czar of all the Russias he could not take a loftier tone."[1]

Indignant though she was, Mary was thrilled to note how England rose to Kruger's challenge. The New South Wales Lancers, which had come over for the Jubilee, and remained for training, immediately volunteered for service in South Africa; other Australian colonies offered troops as well, and Mary felt that Joe's four years of toil with the colonies was bearing fruit at last.

When Joe went to the House on October 17th he was cheered wildly. His major speech was not made until the 19th. Initially he disposed of the Opposition, and laid again the spectre of complicity in the Jameson Raid. Then, too, "Mr. Stanhope had charged Joe and Sir Alfred Milner with having decided months ago to work for war. That was a charge of dishonour which could not be ignored. The quiet, terse sentences, the scorn and contempt with which they were delivered, Mr. Stanhope's heated remonstrance and claim of injury, Joe's suppressed emotion which I doubt if others detected as his wife did, made it a most exciting scene.

". . . [The speech] was an able defence of the policy of the Government, a courageous explanation of its motives, and a frank avowal that in the light of . . . the ultimatum . . . war was inevitable . . . It

126

was nearly seven o'clock when he sat down. Two hours and three quarters had he been, and to the end the House listened with absolute attention and sympathy."[2]

The next day came news of the first serious engagement: the capture of an enemy position in Natal. However, to counterbalance this came news on November 1st of the capture of 1000 British troops outside Ladysmith, in Natal. Hopes that the war would be over by Christmas soon receded. In succeeding weeks Mary rejoiced that Joe had chosen the Colonial and not the War Office four and a half years before. The Boers were not at all the amateur farmer fighters the British had been led to believe. They knew their terrain and fought brilliantly. Lord Lansdowne's management of the War Office was under attack, but the public had confidence in British generals. Despite the fact that Ladysmith, Mafeking, and Kimberley (the latter two in Cape Colony) were besieged by Boers, no one doubted that relieving forces would soon arrive and put the enemy to flight.

Mary felt especially patriotic that fall, for Joe allowed her to christen the battleship *Venerable*. She was given an intricately carved hammer and chisel with which to do her part; for an awful half minute the ship stayed still, then slowly, to her vast relief, slid down the ways. The ship was named for an earlier, famous one; Mary learned the story a few weeks after the launching: "Duncan, lying off the Texel, with his own flagship, the *Venerable*, and only one other vessel, heard that the whole Dutch fleet was putting to sea. He told Captain Hotham to anchor alongside him in the narrowest part of the Channel and fight his vessel till she sank.

" 'I have taken the depth of the water,' added he, 'and when the *Venerable* goes down, my flag will still fly.' "[3]

Joe was readying himself for the State Visit of the Kaiser that fall. All over Europe there was talk of "Mr. Chamberlain's War" and strong anti-British sentiment. The Kaiser was well aware of this, and forced the settlement of the Samoan dispute with England before he came to Windsor. Joe had hopes, destined to blight, of helping form an Anglo-German alliance one day. Though anxious to obtain for England the official neutrality of Germany portended by the Kaiser's visit, Joe did not lightly give up Samoa.[4] In return

Germany ceded many of the Tonga and Solomon Islands, also in the South Seas. In West Africa a neutral area behind German Togoland and the British Gold Coast was fairly divided up; and Britain continued to hold a triangular territory at the mouth of the Volta River.

On November 16th the Chamberlains went to Windsor, where for forty-five minutes the Queen quizzed Joe on the progress of the war. She said she admired all he had done; she seemed undismayed by British reverses, and calm about the future. Mary spoke with the Queen about Lady Randolph Churchill, and her hospital-ship project. The ship and crew had been gathered, and Lady Randolph was begging thousands of pounds from British and American enthusiasts alike. Though Mary wondered with the Queen if enough money would be forthcoming, it was: on December 23rd (the day after she heard of her son Winston's escape from Pretoria Jail) Lady Randolph set sail with the hospital ship for South Africa.

The following week Joe went back to Windsor alone for the State Banquet welcoming the Kaiser. The Government guests were going up and down by special train, as the German retinue was too great to allow other overnight guests at Windsor. The thought of travelling in the thin silk stockings of Court dress was chilly; and Joe copied Lord Lansdowne, borrowing some of Austen's white flannels to wear over his regalia. Mary waited up to hear about the dinner; 150 people had eaten off the Royal gold plate, which was valued at two million pounds. The scene was magnificent, and the Kaiser genial. He was pleased with the Samoan agreement, and, said Joe, his sentiments towards England were "all that they ought to be."[5]

The Kaiser wanted Joe to meet his Prime Minister, Bülow, and Joe made another trip to Windsor two days later. Bülow and he talked agreeably for a long time; then Joe and the Kaiser had a private session of about an hour. The Kaiser was deeply interested in developing his Empire (back at home he was busily enlarging the German Navy) and Joe was impressed: "Certainly he is a man of much more force and intellectual capacity than Princes usually are . . . with all the impetuosity of his character, and the mistakes which he undoubtedly has made, he goes on becoming more and more of a power in Europe; in fact really he is the only Crowned Head to be reckoned with on the Continent."[6]

Joe determined shortly afterward to speak publicly about better-
ing both Anglo-German and Anglo-American relations. At Leices-
ter on November 30th he spoke of his hope for a new "Triple Alliance between the Teutonic race and the two great branches of the
Anglo-Saxon race", but the speech earned world-wide condemna-
tion. The very word "alliance" alarmed Americans; while in Germany Bülow was off on a fresh tack entirely. In the Reichstag, which
had opposed the Kaiser's State Visit, Bülow was winning round an
Anglophobe group. By deprecating England he meant to build up
the German Army and Navy. This double-cross of the Colonial Secretary, who expected Bülow's support, was maddening. Yet Joe
rallied from the attacks of his critics; he put less trust in Germany,
but still hoped for alliance. He now also considered the alternative
of joining Russia and France.

Joe had ventured far into foreign policy. In the Colonial Office
his own work was greatly stepped up by the war. The colonies were
offering troops, which was encouraging to Joe's imperialist views;
but to get the War Office to accept them was another matter altogether. The regulars looked down on the colonials, even after a
shattering week of losses from December 11th to December 16th.
In north Cape Colony the British lost 700 at Stormberg; then Lord
Methuen, leading 15,000 men to relieve Kimberley, lost 1000 at
Magersfontein. Sir Redvers Buller, leading the main army to relieve
General White and his 10,000 at Ladysmith would surely get
through. It was not to be. On December 15th at Colenso Buller lost
10 guns, and had 1100 casualties; he was ready to abandon Lady-
smith, but White insisted on hanging on. Within the week Lord
Roberts, a veteran general, was posted as Commander-in-Chief in
South Africa, Kitchener joining him as Chief-of-Staff.

Right after that "Black Week" of British defeats Joe had to go to
Dublin to get an honorary degree from Trinity College. There were
rumours of Nationalist troubles; stepping off the boat, Mary walked
closely on one side of Joe, and softly urged Hilda, who was with
them, to stay close to his other side. She took no chances on stray
assassins, but fortunately their precautions were needless.

After Colenso troops from Canada, Australia, and New Zealand
began to arrive in force. Joe was convinced Great Britain would win

eventually, but as much by numbers as generalship, for the Boers displayed amazing mobility, great skill with guns, and in trench warfare. At Christmas-time Buller tried twice more to relieve Lady-smith, and made two more retreats. When the new session of Parl-iament opened on January 30th, there was a serious question that the Government might be turned out.

Mary appeared unperturbed; she had her household knitting away on woolly caps and socks for the forces; she was always there to cheer Joe, but she wondered and worried to herself. How long could Ladysmith last? How could Joe handle the Opposition, now declaiming louder than ever against the war? How could the Com-mons be so party-minded in the midst of crisis? Sir William Har-court was even planning to go into the whole matter of the Jameson Raid again. Mary was disgusted. Joe had given his word of honour; how could he say more? She hoped he would refuse to go into the question and would "make his speech on the Imperial lines. There is much to be said about the splendid vigour and courage of the na-tion and the honour which has been won on the field of battle by those who have fallen . . . You will be amused at my having ideas about this speech . . . I am not in the habit of making suggestions to my spouse, and so I suggest to you. I think it not impossible how-ever that the trend of feeling has suggested itself to him as it has to me."[7]

Joe did not disappoint her. In a tightly-packed speech he showed the Empire in action. "We shall have in this war before it is over an army of colonials called to the aid of Her Majesty who will outnum-ber the British army at Waterloo, and who will be nearly equal to the total British force in the Crimea . . . [Our colonial peoples] now for the first time claim their share in the duties and responsibilities as well as the privileges of Empire."[8]

Once again the House rallied to its Ministers, and the proposed vote of censure was defeated by a vigorous majority. Mary was thrilled to see the change in Joe: "He has been very silent and quiet of late—Now his spirits are excellent."[9]

Though Buller still vacillated, crossing and recrossing the Tugela River, there was every reason for optimism with the gifted Roberts-Kitchener team on its way to Capetown. Rather than scattering his forces through the Cape Colony and Natal Roberts planned to march through enemy country, the Orange Free State. Mobility was everything; frontal assaults on the Boer were always costly, so Roberts planned to outflank the enemy, move rapidly, and take him by surprise.

On February 15th Kimberley was at last relieved. Roberts meanwhile had pursued General Cronje's forces to Paardeberg, and was awaiting his surrender. Buller was working up to another effort at Ladysmith. The excitement and tension mounted all over London.

Meanwhile a new enquiry about Joe's part in the "conspiracy against the Transvaal Government" and Jameson's Raid in 1895 was moved by a Welshman, D. A. Thomas, and seconded by Mr. Evans, also from Wales. Mary thought there was an ominous air of expectancy among the Opposition; Evans was a clever speaker, and the Irish grew excited, and broke into ugly yells. Then Joe rose, quietly and calmly, looking pale and scornful. He had no notes, but spoke for thirty-five minutes, demolishing every charge and insinuation. It was a tour de force; at the end of it he rang out, "Let them do their worst!", and there were deafening cheers from his supporters. He turned on his attackers with defiance and contempt. Mary was tired, but triumphant, when Joe finished. Joe had routed them once more.

Only a week later Cronje surrendered at Paardeberg; and Buller finally crossed the Tugela to some purpose. General Dundonald rode into Ladysmith with the second Mounted Brigade, and London nearly went mad with joy: "For three hours there was a solid crowd outside the Mansion House singing, the Stock Exchange sang and sang, and refused to do anything else . . . Lord Roberts is on more of a pinnacle than ever . . . You can imagine the load it lifts for the Government . . . My spouse is more himself than I have seen him for months."[10]

Queen Victoria, who had announced one day that she would have no depression in her house, was overjoyed at the news. The Duke of York tried to keep her calm, and said, "But you know, Grandmamma, the telegram did not say that Ladysmith was *relieved*, it said that Dundonald had entered the town." Her Majesty replied firmly, "George, I will not be dashed."

Mafeking remained besieged, but Colonel Baden-Powell and his garrison there were in good spirits. He managed to send out some letters to his family, describing the beleaguered life. General Cronje had originally surrounded him with 10,000 Boers, now there were only about 2000; while Baden-Powell, counting the men of the town, had about 1200 men. There were 650 women and children in Mafeking, among them Winston Churchill's aunt, Lady Sarah Wilson. She, like her nephew, had gone out as a war correspondent (her husband was ADC to Baden-Powell) and, like him, she was captured. To Baden-Powell's reluctance he was driven to exchange Viljoen, a Dutch horse-thief and spy, in return for Lady Sarah. He protested, with some lack of gallantry, on the unfairness of exchanging a combatant for a woman. The Boer commander threatened to shoot Lady Sarah as a spy, so he had no choice.

Baden-Powell was always ingenious. He thought the Boers were ominously quiet, so stirred them up by sending them a message asking why they had interfered with his telegraph. The bewildered Boers sent out work parties to dig for an imaginary wire. Meanwhile the civilians kept busy till near the end of the siege with horse races and gymkhanas. A change in menu put an end to these amusements. Lady Sarah got out a telegram somehow which ran "Breakfast horse sausages lunch minced mule all well."

That spring of 1900 Australian delegates were in London to present the Commonwealth Bill; Mary presented their ladies to the Queen, and there was great goodwill expressed on this occasion. Joe was in a tight diplomatic spot and needed all the help he could get. He took issue with one clause of the Bill (which would be the Constitution of the six federated Australian colonies) which restricted appeal to the Court of Privy Council. Joe hoped ideally for an unrestricted right of appeal such as prevailed between the Privy Council Court and the Dominion of Canada. The strong nationalist spirit of the Australians seemed to preclude this. At last a compromise was reached: all Imperial matters must be referred to Westminster, those purely Australian would be settled in Australia. With Australian troops fighting bravely in South Africa, it made dramatic Queen Victoria's signing of the Commonwealth Bill on July 9, 1900.

That spring was bitter-sweet for Mary. Joe was more himself, and the tide of war was turning, but with every letter from America she heard of her father's decline. On May 6th the Chamberlain household was in a flutter, for Ethel was engaged to Lionel Richards, a young barrister who had been at school with Neville. Mary worried sometimes about Joe's daughters, and feared they were too devoted to their father to marry; perhaps the others would follow Ethel's good example.

Early in the evening, in the midst of the excitement, came a cable for Mary. Papa was dead of pneumonia; she was 3000 miles away and could do nothing. She would not spoil Ethel's happiness; miserable as she was, Mary managed to keep on going mechanically. During her engagement and long separation from Joe she had learned a hard lesson: no matter what reverses you struck you had to keep going, talk, seem cheerful, and plan your affairs. Joe certainly knew this: his political career was forged in a time of private sorrow. Even now, when they were so perfectly happy at home, political strains took their toll on him. When Joe had one of his headaches, or was down with gout, he ignored it as much as he could. And the public criticism was an inevitable part of politics. If Joe was caricatured more than many, he had at least a sharper tongue to deal with his assailants.

Mary cancelled her engagements, answered notes of sympathy, and tried to rally from her father's death. All Joe's children, though they found it hard to express themselves, showed their affection for her in this difficult time. Mary set to work planning Ethel's wedding. In mid-May came the news of the relief of Mafeking; at the end of the month Lord Roberts marched into Johannesburg. Pretoria was next in line; when it fell on June 5th Joe began to speak of the dissolution of Parliament. The Government had been in five years, and so must call an election within the year. A General Election held on the crest of Lord Roberts' victories would surely swell Unionist majorities.

In March the Presidents of the two Boer Republics had turned down tentative peace proposals flatly. Kruger and Steyn continued to speak of their sovereign and independent Republics, and demanded that those British subjects who had fought with them, rebels from the Cape Dutch population, should go unpunished. In May the Government policy was announced: annexation of the Boer Republics. The threat of disfranchisement of the Cape rebels for life, coupled to this policy, caused the Dutch Ministry at Cape Town to fall. A British one was formed, which Joe hoped could work in a conciliatory spirit with the Dutch. Milner wanted to suspend the Cape constitution, but once more Joe pressed for moderation.

Mrs. Endicott reached Highbury late in June. By then hopes for an early dissolution were almost gone. Rebellion in Ashanti, and the rising of the Boxers in Peking, with the siege of the foreign legations, for the moment overshadowed South African concerns. Joe was in town; Mary and her mother shopped for Ethel's wedding, went for drives, and sat outside in the garden. Mary was tireder than she realized, and Mrs. Endicott persuaded her to take a little jaunt to the Continent. Mary did not want to leave Joe just then; both ladies were strong-minded and tactful, so the holiday was arranged, but postponed until September.

Parliament held its last session on August 8th; between then and the dissolution on September 17th, Joe took what rest he could manage. For the "Khaki Election", whose issue was South Africa, was really a one-man show. The vote would be for or against Joseph Chamberlain, Colonial Secretary. His enemies were stirring even at the end of Parliament, preparing to heap slander on his head. He would fight back unsparingly; all the future of Empire, he believed, hung on a just South African settlement, by the Unionist government continuing in power.

Though Joe would have liked Mary beside him in the campaign, he always heeded Endicott warnings against over-doing; so he saw her off with Mrs. Endicott, and wrote her daily about his fight. It was terrific: he hurried about, night after night, addressing huge crowds. The Liberals were divided, and no one of them could match his speeches. Time and again he had decried "pro-Boers" or "little Englanders"; Joe went after them harder than ever now. His colleagues' speeches were pallid by comparison, and inch by inch Joe gained his ground.

Mary, out rowing in Switzerland with a sailor-hat upon her head, and looking to her mother like a girl of eighteen, kept her heart in two places. She was a perfect travelling companion, enthusiastic, and thoughtful as ever. She was pleased to see how Mrs. Endicott perked up with sight-seeing; for she had been much at home during the five years of Papa's illness. Mary wrote to Louise that she had a faint hope of persuading her mother to take a winter journey on the Nile.

Yet no day passed without her settling down to write Joe words of encouragement. She thought of him, puffing on his cigar, getting down a book, taking notes in the library. Though they had been apart only three weeks, the trip seemed long to Mary, away from Joe; he wrote right after she had left, "It is only a few hours since I said good-bye, but already it seems a long time."[11] Seventeen times in a fortnight he had spoken; the polling had started, and clearly the Unionists would have a large majority. Reading over Joe's speeches, Mary almost saw him in the room with her. Accused of letting social reforms go by the board, Joe answered, "I am not dead yet." Urging his listeners "not to think of persons or parties, but only of Imperial interests", Joe adopted as a rallying cry the words of the Mayor of Mafeking, "Every vote given against the Government is a vote given to the Boers."

His detractors could not succeed. They dug around trying to establish that he and his near relations had munitions investments, saying that the war was a chance for the Chamberlains to line their pockets. Joe did not mind an honest fight, but he detested innuendo. Mary and his children were indignant at the charges. To their relief the Unionists got in with a majority of 134. Joe and Austen travelled to Italy, where they had a well-earned holiday. Mary, reunited with her husband, realized how long it had been since he had rested. He was sixty-four, and had been speaking or writing for the campaign every day for weeks. There was the war, and the Boxer Rebellion, and dozens of other concerns for him, great and small; yet Joe was resilient and cheerful. At Rome, Mrs. Endicott and Austen went down with fish poisoning; Joe and Mary, cheerfully exempt, went sight-seeing. They returned to England ready to take up where they had left off.

Joe's enemies started in again as soon as Parliament opened. Though the first session was less than two weeks long, there was a "conspiracy of insinuation" ably led by Mr. Lloyd George. Both Joe and Austen spoke in vindication of family honour and investments. Lloyd George moved that Crown Ministers and those holding subordinate office in any public department should have no direct or indirect interest in companies competing for Crown contracts. This was rejected. Arthur Balfour satirically stated the Opposition's case, "Wanted, a man to serve Her Majesty with no money, no relations."[12]

Mary was completely disgusted. For decades Joe's family had been in Birmingham manufacturing. He had come there from the family shoemaking business in London in 1854. Now "those men" made it seem that he was in politics for financial gain; one of the hardest things to take was *Punch*'s gibe: "The more the Empire expands, the more the Chamberlains contract." Joe had sold out many of his holdings at a loss when he took office. Fighting a war he had hoped to avoid, he had also to fight the Opposition which implied he was making a good thing out of it himself.

Mary had continued scheming about Mother's trip up the Nile; her Uncle Augustus Peabody and Uncle Powell Mason agreed to rendezvous with Mrs. Endicott, Beatrice, and Hilda for the trip to Egypt. At last it was all settled, and Mrs. Endicott led the procession, with a full complement of shawls, parasols, pills, and potions. From her Continental travels she was used to bad coffee, damp sheets, and profiteering hotel managers. Egypt, even with all Mary's elaborate descriptions of it, was an unknown quantity. At Mrs. Endicott's first interview with her dragoman, Ali Hassam, a tall dark-skinned Egyptian in blue knickerbockers and embroidered jacket, he bowed before her, took her hand, kissed it and carried it to his forehead. Then, turning to the others as if he feared they might be hurt at not receiving the same mark of his esteem he explained, "She my lady—same as my mother." After this, added Hilda gleefully, "You should have seen Mrs. Endicott jump up as soon as he left the room, and go to wash her hand!"[13]

The greatest public event Mary was involved in that year was the luncheon welcoming Lord Roberts back from South Africa. Kruger had departed for Europe; and Kitchener was left to mop up the commandos. It was not realized at first how long his struggle would go on. Victory seemed to be just around the corner, so the luncheon was a real gala. Lord Lansdowne had succeeded as Foreign Secretary in Salisbury's new Cabinet, and Mary sat next to the new Secretary of War, Mr. Brodrick, who remarked, "Do you realize what an historic luncheon this is? Certainly you and I shall never witness such another. I don't suppose since the Duke of Wellington came home that there has been anything like it."[14] Happily, Mary could not foresee the two World Wars through which she would live; looking round at all the Royalties, Ministers, and Generals assembled, she entirely agreed with Brodrick.

The peace which was expected so soon did not come about until May 31, 1902. Meanwhile Kitchener waged a thankless and frustrating war. In the hope that destroying Boer homesteads would destroy the burghers' will to fight, farms were burned, women and children were interned; but the battles dragged endlessly on. The commandos, having homes no longer, lived off the land and determined to fight to the death.

Meanwhile a natural, but unlooked-for, event put the whole Empire in mourning. After an illness of a few weeks, on January 22nd, 1901, the eighty-two year old Queen died. Joe had seen her at Osborne on the tenth; she had looked well and talked much as usual. He was the last of her Ministers to have an audience with her. As he reviewed his career, he could see what a long road he had travelled from the "dangerous Radical" to the "favourite Minister". The Queen had been especially fond of Mary; both the Chamberlains found it hard to think of her gone.

All London was in black mourning; everyone looked sad, and it was hard to get used to saying "God Save the King". The Queen's dream of Empire, happily, had coincided with Joe's. She admired his work, and liked his wife; the two sentiments could not help but reinforce each other. Joe's early Radicalism had been alarming, and his marriage to an American girl was not in itself a recommendation. The Prince of Wales's set of beautiful, daring, and frivolous women included some Americans. They were not in high repute at Court. Mary, on the other hand, the Queen found pretty, and more important, "very ladylike with a nice frank open manner."[15]

As the Queen had emerged from the isolation she chose at Prince

Albert's death, Joe had moved toward the Conservative alliance, formed his views on a federated Empire. He became a Crown Minister; and Mary stood naturally and gracefully beside him. She was charming, devoted to husband and home, yet with great self-possession in society. Chamberlain outshadowed the aging Prime Minister, and to his visions the Queen assented. She saw, by his efforts, the Australian Commonwealth come into being; and she died quite confident in the success of the South African War. She had ruled for sixty-three years, and latterly as she became the Empire's symbol, Joseph Chamberlain became her foremost Minister. Truly, things could never again be the same.

The new King summoned the Privy Councillors the day after his mother's death. The bluff and cheerful man, soon to be known as "The Merry Monarch", picked his phrases with tact and delicacy. He explained that he was taking the name of Edward, for there could be only one Albert, his father.

It had been so long since a new Sovereign had been proclaimed that there was great confusion over the proper ceremonies to observe. As the Queen wanted a military procession through London, and burial at Windsor, her body was brought by yacht from Cowes, then taken by train to London. The procession was held on February 2nd, and a Memorial Service in Westminster Abbey. Meanwhile the Court, Ministers, and royal relatives waited at St. George's Chapel, Windsor. There was a delay; Mary later learned that "one of the artillery horses attached to the gun carriage refused to take [a very steep hill], then became restive and unmanageable, so that the whole team had to be unharnessed. Fortunately there was a guard of Bluejackets on duty, and they came to the rescue, and so the Queen was drawn up the hill to the church by her own sailors . . . On the green the troops were drawn up standing with arms reversed and bowed heads. In the doorway the coffin was borne shoulder high by Guardsmen, their officer in his bearskin towering above all near him. Immediately behind came the gentlemen of the Household, bearing a frame on which was laid the gleaming white satin pall . . . and on which were placed the Royal Standard, the jewelled golden crown, the orbs, and insignia . . . After them came the mourners headed by the King with the Emperor William on his right [at his grandmother's death the Kaiser turned briefly from his own ambitions and went to work sorting condolence letters and helping the Household through the maze of detail connected with the Queen's funeral] and the Duke of Connaught on his left . . . Immediately behind came the crowned heads who were present, and the representatives of all the civilized countries in the world."[16]

The service for the Queen was the same as for anyone else; when it was over, and they had been given lunch, the Chamberlains returned to London. That evening as they sat over dinner came a message from the Belgian Minister who wished to know if they would be at home next day, a Sunday, the King of the Belgians wished to call on Mr. Chamberlain. Mary was in dismay. The house was in dust sheets, they had only planned to camp out in it for one night. The library was in a hopeless clutter, the morning room was too small, so at first light Sunday the parlormaids were up putting the drawing room to rights. The furniture was polished, two roaring fires were laid, and by good luck Mary had some fresh flowers. At noon all was ready, but no King! One o'clock, and one-thirty passed. At five minutes to two Mary was on her way upstairs before lunch, convinced the King would not come till afternoon. There was a violent ring at the door. Joe greeted King Leopold in French. Mary hastened to the top of the stairs to add her welcome.

"We had a grand bowing and scraping and much gesticulation over getting into the Drawing Room. 'Je vous suivrai, Madame' so in I had to march. At last we got seated. The conversation was in French, so you can imagine that my part in it was limited. The King is an outrageous flatterer and kept on repeating to Joe his admiration of his strength, his scorn of attacks, and his fulfillment of his ideas in administering the Colonial Office . . . He talked on, and was very pleasant and stayed and stayed. At last he said, 'But it is late and I am keeping you from your lunch.' Awful moment. I felt I must ask him to lunch, and visions arose before me of our limited menage and its effect on the cuisine. However, the same thought struck Joe, so he did it, and I seconded it with a shrinking.

"He considered a moment, and said he was much obliged, but the King of Portugal was waiting for him at the Palace and he must go back (poor King of Portugal, it was then twenty minutes of three!) but he would take a glass of wine with us. So off Joe rushed to order it up, while the King got up as if he expected it to appear through the floor, and I had to engage him in conversation during the interval, which seemed interminable . . . Having poured out three glasses I gave one to him and we all three solemnly stood up, clinked our glasses, and drank each other's healths in the most approved fashion, and then after many more complimentary remarks His Majesty took his leave. I accompanied him to the top of the stairs, and Joe to the carriage. As the latter turned to come in to the door he saw our next door neighbor Mrs. Waring with her curtains well drawn back gazing out with much enjoyment!"[17]

The Chamberlains went back to Highbury, with sighs of relief, before the opening of Parliament. This was an occasion when ladies came in black evening dress with jewels, the peers wore scarlet and white robes, and the King was got up as a Field Marshal, with a red and ermine mantle. Queen Alexandra, though in black dress and full veil, had a similar mantle and the Koh-I-Noor diamond, among others, to relieve the gloom.

His Majesty had some difficulty maneuvering the Queen to the throne, and his bow, though dignified, was portly rather than graceful. Then the King read his speech, and after the ceremonies were over, proceeded away with his Queen. Mary and Ida, who had been in a gallery, made a rush for their carriage. The Portuguese Minister took them in tow; he said he had got out ahead of the others because he felt very ill. They stationed themselves right behind a group of Grenadier Guards and had a good view of the gilded coach driving by with its royal occupants. The King smiled as he recognized them; the Minister and the Chamberlain ladies bowed, and the encounter was over.

When Mrs. Endicott got back from Egypt she fell in with a pet project of Mary's: having her portrait painted by Sargent. She claimed this was hopelessly extravagant, and she was not unreasonable: the finished work, with frame, was billed at 812 pounds. But she yielded to entreaty, and through the spring sat for Sargent. In the fall the finished portrait came to Highbury, where for some time it reposed in the Great Hall. Mary was delighted to see her mother "seated in front of a splendid red curtain, her figure full of grace

and lightness, her face sweet and thoughtful and tender, her hands
all her own . . . Everyone in the family came round to say, 'It grows
on me, Mrs. C., I like it more and more!' "[18]

Presently the portrait was packed up and sent to America, where
it hung in the Marlborough Street dining room. At the other end of
the room a portrait of Mr. Endicott, done as Secretary of War, continued to mount guard at right angles to his ancestor the Governor,
whom he markedly resembled. The Sargent picture aroused most
comment; all Boston was being painted by him, and many self-
styled art critics were about. Mrs. Endicott was portrayed as she
was, stalwart and uncompromising; William grew indignant at controversy over the picture: "Mother's portrait represents an ideal, I
believe, of a dignified, well-bred New England woman, which apart
from the person appeals to the imagination. After one has lived
with it I do not see the pained expression people talk about—serious, yes—but what does life teach us with all its trials if one has to
shrink from everything that suggests seriousness and experience.
That is its great value to me, and I would not have it otherwise."[19]

Mary was inclined to agree. Her mother could always steady her
when she felt impatient. In her letters, and better still, in her visits,
she was sympathetic and helpful. Mary was gentle not by nature,
but by training. Her mother's long visits helped her get through the
varied demands on her days. Joe always welcomed Mrs. Endicott,
for she was invariably tactful. She always admired her surroundings.
At Highbury, the gardens made this easy, but in damp, foggy,
winter-time London she could comment pleasurably on the sheep
grazing in Hyde Park, or the pattern tree branches made against
the wintry sky. Mrs. Endicott admired Joe's work, was kind to all
the young Chamberlains, yet did not intrude herself on their affairs.

In the summer of 1901 Joe's spirits were boosted by the first con-
ferral of degrees at Birmingham University. The University was entirely his brain child. Since he had taught evening and Sunday
classes in French and arithmetic as a young man, Joe had seen the
desire of the working-man to better himself. Mason College, found-
ed in Joe's mayoralty, gave a fair scientific and technical course, but
no humanities. Joe longed for a real university, and appealed far
and wide for funds. Andrew Carnegie sent £50,000 to endow the

sciences; and local friends and businessmen were approached, as
well as total strangers. He had in the end over £400,000 subscribed,
and there was gathered a group of eminent professors. Joe planned
buildings, studied curricula, and insisted on high standards in everything.

Yet this was only one of his projects. Joe had also encouraged the
Royal Society to study tropical diseases, and helped found the London School of Tropical Medicine. He also actively sponsored the
Colonial Nursing Association. Mary knew from her hours of letter
writing and interviewing what it took to raise £5,000 for this cause;
yet here was Joe, running the Colonial Office, with all these other
claims on him as well.

In 1901 Joe was put in charge of the South African internment
camps. There was an outcry against conditions there, and with
Milner he managed to reduce the death rate spectacularly. But the
Opposition blamed the Government for poor conditions there, as
for the war itself. To counter their outcries, the Unionists organized a huge meeting at Blenheim.

There were 3000 gathered for lunch. The Duke and Duchess of
Marlborough were the hosts; they sat with the M.P.s and dignitaries
under a marquee while Joe and Arthur Balfour made speeches. The
Chamberlains stayed overnight, and Mary, studying the whole
scene critically, could find no fault with the arrangements. Consuelo Vanderbilt had entered unwillingly into a classic American
money-English title marriage, but as a hostess she played her part
perfectly. Guests were well fed, housed, and pleasantly entertained.
In the library was a huge organ (contributed by the Vanderbilts—
with shimmering tin pipes and florid decorations it caused a modern sightseer to exclaim, "Coo! looks like a bloomin' weddin' cake
gone wrong!") and the organist from the Birmingham Town Hall
had been imported to play on it at all hours.

After Blenheim Joe had no real rest. Milner came home hoping to
draw up plans for reconstruction in South Africa. But the Government felt the guerilla warfare must be completely over before this
could begin; by the spring of 1902 there were ten times as many
British as Boers in action, and Kitchener's hard methods were
wearing the commandos down at last.

Bülow had continued to keep England dangling in the hope of an alliance. But a speech of Joe's in October, 1901, and the German reaction to it, caused the Foreign Office to declare all hope of an alliance ended. Joe was justifying Kitchener's tactics and touched on the "barbarity" of other nations faced with irregular resistance. Bülow seized on mention of the Franco-Prussian War and demanded an apology; but was assured officially no offence had been intended and no apology was needed. In England those who knew how Joe had worked for German friendship felt him badly used. Bülow meanwhile cunningly decided to use the anti-British sentiment rampant in Germany to his own use. He delivered a speech insulting to Chamberlain on January 8th. He hoped thus to get the Reichstag to approve the expansion of the Kaiser's cherished navy.

The German move backfired. British opinion was outraged, and rallied to the Colonial Secretary. At the annual Jewellers' Dinner in Birmingham on January 11th Joe answered Bülow's rebukes with self-control but unmistakable firmness, ". . . What I have said, I have said. I withdraw nothing. I qualify nothing. I defend nothing. As I read history, no British Minister has ever served his country faithfully and at the same time enjoyed popularity abroad. I make allowance for foreign criticism. I will not follow the example that has been set me. I do not want to give lessons to a Foreign Minister, and I will not accept any at his hands. I am responsible only to my own Sovereign and my own Country-Men."[20]

With this speech Joe became the man of the hour. He had stood up to Germany in good English fashion. He and Mary went to Windsor for the first time in the new reign; both King and Queen were pleasant, and their daughters Princess Victoria and Princess Louise both mentioned Joe's speech, the former asking, "Did it not make you very proud of him?"

Mary was pleased at how comfortably they fitted in on this visit to Windsor. The King and Queen seemed more human than she had ever suspected them. They had waited so long; the Queen especially seemed like a child with new toys as she showed off her possessions. She pointed to a bit of Sèvres china and said, "I am so afraid a housemaid will break it! But then, one only has these things once in one's life, and one may as well enjoy them!" Joe's first grandchild, little Hilda Mary Richards, had been born during the summer; so Mary was able to have grandmotherly chats with the Queen. The latter was lamenting the loss of her grandchildren after the Duke and Duchess of York carried them away on their return from their Australian tour.

In confirmation of Joe's answer to Bülow the City of London honoured him with a luncheon on February 13th, 1902. As he was a member of the Cordwainers' Company he already had the Freedom of London; so the next best thing they could give was an address in a gold casket. Joe and Mary drove in an open carriage on a bright windy day to the Guildhall. Aldermen there conducted them, through a fanfare of trumpets, to the Library, where the Lord Mayor of London awaited them.

Fifteen Cabinet members were on hand for the speeches and the luncheon; Joe was almost overcome, for he had thought that one or two might turn out. The most touching moment of all came at the luncheon when Arthur Balfour was asked to make an impromptu speech about Chamberlain; it was natural and charming. Mary realized, as they drove home through the crowds that "such an event does not come to many men . . . The City of London . . . has reserved such a ceremony for those who stand high in the nation's estimation and Kings and Princes have felt it an honour to receive such a mark of its favour. To Joe there is a personal feeling about it, coming as he does of a family which for generations took part in the city life, which makes him prize it as no other appreciation of his work would be prized."[21]

The tribute did make Mary think a little about the years she and Joe had been through together. Though she had been married thirteen years she still thought of Joe's daughters as "the girls"; it was a new sensation to play Grandma while Joe sat cross-legged beside "The Cherub", his granddaughter, and she snatched at his sparkling eyeglass. Sometimes Mary brooded a little about not having children of her own. But if she had had them, how could she have been so companionable with Joe's, and how could she have been so constantly with her husband? Mary spoke seldom of the family she might have had; the new baby did seem like her own grandchild; and the whole family was so absorbed in her antics that a tea-time visitor observed tartly, "I see you have all got it very badly!"

On May 31, 1902, came the long-awaited Treaty of Vereeniging, ending the war, and a week later there followed a Thanksgiving Service at St. Paul's. The peace seemed a fitting Coronation present for the King. Colonial contingents began to arrive, and on June 23rd Mary and Joe gave a reception for 218 dignitaries. William, Louise, and Mother were all on hand; Mary was radiant, and the house, filled with pink and red roses, looked splendid. Next day came stunning news. The King had appendicitis, and was to be operated on. The Coronation was indefinitely postponed, and the country held its breath. This was a grave ailment, an unfamiliar operation. Parties were cancelled, and householders sadly inspected their expensive decorations and waited anxiously for news.

The good news of the King's recovery had scarcely been received when catastrophe brushed close to the Chamberlains. Joe, leaving his office on July 7th, was in a bad cab accident. The cab horse shied at some street decorations and fell; a heavy pane of glass smashed over Joe's head. Luckily his high silk hat took most of the blow, but he was badly cut and bruised and lost a great deal of blood. Mary was out driving with her mother when they saw a news poster about the accident. Rushing to Charing Cross Hospital she found Joe, stitched and bandaged, sitting up in bed smoking a cigar. Though this was reassuring, he was dizzy and confused when he came home two days later, and was ordered two weeks' complete rest.

The accident came at a crucial time politically. Mary was torn between obeying doctor's orders, while Joe fretted; or letting him talk, write, and make decisions, and perhaps harm himself further. Finally she had to compromise. Lord Salisbury, his powers failing, finally resigned on July 11th. The same afternoon the King summoned Arthur Balfour. Balfour wanted to consult Joe and the Duke of Devonshire before accepting. He called at Prince's Gardens; Mary led him upstairs and woke her husband. She insisted, though, that Joe dictate, rather than write, his farewell letter to Salisbury.

There had been much discussion about Joe's succeeding as Prime Minister. Early in the spring he had come out against it, saying his work with the colonies was not done, and that he was quite willing to serve under Balfour. On July 14th it was unofficially announced that Joseph Chamberlain would remain at the Colonial Office. Two days later he went to the first Cabinet meeting.

Then, to Mary's relief, they got off on a three day cruise on the *Enchantress*. It was little enough of a break from work; but Mary hoped that Joe's rugged nature would somehow absorb the blow it had received. The Colonial Premiers were gathered in Conference, and Canada raised a momentous issue: reciprocal Imperial Prefer-ence. Joe would study this carefully in months to come; now it was only one of the problems he faced.

The Boer Generals were another. Botha, De Wet, and De La Rey, the new leaders in South Africa, journeyed to Europe ostensi-bly to raise money for destitute burghers' families. Really their "ap-peal to the civilized world" was as much for sympathy as money. They hoped to maneuver somehow a new peace settlement.

Joe was prepared to talk with them informally, and Kitchener felt it would do them good to go to the Coronation Naval Review, held in mid-August. So the generals were put on a launch and taken out to the *Nigeria* to meet the Colonial Secretary. It was an awkward meeting. Joe waved at the fleet and invited them to watch "their ships" with his party. The Generals mumbled that their clothes were not smart enough and went ashore again. Joe was dis-gruntled and encamped at Highbury, waiting for the Generals to "climb down". He would not meet them at his office until they gave him a list of what they wanted to discuss. They finally got together on September 5th.

Meanwhile Joe had been hatching a plan which Mary highly ap-proved. Eventually he wanted to tour all the self-governing colonies personally; he felt now would be a good time to go to South Africa. It would be a good-will mission, aiming at the reconciliation of Briton and Boer; but he would also get in some practical words about South Africa's paying her share of the war. Such a tour by a Minister was unprecedented, but both King and Cabinet approved the tour.

Even though Joe would be speech-making constantly in South Africa, it would be a change of scene, and he would have the long voyage out to relax him. He needed refreshment, for he had had to fight hard for many things that year, not the least being the Education Bill of 1902.

There was long and bitter wrangling over this; Nonconformists were indignant at the thought of taxes going to support denominational as well as public schools. Joe had suggested compromise, but while he was recovering from his accident his amendment had been struck out. He feared the Bill might ruin the Government, and Mary had seldom seen him so gloomy as he was in October about the prospects of the Bill: "An honest attempt to make things easier and better than they are both for Churchmen and Nonconformists it pleases neither, and for the Liberal Unionist party it promises to be disastrous . . . Joe thinks that the party is really on the verge of being broken up by it. Once broken it will not re-unite, and he fears it is now too late to save it."[22] These were ominous rumblings, but Joe did all he could for the bill, speaking for it in Birmingham, and winding up the Government debate in November.

Mary meanwhile was planning their trip. The King wanted them to go out in the cruiser *Good Hope*, money for which had been voted by the Cape Parliament. They would go first to Natal, which had borne the brunt of the early part of the war, and been unswervingly loyal. Disembarking at Durban they would journey, chiefly by train, for two months through the four colonies, finishing at Cape-town. The trip was bound to test her diplomatic resource as well as Joe's and Mary armed herself with the stout volumes of the *Times* history of the war to read on the way out.

Her principal problem was clothes. She must be fresh and attractive through mid-summer heat, dust, and rain. She ordered sturdy and practical travelling dresses and suits, which were stylish as well; they would be surmounted by a voluminous silk dust coat. There were light and pretty clothes for dinners and receptions: her favorite was a white batiste garlanded with roses. In all she had twenty-six dresses, and she felt almost as encumbered as Queen Elizabeth on her travels.

Just when she was busiest with last minute arrangements—she *must* have new gloves, and she was longing to visit Ethel and the baby, too—there was a Royal Command for Mary and Joe to come to Sandringham. Mary was curious about it, especially as she would be meeting the Kaiser for the first time since 1889. They arrived for tea, and found the King's grandchildren playing about in the Hall; presently the King, Prince of Wales, and gentlemen of the Household went off to meet the Emperor at the station.

"We all naturally joined in a circle, and the Emperor walked round it, the King presenting the gentlemen and the Queen presenting the ladies. When he reached me he showed that he was the possessor of the traditional Royal memory, for on this point there could have been no one to prompt him. He said, 'The last time I met you was at Hatfield.' We were all much impressed by the force of his grip (it was the 'mailed fist' indeed). That night at dinner I . . . sat next His Imperial Majesty, an honour due no doubt to the scarcity of ladies among the guests . . . I found him most agreeable, and conversation flowed with the greatest of ease. Of course he talked a good deal to the Queen, but she is so deaf that I got my full share of him. He told me about Prince Henry's visit to America, and his account of the beautiful decorations of the dinner tables in New York and how well arranged things were there, and how he meant to have his tables done in the same way . . . My only embarrassment was caused by his persisting in addressing me as 'Ma'am' which, in consideration of the presence of Royalty, was very trying. However, it was natural enough for him, as a direct translation of Madame, and it was not my affair."[23]

It appeared the Kaiser was fond of practical jokes. They had spoken of table decorations. His eye roved to the cloth runner in the middle of the Sandringham dining table. The plates were cleared, and as usual before dessert a footman went round to the bottom of the table to remove the runner. The Kaiser turned to Mary, saying "Look what I am going to do!", and put his hands firmly on the end of the cloth. The footman pulled and pulled; nothing happened. Then suddenly the Kaiser removed his hands, and the poor man tugging away at the other end flew back and only just managed not to fall over. With this jest the German Emperor was well pleased; Mary saw the "mailed fist" in a new light.

The next day trees were planted honouring the King's birthday, and the guests gave presents. Then they toured the greenhouses and stables; the race horses Persimmon and Diamond Jubilee, and some of their colts, received carrots from the Queen. At dinner that evening Mary sat on the King's left, and he told her how pleased he was about their trip to Africa. He was very hearty about the cruiser taking them, "Quite right, quite right that Mr. Chamberlain should go out in that way."

Before leaving England, Birmingham feted Mary and Joe at the Town Hall. On their return to Highbury, 4000 torch-bearers lined their route. It was a wildly picturesque scene, flames on either side and following them, and a constant stream of cheers from the crowd. "What they had come to see was Joe, and when he stood up in the carriage . . . every eye was lifted to his face. 'There's Joey.' 'Look at 'im now,' ' 'Ere comes our Joe.' 'Wish you a pleasant journey, Joe.' "[24]

At Cannon Hill Park, where a fireworks display had been arranged, the Chamberlains' escort left them. The suggestion had been tactfully declined that a group of students should unhitch the horses and drag the Chamberlains home themselves. Mary was glad of the quiet which fell after that tumultuous evening. She was quite overcome, for Joe had paid her rare public tribute when he said, "during fourteen years of arduous and sometimes excessive strain, she has sustained me by her courage, cheered me by her gracious companionship and I have found in her my best and truest counsellor."[25] It was hard for him to speak like that, and Mary had had all she could do to remain mistress of herself, hearing him.

Their send-off from Portsmouth was splendidly ceremonial. Family, friends, and some of the Cabinet rode down on a flower-garlanded train to say good-bye. In mid-afternoon the visitors left the ship, and the *Good Hope* "steamed out—the sun lighting up the ships in the harbour, marines in their scarlet uniforms saluting from the deck of a man-of-war, our band playing and theirs responding."[26] In the month-long voyage ahead Mary would see Joe more relaxed than for years; he put the year's troubles behind him and looked forward with eagerness to the journeys ahead.

CHAPTER XII

"Much Have I Travelled in the Realms of Gold"

JUST at first Mary could not appreciate the comfortable quarters Admiral Fawkes had turned over to her and Joe aboard
the *Good Hope*, for as they reached the Bay of Biscay, it proved
true to its stormy reputation; Mary spent thirty-six hours in her
cabin while the ship dipped and plunged. She was consoled when
Joe, who was fit as a fiddle, told her that of twenty officers only six
had appeared in the ward-room for dinner.

Once recovered, Mary was delighted with their routine. There
was a special boudoir for her, a little cabin on the after bridge fitted
up with carpet, flowered armchair and sofa, and writing table. They
dined with the Admiral, his Flag Lieutenant, and the Captain; the
midshipmen came two by two to join them at breakfast, and the officers to dinner. The three-man staff Joe had brought from the
office ate in the ward-room, and it was not long before they all felt
at home on board ship.

The party stopped for two days in Cairo, where Joe talked politics with Lord Cromer. The excursion naturally included a visit to
the pyramids: the ship's chaplain, a former champion runner,
sprinted to the top of the Big Pyramid, leaving four of the five Arabs
who were with him far behind!

On December 13th there was the traditional "Crossing the Line"
ceremony. Father Neptune appeared in a red robe with trident saying he would soon be giving the Chamberlains the freedom of the
seas, and initiating those young men he had not seen already.

In due course an entire Court appeared with Neptune; Mrs. Neptune gave Mary a coral bouquet, and her husband read an address
to Joe, then invested him "with the highest order of the sea, the
Order of the Sardine; then he conferred on me the Order of the

Bloater, pinning a pink fish tied with a blue ribbon to my dress, and suspending a blue fish round Joe's neck. Lastly we were made free-men of the sea by anointing us with water on the forehead (so Joe was spared the ducking)."[1]

The procession then continued on to a huge canvas bath which had been filled with three feet of water; the victims were lathered and shaved with a whitewash brush and huge wooden razor, then dumped unceremoniously in to splash. Mary and Joe looked on from the bridge, there was much laughter and shouting, and even the Major of Marines, who offered £25 to be let off such an undigni-fied proceeding, did his part with éclat.

Two days later the Chamberlains landed in Mombasa, in the East African protectorate. This was under Foreign Office jurisdiction; the community was a bustling one, and there was a luncheon for ninety at the Law Courts. The men wore white drill uniforms and sun helmets, the ladies their European finery; they contrasted bril-liantly with the rich green of the tropical trees.

That same afternoon they set out on a special train for the interior on the Uganda Railway. At one station were gathered a group of Somali children under the care of two lady missionaries; one of them presented Mary with a bunch of roses. The rich foliage soon gave way to scrub bushes and trees; Mary was reminded of New Hampshire wastelands she had been through. After tea Sir George Whitehouse, the Engineer and Manager of the Railway, suggested that the Chamberlains ride on the cowcatcher of the engine. There was a comfortable seat installed there, and they sped on while the sky filled with the rosy light of sunset.

Next day they had their first look at some game—in the course of the journey they saw antelopes, hartebeest, wildebeest, zebras by the score, ostriches, and even a rhinoceros. To Mary's great disap-pointment she and Joe missed seeing in all five lions that the others had a glimpse of. For a day and night they stopped off at Nairobi, which was "a most flourishing settlement which has only been in existence four years, but which is rapidly becoming a place of such importance that more than half the white population is already liv-ing there. The Railway has its headquarters and works there, and for the Administration of the Protectorate it is an important centre

—so when we arrived at the station, gaily decorated in our honour, we found a group of ladies arrayed as if for Ascot, and a larger group of gentlemen looking very nice and cool in their white drill clothes and helmets—the universal uniform, naval, military, and civil, of the East.

"It was a picturesque scene as we emerged to drive to Sir Charles Eliot's [the High Commissioner]. A mushroom town of corrugated roofs, surrounded by hills on all sides, bungalows on the higher ground surrounded by bright little gardens—a long straight road . . . with five triumphal arches . . . pennons of red, white, and blue and palms fluttering in the fresh breeze—the road lined with police (Indians in khaki uniforms and red turbans) and wild half-naked savages, the Masai, decked in all the glory of wonderful head-dresses and war array. I got into a ramshackly vehicle with Sir Charles Eliot, but the horses, unaccustomed to bands and crowds, preferred not to move . . . so we ignominiously descended and got into Sir George Whitehouse's American buckboard. About halfway down this road the motley procession of mule carts, horses, jinrickshaws, handcarts, etc. came to a standstill—a lady from an outlying district rode up on horseback and presented me with a bouquet . . . and the Indian community, merchants, etc. presented Joe with an address in a silver casket, which he duly acknowledged.

"Then on we drove, and made a circle on the hill to see the view. It was very pretty, distant mountains encircling a plain in which was the little town, while dotted about were the houses of the various officials. All of a very temporary description, with one or two exceptions, but what struck me much was the way in which all were striving to gather home surroundings about them. Roads were being made, gardens laid out, a Club was started, and all were vying with one another to make life as pleasant and as natural to their own habits and customs as could be under the circumstances . . . When we saw the children, some of whom had been born there, looking as rosy as in England, it was the best sign one could have that it was a white man's country . . .

"A large luncheon under a marquee was given by Sir Charles Eliot in the garden of Mr. Ainsworth, the Sub-Commissioner or Resident at Nairobi. Everything was very nicely done, the table covered with a profusion of English flowers which do extremely well here, and again a menu which was a surprise in the heart of Africa. They have been most successful in Nairobi in raising English vegetables, and it promises to become an industry of some importance, as they are beginning to send them to the coast and Zanzibar, even to South Africa."[2]

After lunch the Masai warriors gave a war dance. Mary was intrigued by these fierce tribesmen, who live in war on raw meat and blood, though in peace on milk and maize. They came and gave Joe an address in a silver box; this civilized gesture contrasted strangely with their dance. Garbed scantily in brown cloth they had shields, and wild head-dresses, some of lions' manes; they wore frills of ostrich feathers round their necks, had jangling metal at the knees, and carried spears and wooden knob-kerries. Their hair was twisted into ropes, held together with red mud. They pranced and shrieked and jangled that afternoon, and again that evening by torchlight; the Chamberlains watched in wonderment, and thought life on the train quite tame by contrast.

They travelled 521½ miles along the Uganda Railway in all, and were constantly surprised by the scenery. The Kikuyu country had cultivated fields, then they got into the forest with huge trees, and tangled jungle creepers beneath. There were vast stretches of mountain country, with steam pouring out of volcanic rock; then there were grassy uplands and tree-filled hollows so like Sussex it was hard to believe they were within a few miles of the Equator, and 8000 feet above the sea. It was not hot; the air was so fresh they slept comfortably under several blankets. Mary thought it had meant a lot to the East African settlers to have them come; and Joe was fascinated by the railroad, having been a strenuous advocate of it from the first.

At the end of the week they came down to the steamy coast, and dined at the Mombasa Club. The streets were illuminated, and torch-bearers accompanied the Chamberlains down to the pier. Then, under a canopy of stars they were rowed out over the dark waters to the cruiser *Forte*. This carried them overnight to Zanzibar Harbor, where they re-joined the *Good Hope*. Joe and his staff, with the Admiral and his officers, were to be received by the Sultan of

Zanzibar; but being a lady Mary had to proceed separately. She drove with the Acting Consul's wife in one of the Sultan's carriages (stiflingly lined with red velvet!) and they met the Sultan. He was very young and boyish, as his father had only recently died, and he was fresh out of Harrow. Mary thought him quite dignified, though his entourage thought him very gauche and shy as compared with his father. He was dressed in white, and had a gorgeous red-and-gold belt, a flowing black garment over the white, and on his head a red-and-blue turban. After a short conversation the ladies were led to the piazza and given coffee and sherbet. There they could see the gentlemen, but not themselves be seen.

"The Sultan had sent his State Barge for Joe . . . with twenty black oarsmen, dressed in crimson and green and gold. The Admiral's barge followed, and they all walked in procession across the Esplanade.

"From a corner behind a Venetian blind we were able to look into the long room where the audience assembled. The Sultan sat in the middle with Joe on his right, and all the Europeans; on his left the Arabs. These last sat motionless in silence, while coffee and sherbet were served to the Europeans. It being the fast of Ramadan none of the natives took anything. At the end of ten minutes they took their leave, and after a short time the Sultan came out on the piazza . . . divested of his state garments . . . He showed us the Baraza Room, a curious medley of handsome Eastern things and bad European ones, then we went into a smaller room to see his wife.

"She is a mere child, being only twelve years old, but of course dressed and veiled like a woman. [She and the Sultan's married sister] were gorgeously apparelled, a sort of narrow skirt of dark blue and gold, and around their shoulders wound a mantle of reddish gold tissue . . . heavy gold bracelets on their arms and necklaces of gold and pearls . . . a curious sort of open mask took the place of the Egyptian yashmak. It is almost triangular in form—a band of gilt and spangles passing across the eyebrows and again below the nose, leaving the eyes and the lower part of the face exposed.

"The little lady was all smiles, shook hands very nicely and greeted me in Arabic. It was funny to see her appealing look to her husband to see what she should do next . . . I made several attempts to converse with the Sultana, but it was difficult to know how to interest her, and after he [the Sultan] had interpreted my attempts he said, 'You know, she is only a child,' so after that I felt I had discharged my responsibilities sufficiently and talked to him.'"[3]

The Chamberlains, after lunching with the English community, went for a drive to cool off. They drove into the interior, among cocoanut and clove trees, and thatched native huts. In rosy twilight they returned to the harbour. As the Zanzibar channel was treacherous the *Good Hope* had moved seven miles out to sea. So Joe and Mary climbed into the Sultan's barge, and a launch towed them smoothly over an amethyst sea. Night fell, and they studied the stars, marvelling to find them all reversed; the Great Bear, turned upside down, appearing just above the horizon.

On Christmas Eve there was a farewell party on shipboard; next day Mary and Joe made the rounds of all the messes, admiring the flags and paper flower decorations; and at each table accepting a slice of plum duff. In the afternoon there was a display of gymnastics, then a quiet dinner, and a last farewell gathering on deck, and the Chamberlains said good night.

Next day they went ashore at Durban, and were greeted by the Governor and Premier of Natal. Their two days in the city were a good foretaste of things to come. Following a welcome at the Town Hall, Joe addressed a luncheon gathering; he urged reconciliation of the two white races under the British flag. Upon this depended self-government for the two colonies; not until they had self-government could there be South African federation. He warned that it would take time, patience, and good-will; grievances could not be waved away. After the speech the street crowds greeted Joe almost as if he were at home, "There 'e is!", "What's the matter with Joe? 'e's all right!", and shouting and cheers as the Chamberlains went by. The next night Joe spoke impromptu on his other great theme: the duty of colonists to accept the obligations as well as the privileges of Empire.

From Durban the Chamberlains went by train to Pietermaritzburg, stopping along the way at flower-decked stations. Pietermaritzburg, with its primitive houses set in a hollow surrounded by hills, was very much like Omaha as Mary had seen it in 1885. In fact she thought constantly of the American West in this country; except that the towns were built of corrugated iron, not wood. There were delegations coming to see Joe every minute between breakfast and dinner; he was so busy that Mary had to go alone to a large garden party given by the Mayor and Mayoress at Government House. If this was the sort of pressure they were going to put on Joe it was too much, and Mary did not hesitate to say so.

Journeying on, they stayed overnight at Colenso, where more than a hundred Zulu warriors put on a blood-curdling war dance for them. After this they climbed into a mule wagon, rather like the Army wagons Mary had ridden in at Fort Leavenworth, and drove to the battlefield. Having looked over the terrain they went on to Ladysmith, where Joe gave a speech in thanks for the address presented to him there. The tree-lined main street, with its small houses with wide piazzas, was much like New England; but the shattered tower of the Town Hall gave eloquent witness to the siege sustained by the town.

Driving out by mule wagon to see Spion Kop, eighteen miles from Ladysmith, the Chamberlains had their first real view of the veldt, with rolling green and distant hills, and clouds hanging about the bold range of the Drakensberg. At the foot of Spion Kop both English and Dutch farmers had gathered to greet them; a lady offered Mary her horse and though it felt like riding up the side of a house, the horse managed all right. They paused to see the long line of trenches, then rode down again towards evening. At the Town Hall that night the Stars and Stripes were flying beside the Union Jack.

Next day it was on to Pretoria by train. At the last station in Natal the Governor and Prime Minister got off, and Lord Milner, the High Commissioner, and Sir Arthur Lawley, the Lieutenant Governor, of the Transvaal boarded the train, and accompanied them into the colony.

It could have been an awkward meeting, for Joe and Milner had clashed many times about the Cape constitution. Milner, and many Cape loyalists, wanted to suspend it entirely, and change the colony to a Crown Colony. This was because the Bond, the Dutch nationalist party, controlled the Parliament and it seemed would permanently obstruct British progress in South Africa. Milner, exhausted by years of strain, had been ready to resign; he was delighted to have Joe on the spot to see things as they really were.

Mary was surprised not to see more evidence of war in the veldt country they were passing through. Houses had been destroyed, but tents had replaced them; here and there were block houses with tin cans strung along a wall which had been used to sound the alarm. They made several stops; at Volksrust the son of General Joubert, the old leader of the Progressive Party whom Kruger had made Commandant General at the start of the war, was introduced. At the stop after that tea was served, and Mary was given an ostrich-feather fan; many Dutch names were among the donors; and a Boer woman had baked the brown bread served at tea.

At Pretoria a surprising gathering took place at the Lieutenant Governor's garden party. "One hardly expected a few years ago that we should be greeting a group composed of Generals Botha and De La Rey and old Piet Cronje, who stood and gazed at Joe with quite a kindly expression, notwithstanding the term he has served at St. Helena as prisoner of war . . . Several addresses were presented to Joe, who made a short speech in reply, otherwise it was a purely social function, and we had as our chief duty to assist Sir Arthur Lawley in receiving. My supply of gloves will soon come to an end with all this hand shaking, to say nothing of my hand, for the Colonial grip is strong . . .

". . . The chief and historic interest of the visit, however, was the meeting which took place on the last morning in the building of the Volksraad. Think how we should have been astonished if anyone had told us three years ago that Joe would preside over a large gathering of Boers in the Raadzaal at Pretoria! Many of the audience being ex-members of the Raad, and of the Government of Kruger! . . .

"The Hall, which is arranged with rows of semi-circular seats and desks facing the chair, as in the House of Representatives, was filled—a motley assembly of Boers, from the carefully dressed men of the world to the rough farmer from the distant veldt, with his unkempt beard and haystack head and shabby ill-fitting clothes—all the intervening grades were represented. It was a moment worth seeing when into this strange meeting Joe walked, followed by Lord Milner and Sir Arthur Lawley and the staff. As he took his seat in the front . . . he was applauded by the stolid company, at the lead of Botha who had conducted them in, and then had taken his seat among the Generals. As Smuts rose to present the Memorial which had been prepared, one wondered what was in the minds of those who had witnessed such different scenes in that self-same spot, in the old days when Kruger, who had no right to sit in the Lower Assembly, used to come down and take up a position on the side of the Speaker's chair, and stay there until the Raad did his will . . .

"Smuts, a trim-looking young man, spoke extremely well, and nothing could have been better than his manner. His fellow Boers punctuated his remarks with signs of approval, but one was struck by the fact that they were much less articulate than a similar audience in England would have been. Of course the speech re-iterated the various demands which have been made, laying great stress on amnesty for our own rebels. Then Joe rose to reply—he opened his speech with a few friendly sentences, in his most conciliatory tone and manner—and I think that his words were appreciated, judging by the expression of those who listened—but as he went on speaking as firmly as they had done to him, maintaining our position with firmness, the faces fell. All the same the speech was well received, and I think the Boer farmers were surprised when they were faced with him to find him human after all, and not the ogre they had had pictured to them."[4]

Joe scolded the Boers in his speech for not appreciating the ten to fifteen million pounds the British had already spent in post-war rehabilitation, when they had made so much of £100,000 given by the Europeans in answer to their "Appeal to the Civilized World". He defended the Vereeniging Treaty as the charter of the Boer people, and declared the British would not be pressured into amnesty for rebels in the Cape and Natal, reminding the Boers how harshly they had treated rebels from their own cause. Smuts had closed avowing Boer loyalty; Joe finished with his hopes for reconciliation. When he left the chamber, General Botha led the applause.

The Chamberlains set out for Johannesburg, pleased with events thus far. The generals had been lobbying against them for months;

now Schalk Burger, their leader, had counselled against further resistance.

At Johannesburg Joe addressed a crowd of 10,000 at the Wanderers' Club. It was a critical meeting, for the Transvaal Government would be asked to contribute towards the war's cost, and Johannesburgers, exposed by Kruger for so long to taxation without representation, were apprehensive. Joe was dextrous in winning over the crowd. There had been welcoming addresses, and a bouquet for Mary. Then Joe got up and expressed his "appreciation for the patriotism and gallantry which the Johannesburgers had shown in the ranks of the Imperial Light Horse, which all agree was the finest body of irregular troops in the war."[5] Skilfully he led them on; having praised their courage in war he continued, "It has been said that you are prepared to repudiate your share of the expenditure which has been incurred in this war . . . that you and you alone in the British Empire, will fail in your duty." A voice cried "Never!" And Joe: "I will wait and see." Cheers swept the crowd, and the stage was set for the work Joe had come to do.

They were staying at Milner's house, "Sunnyside", in the suburb of Park Town; here Mary saw Joe continually absorbed with delegations. Even at lunch people had questions for him; so Mary insisted that he have a quiet tea with her. Then he had to write out despatches and telegrams, and every evening there would be an important dinner party, after which the secretaries would be summoned for more work.

Sir Percy Fitzpatrick, leader of the mining interests, held a garden party one afternoon. Joe had conferred at length with him, and agreed that the Imperial Government should grant an investment loan of thirty-five million pounds, for settling a larger British population on the land, extending the railways, and paying compensation claims; while in return the business leaders would contribute thirty million pounds towards the war debt. Matters being so agreeably settled, Mary tried her hardest to be pleasant at the party; she was pleased by the ladies' clothes here, for they were as elegant as those in London.

There was another pleasant party at Lord Milner's, but Mary had to rest her right hand after a week of Colonial hand-shakes, which brought on some aggrieved murmuring in the newspapers. In two weeks Joe and Lord Milner had been over most important questions: compensations for war damages, the labour shortage in the mines, competent Crown administration, the investment loan, and the war contribution. Most important, Milner, though worn out and anxious, was willing to stay on in the Transvaal.

Mary and Joe had both been prejudiced against Johannesburgers in the past. When they left, their impressions had become favourable. Dinner party conversation at Sunnyside was not always of general interest, but Mary had drawn out several experts to discuss mining, and found them quite enthralling. She had met several Americans, "all of the first order of intelligence and energy, some of them gentlemen, others who have risen by sheer ability."[6] And the American ladies in the city had given her a garden party, presented a golden purse, and ordered the band to play "Hail Columbia", "The Star Spangled Banner", and "My Country 'Tis of Thee."

After all those official functions it was a welcome change of pace to go trekking into remote regions to visit Boer farmers. They stayed in Potchefstroom in a pleasant house lent by its Dutch owners. They visited the nearby Dutch Land settlement, "a large farm owned by a syndicate, and allotted to various Dutch farmers, in especial amounts according to their means . . . [Our visit there was] a most unexpected experience. Quantities of Boers met us at the border of the farm and we drove under a triumphal arch of welcome. Escorted by the cavalcade we drove on, and then fancy our astonishment when we found them removing the horses, and we made the final stage of the drive, drawn by Boers old and young, all smiling and waving and enthusiastic. Who could have foreseen that such a thing could ever happen to Joe and me?"[7]

The next day they moved to Ventersdorp, where General De La Rey was on hand to greet them. Following that they trekked forty-two miles and camped in Lichtenburg. It was tenting with a difference. Mary and Joe had a large bedroom with four doors and mosquito netting, a big brass bed, carpet, and bedroom furniture, with a dressing room attached. Besides this they had a sitting room and dining room of their own; all round them ranged the rest of the party in somewhat less elaborate quarters.

General De La Rey made the Chamberlains welcome; Mary was impressed by his wife, who was "a typical Boer in appearance, of the rather French type—short, thick and genial, and after having talked to her for a couple of hours I came to the conclusion that she was a woman of much ability. These Boer women, unlike 'the world' as their appearance may be, have great power over their men, and it seems to me almost more important in the interest of the country to make friends with them than with the men . . . The wonderful thing is to find how ready they all are to talk of the war and how little bitterness they show in speaking of their losses.

"The meeting of burghers under the trees at Lichtenburg was very typical . . . At first I thought some of [the farmers] looked a little sullen, but as Joe addressed them, and then General De La Rey also spoke they became more animated, and ended by applause.

"Then Joe interviewed the predicants who were gathered there for a synod. That, too, though more difficult, passed off well. The ministers of the Reformed Church are perhaps one of the most difficult elements of all for they are very bitter against those who surrendered before the close of the war, and who came to our aid as National Scouts—and in some cases have refused them the sacraments of the church . . . I hope Joe may have been able to smoothe matters with them."[8]

Mary's favourite moments on trek were at sunset. All day the clouds chased each other over the rolling veldt. At evening they heaped up, red and purple, against the sun, or sometimes in soft shades of yellow, green, and pink. Then night fell, wonderfully deep and calm. They would sit outside their tents, picking out the constellations. Noise and battle seemed far off in those evenings. But it was the rainy season and they had several terrific storms when the wind blew, rain cascaded, and dust swept through everything they owned. Lying awake one night and listening to the tent pegs rattling, Mary wondered if they would hold. They did, but when the Chamberlains reached their next camp they found that twenty-seven of their city of tents had collapsed in that storm!

Proceeding towards Mafeking, the Chamberlains were joined at the border of Cape Colony by a detachment of Cape Police, the Governor, and the Prime Minister. As they drove along General

Baden-Powell pointed out the lines of defence and told stories of the subterfuges he had resorted to to make the Boers think his forces were stronger than they really were. Having Baden-Powell beside them, telling siege stories, brought the war closer; a wild thunderstorm bathed the scene in lurid light.

They reached Kimberley after a long day's train ride. Here, in the great diamond-mining centre, there was an elaborate welcome; even at the station many of the welcomers wore evening dress. Next day, when it was ninety-seven in the shade Chamberlain received addresses of welcome, and Mary had three addresses of welcome, and a box of fifty-three uncut diamonds given her by Kimberley's ladies. That afternoon they went over three of the De Beers mines and Joe let Mary carry home some samples: five good-sized and beautiful diamonds.

The mines impressed them; the white workers had a model village with gardens and a vinery, and the native compound was also fresh and new with its own store and hospital. Rhodes had made his way to fame and fortune directing the De Beers monopoly; Mary was impressed with the monument to his success.

Next they trekked through Orange River Colony, stopping at farms to talk with the farmers and their wives. They found hospitality everywhere; even though their hosts might be glum at first, they always parted friends. The Lieutenant Governor accompanied them through a dustier and browner veldt than they had seen in the Transvaal. Mary was swathed in blue veils, and carried a parasol; but even Joe, who was near-sighted, could see how brown and sunburned she was getting. She was almost bronze, and laughingly assured Joe she would probably stay that way.

At Bloemfontein Boers and Britons alike streamed four miles out to welcome them. Mary was relieved to find that as the Lieutenant Governor was a bachelor she would not have to go on a series of calls, visits, and drives, to please an eager hostess. She was free to perch in a corner and listen to the men talk. Their host, who had spent years in Rhodesia and the wilds of Africa, amazed her with his tales. She had a chance to marvel at Joe also; she had never doubted his purpose, but he had been working eighteen hours every day steadily, and she couldn't see how he managed it. He gave all his callers his most critical attention. Though he was almost as thin as he had been after the cab accident his general health, like her own, was blooming. And there was so much to vex him. At Mafeking and Kimberley, for example, he had run square into the loyalists' anxiety to avoid Bond domination by being annexed to the Transvaal. Joe said firmly, "It is like marriage. You take self-government for better or for worse."[9]

Now in the Government House ball-room with Lord Milner, who had re-joined them, Mary heard Joe attack an extremist Boer deputation. They had presented charges of British violation of the peace; Joe decided to read their spokesman, one Dr. Hertzog, a lesson. "For two and a half hours a most animated discussion took place, and we sat in breathless interest. Dr. Hertzog always seeking to confuse the issue, and Joe bringing him up . . . and even refusing to hear him unless he would give him a direct answer . . . When it was over many of the most prominent men present either came to see the Lieutenant Governor or wrote repudiating the terms of the address, and excusing themselves for having signed such a document . . . It is rumoured that [it] was really framed in Cape Town by the Afrikander Bond, and foisted upon the Boers of Orange River Colony."[10]

They left Bloemfontein in a climate of optimism. Joe's star-gazing at the southern constellations gave him a happy simile for his speech: ". . . And so it is with your South African problems. They are the same questions as those with which we have been familiar for a long time, but somehow or other, in the atmosphere of London they appear to be different from what they are in the atmosphere of South Africa."[11]

Lord Milner joked with Mary about her conquest of some old Boers. She had circled the room during a reception, shaking hands with all she met; next day she had word that "Mrs. Chamberlain had greatly pleased them, that they were all going about the town saying she was so charming that they were going back to tell their wives that they ought to be like her."[12]

The train journey through Cape Colony began well. They were received well at Grahamstown and Port Elizabeth, but at Graaff Reinet they met out-and-out Boer hostility for the first time: "Two thirds of the houses we passed had stolid impassive groups on their *stoeps*, who vouchsafed no sign of welcome, while the remaining third were waving handkerchiefs and flags and bowing with all their might . . . Here even in response to our bows few hats were raised, though now and then a reluctant dame gave a grumpy nod, or a shaggy farmer pulled at his hat brim in a grudging kind of way. Their curiosity was too great to keep them within doors, but they could not bring themselves to greet us, *even though they were the citizens of a British self-governing colony* [italics mine]."[13]

Joe spoke plainly in the town, pointing out that many of its citizens had joined the enemy forces. The rebellious elements must not continue to stir up trouble for the loyalists. Joe had asked in Port Elizabeth that the Bond leaders abandon thought of a separate Dutch Republic. When he left Graaff Reinet the Bond Secretary, Mr. De Waal, travelled with them. His speech at Middelburg seemed to answer that demand. He supported boldly reconciliation and allegiance to British rule; this seemed such a good omen they could gloss over the "disaffection" in Graaff Reinet.

Journeying through the most desolate stretches of the Karroo (Cape Colony's term for the veldt) people seemed to rise out of the earth to greet them. When the train stopped for water they would find whole families, complete with babies, who had driven fifteen or twenty miles to greet Joe. Often they had a grievance, but often, too, they wanted to thank the Chamberlains for coming to Africa.

They visited a prosperous British farm; and though the day was sunny and warm Mary insisted on putting heavy coats and rugs into their cart. They spent a happy day hearing how their host had hidden his animals from the Boers in the war, and when it was time to go all Mary's fussing about the weather paid off; Joe called her a mollycoddle, but he was glad of all the blankets they had brought!

Mary got up at dawn the next morning to watch their approach to Cape Town, "We came down faster and faster into a fertile and smiling land of fruit and flowers and cosy farmhouses, their white-washed walls and thatched roofs nestling amid groups of fine trees under the hillsides, surrounded by green fields and looking as if they had been established there for years—in strong contrast to the corrugated iron houses with their bare surroundings of some of the places farther north.

"As we approached a station at 6.45 a.m. I poked my head out and saw a crowd, and ladies in gay garments with the inevitable bouquet. Fancy my dismay, for I was in my dressing gown and Joe was still asleep. I had just time to retreat to my stateroom, from which I sent a polite message of regret that we could not appear, and Lord Monkbretton who was on the cowcatcher received the address and bouquets and huge baskets of delicious figs and grapes and peaches on our behalf."[14]

It was hot and sunny; but the Chamberlains looked cool and elegant when they stepped out in the old Dutch village of Paarl: Joe in grey frock coat, and Mary in white muslin with red toque and sunshade. Paarl was not reconciled, but the inhabitants were more dignified than those of Graaff Reinet. Much of the population simply went indoors. At the Mayor's garden party only a quarter of those invited actually came. Mary was just as glad, for Joe was exhausted, and needed to save his strength for the final week in Capetown.

They stayed outside town with the Governor at his summer place, Newlands; every day the Governor and Joe drove in for conferences, luncheons, and deputations. Mary dutifully went round with the Governor's lady to meet people: she went to a garden party, laid a cornerstone, and attended an agricultural show. Their only diversions were a Sunday spent with the Naval Commandant down the coast at Simon's Bay, and a visit to the Government wine farm at Constantia.

Joe had desperately hard work to do. A session with the most influential man in the Dutch community, Jan Hofmeyr, showed that De Waal's assurances were far from being realized. Hofmeyr sought, in return for a larger defence contribution, an amnesty for rebels. Joe saw how dangerous it would be to bargain. He wanted now to bridge the gap between the Bond and the Progressive Party in the Cape. On February 21st, 1903, Hofmeyr came to present an address, and followed it with an important speech. He declared his group would co-operate to the fullest extent in reconciling both European races under the British flag. Though the Progressives were suspicious of the Bond's good faith, Joe warned them not to reject it lightly. After some deliberation the Progressive leaders came around, and Mary watched the proceedings of the Farewell Banquet on February 24th in relief.

"It was a great sight . . . when Joe rose to speak a thunder of applause—then as he proceeded the great audience listened breathlessly . . . He made an announcement that the progressives . . . were prepared to accept the assurances given by Mr. Hofmeyr . . . It was the final success of the tour . . . the curtain was rung down, and the audience turned away, well pleased with the chief actor while I, his wife, laid my head down in peace that night, happy in the thought that his labour was finished in that arduous task, and proud in the belief that the work was truly and faithfully done."[15]

The Chamberlains embarked on the R.M.S. *Norman* for the long voyage home. Now that the strain was over Joe came down with a full-scale cold, and gout as well. Fortunately he could walk when they reached Madeira, for here to their surprise the Portuguese Government turned out in full array to welcome them to the island. They had tea, toured through fields of flowers and sugar cane, and bought some wicker chairs; then they started on the last lap home.

On March 14th they were welcomed home in force at Southampton. Joe was still in his bath when a group of constituents came on board with the medical officers. Then came the family, followed by the Mayor and Mayoress of Southampton. Then they boarded a special train for London. Austen, who had advanced from the Admiralty to Financial Secretary to the Treasury, and then, under Balfour, to Postmaster-General, had Cabinet affairs to report. The girls exclaimed over Mary's tan, and she shivered over the wintry landscape. After the summer heat of South Africa it was hard to accept the grey chilliness of England.

Mr. Balfour and most of the Cabinet were at Waterloo Station; so were the Colonial Office staff, and then, late and breathless, the Duke of Devonshire hurried up; he had gone to the wrong platform first. There was a crowd outside the door at Prince's Gardens, and welcome quiet indoors. Next day Joe went to report to the King, and Mary celebrated her thirty-ninth birthday by receiving streams of callers.

On March 20th the City of London presented its congratulations with ceremonies at the Guildhall and a luncheon at the Mansion

House. Joe was cheered as a peace-maker, and Mary who had been beside him through so many dark days, when the whole blame for the war was heaped on his head, took great satisfaction in this. In the two months they were in South Africa Joe had been to twenty-nine towns, delivered sixty-four major speeches, received eighty-seven deputations, and given over two hundred and fifty interviews. The Lord Mayor made complimentary remarks about Mary, who blushed at Joe's acknowledgement: "The Lord Mayor justly associates my wife's name with mine. Of my personal obligations to her this is no time to speak, but so far as the nation is concerned, she is entitled to some share of its gratitude in the work of reconciliation in South Africa. Her kindness, sympathy and interest made friends where I might have failed."[16]

Mary talked to both King and Queen about the tour. It was clear that though many problems remained, Joe's tour had had a profound psychological effect. The Boers had seen him not as an ogre, but as a human being. Mary, watching Joe, saw that he paused not at all. The spotlight of acclaim played briefly on them both. Now, said Mary firmly to her husband, she must disappear into the background again. The Colonial Secretary smiled, and bent to his work. At his office, in his library, and walking round the gardens with Mary, he was maturing a new plan. In a few months' time there would emerge, with the most profound results for his country, party, and family, Joseph Chamberlain's campaign for Tariff Reform.

CHAPTER XIII

In Sight of the Promised Land

JOE had been settled in his mind about Imperial Preference before he left for South Africa. A nominal duty on imported corn, of a shilling per quarter, had been revived to help the budget deficit of 1902. Canada had made it clear in the Coronation Colonial Conference and after that England should rebate duties on goods imported from the colonies, who would reciprocate on British goods. Ritchie, who had succeeded to the Exchequer when Balfour took office, was suspicious of colonial preference. He though it meant all sorts of new tariff walls must be raised against foreign goods. Having developed a budget surplus, he persuaded the Cabinet to remit the corn duty entirely, not only for the colonies; Joe regarded this as betrayal.

Tariff Reform now appeared vital to Joe as the means of imperial union. He saw the nationalist spirit of the self-governing colonies; and believed preference was the way to get free trade with the Empire. Far from bringing hardship to the workers, tariffs on foreign goods would benefit them. The difference in prices would be slight. For example, the corn duty meant that each four-pound loaf of bread cost about half a farthing more; this increase could be balanced by reducing taxes on essentials like tea and sugar. England was a dumping-ground for foreign goods; tariffs would benefit home industries.

Late in the spring of 1903 Mrs. Endicott had arrived for her annual visit. Tactful and unobtrusive, she could not help seeing that Joe was approaching a crisis in his career. He had struggled to keep the Unionist alliance intact, had supported the Education Bill, even though he thought it meant trouble ahead. But the social reforms, pledged in previous campaigns, had been slow to come. There was a new codification of the factory laws, dealing with safety and sanitation; but the old age pensions scheme was incomplete; and the Licensing Act, designed to promote temperance, was still in the future. Though Joe was still the champion of the working classes, he now thought of reforms on a larger, imperial scale.

The summer was trying for the Government. A report was issued which publicized glaring waste, inefficiency, and blunders in the conduct of the war. And the Cabinet was sharply divided about tariffs. Joe insisted that Colonial preference meant taxing food. His opponents insisted, with telling effect, that this meant "dear food". Balfour liked the idea of fiscal union with the colonies, but disliked the tax on food. In South Africa Joe had declared himself "a missionary of Empire"; Balfour supported him in spirit, but not particulars.

Mary, who saw the storm coming up, persuaded her mother to extend her visit through September. The family at Highbury had a pretty fair idea where the crisis was leading; but when Mary and Joe returned from London they brought momentous news. Ritchie and Lord George Hamilton, the convinced free traders in the Cabinet, had resigned; two others presently followed them. Joe meanwhile said he could not in conscience remain a Minister in a Government which would not declare a tax on food. He strode into the room where his family had gathered, and abruptly announced his resignation.

Like the others, Mrs. Endicott was stunned at first. "We fairly gasped. He then explained the whole situation. Mary came to my room and we talked late into the night. She calm and clear that he had done the right thing, and that Mr. Balfour had shown his strength in agreeing to the plan and policy he had proposed . . . Mr. Chamberlain has once more shown his power of self-sacrifice, and placed himself where nobody can honestly assail his motives. He has risen to the highest plane of patriotism, and I honour him for his position, never so great as now."[1] William, hearing the news, felt the same way, and wrote to congratulate his brother-in-law: "It is splendid for a man to live so entirely up to his principles, which must in the end command the respect of friend and foe alike."[2]

The Duke of Devonshire hung on the fence for a time, then he too resigned, and set about forming the Free Food League, the opposite number of the Tariff Reformers. Balfour's position was badly shaken. On October 9th, when Joseph Chamberlain surrendered his seals of office at a meeting of the Privy Council, Austen Chamberlain received his as Chancellor of the Exchequer. The son's task would often be a sorely trying one: he must be go-between between his father and Balfour; pressing the aims of tariff reform where possible, he must always be loyal to the Premier.

Mary's espousal of this latest, greatest cause of Joe's was as natural as breathing. He had had a vision, and he was right—as always, Joe's enthusiasm spilled over onto her, and easily convinced her mother of the soundness of his action. She set off with him to Glasgow where he opened his campaign, outlined the new taxes he favoured, and emphasized that the workingman's cost of living would not be going up.

Joe spoke later in October at Newcastle, Tynemouth, and Liverpool, but his most famous speech was on home ground, at Birmingham, November 4th. Sixty years later there are still those who recall the famous illustration of the "Two Loaves". For some weeks a flamboyant poster had caught Birmingham's attention: it showed one huge loaf of bread, made under free trade principles, and one tiny one, allegedly the result of the "protectionist" tax on corn. Thus vividly did the Free-Fooders claim the tax would ruin the workingman. Joe was more nervous about his Birmingham speech than Mary had seen him for a long time, yet he carried it off triumphantly. As he reached the topic of the poster, his tone grew richer, and more dramatic; he declared: "I have had the curiosity to inquire what would be the exact difference in the size of the loaf if the whole tax which I propose to put upon corn were met by a corresponding reduction in the size of the loaf. I asked my friend Mr. Alderman Bowkett [a baker in New Street, Birmingham] to make me two loaves in order to test this question."[3] Then, with a flourish he unwrapped a parcel which had been prominently displayed on the platform, and held aloft two loaves, almost identical in size. Mary was as delighted as the crowd. One loaf weighed slightly less than the other, but the difference was imperceptible; the object lesson was unmistakable. The big and little loaf poster was killed in Birmingham, at all events. The audience called out to see the loaves again; Birmingham was backing Joe, and his triumph was complete.

Though she said little about it, their new life, out of office and on the missionary trail, changed Mary's life almost as much as Joe's. Now it was Austen who was bidden to Sandringham, though it was nice to hear that Joe had been asked about, in a very friendly way. Even though it was a pleasure to see Austen going ahead in politics, after long years of training, it was still an anti-climax. The Chamberlains went to a State Banquet at Windsor honouring King Victor Emmanuel and his Queen. Mary described the gold plate service, the jewelled lady guests, and the splendour of the red-and-gold-clad Beefeaters as vividly as always, but the dinner was a farewell. In December Joe gave his last dinner for the Colonial Office staff; Mary busied herself sorting out mementoes of the South African tour.

She hoped that out of office Joe might get some relaxation, for he had admitted that his project was a long-term one. But he was attacking each day as if it were his last, and she realized in dismay how worn out he was. To her delight he agreed to a trip up the Nile. They set off for Cairo where they stayed at the British Agency with Lord Cromer. He arranged a ten day trip for them by government steamer; the time spent idling in the sun was good for both of them.

The Chamberlains went on to Naples, thence to Sicily. Mrs. Endicott nervously expected to hear at any minute that they had been captured by "brigands". But Joe and Mary wandered among churches and temples for two weeks unmolested, then returned safely to London.

Joe was inclined to take his Parliamentary duties lightly, and Mary encouraged him. He concentrated instead on making speeches for Tariff Reform; at one fund-raising dinner over £25,000 was subscribed to the cause. But Mary would not let him go at things too hard for long; in the autumn they took another holiday through Switzerland, Austria, and Italy.

A continuing anxiety since the birth of her baby was Ethel and her health. She suffered from tuberculosis and a house by the sea had not helped. As she grew frailer, the doctors decided she must go to Switzerland without even her husband to comfort her. Thinking of Ethel, lonely and miserable at Christmas-time, Hilda decided she must have some family with her, and went out to join her in early January. She was barely in time; they were happy together one day, and on the next came a crisis, and Ethel was gone. At Highbury Mary had the cable with the news of Ethel's death; she had to break it to Joe and Beatrice, Ida, and Austen. It was a dreadful day. Mary felt she had lost her own child, so many years had she loved and been anxious over "little Ethel". At least she would not not have any more pain to bear. Unhappy as he was, Joe could acknowledge this; to Mary's relief he was able to talk about his lost daughter. He did not retreat; he read aloud from the burial service to his remaining children, and they shared their sorrow. In the shadow that fell over them, the Chamberlains drew closer together than ever.

In the autumn of 1905, refreshed by a trip to the Continent, Joe stayed up every night for a week till two or three in the morning working on a speech to his constituents. When it was over, he said he was not at all tired. This was more than could be said of the Unionist Government. Balfour urged party unity, but in vain. The agitation mounted for a General Election, and on December 4th Mr. Balfour handed in his resignation. The Liberal Opposition leader, Mr. Campbell-Bannermen, took office, and Joe made plans for his campaign.

In less than a fortnight Joe planned a dozen speeches, while Austen had nineteen scheduled. Neville again got in some practice in public speaking when he spoke on behalf of Jesse Collings. The Birmingham polling date had been fixed very late, January 17th; before then the vote from other cities indicated a sweep for the Liberals. Mr. Balfour's candidacy was defeated at Manchester on the 13th, and in the days that followed came news of other Unionist reverses.

Mary and Joe left in an open carriage for the polls on Wednesday the 17th. They were bundled in furs against the cold; Joe held his cigar at a jaunty angle, and after he had voted they drove about, nodding and smiling encouragement to the Birmingham crowds. That evening they heard that he had been returned with a majority of 5079, but elsewhere the Unionist debacle was complete. A few days later Austen came off with a majority of 4366. Apparently Joe, though his party was a battered remnant of its former self, had lost none of his own position. What pleased Mary so much was how well he stood up to campaign rigours. Of course he was dismayed by what had happened to his party; he wrote his mother-in-law:

"To have remained standing while this blizzard was uprooting all my friends would have been a marvel, but to have secured the decision of the whole city and the surrounding suburbs with increased majorities was indeed a triumph which has amply rewarded me for all my exertions.

"In other respects the disaster has been complete and phenomenal. I expected an unfavorable majority of 100, but I had no conception of such an unprecedented revolution . . . It is clear that the rejection of my advice by the late Government accounts for much. The Education Bill, which deeply offended the Nonconformists lost us many seats . . . If Balfour had resigned two years ago we might still have been defeated, but we should not have been overwhelmed as we have been by those who thought that we had overstayed our welcome.

"My special interest—that of Tariff Reform and Imperial Preference—has not suffered, I think, so much as my opponents would like to make out, but its success is postponed indefinitely, and there is still a big fight before me. Many of my friends, not always discreet . . . would like me to compete with Balfour for the leadership, but this I will not do, both on personal grounds and also because I feel that without his influence I could not hope, in what remains to me of active life, to restore the Party to its old efficiency and predominance."[4]

Just before the Chamberlains left London for a holiday Balfour came to dine, but Mary observed disgustedly, "the leopard would not change his spots." He was still not willing to push the cause of Tariff Reform. Joe felt the Unionists might well have more than 150 seats in the House if he had boosted their cause earlier, but Balfour was inclined to be more cautious than ever. It fell to Austen to reconcile Joe with Balfour; he drafted most of the "Valentine's Day letter" in which Balfour accepted the notion of fiscal reform, a general tariff on manufactured goods, and a small duty on corn as "not in principle objectionable." This was a great relief, not only to Austen but the Unionists generally, for "Father is leading the Opposition till Balfour returns to Parliament, and opened the ball exceedingly well yesterday. But the majority in the House is insolent and overbearing, and we shall have much to endure. But now that Balfour and he stand shoulder to shoulder, all will be well. That they should have separated would have been a catastrophe, and at one time it seemed an inevitable one. Thank goodness that they and we are spared that."[5]

Both Joe and Austen were exhausted by the struggle with Balfour; Mary and Joe presently went off to the Riviera for sunshine, but Joe, though he got over his influenza, had an attack of gout, and foreign climes rather backfired for him. For his son they had a very different result.

Austen made a slow and painful progress to Algiers; once there his aches and pains seemed to leave him very promptly. He wrote home in May that he was riding every afternoon, and had actually been made to *dance* twice! This was astounding news; but more was to come. At forty-two, Austen, with the same promptness as his father had shown, fell completely in love. Ten days after meeting Ivy Dundas, daughter of a retired Army officer, he was engaged to her; he felt like a twenty-five-year-old, and as he walked down the street was convinced the whole world must know him for a happy man!

Mary was overjoyed, as was Joe. They had hoped so long Austen would marry, and here he was doing it at last. It seemed no time to Mary since she had been a bride. Sitting at Highbury with Joe that June they spoke of Austen's wedding, and also of Joe's birthday. Birmingham was planning a huge celebration to mark his thirty years in Parliament, and his seventieth year of life.

Though he was still tired, Austen's happiness rejuvenated Joe. And the tremendous tribute from Birmingham was overwhelming. On July 7th the Lord Mayor gave them luncheon, and there followed a triumphal tour by motor-car. Eighteen miles Mary and Joe were driven, and all the way the streets were lined with cheering crowds. They stopped in six parks to receive addresses, flags waved, and people shouted approval. Next day came Joe's birthday and telegrams and messages of congratulation poured in from all over the world. Joe's speech in Bingley Hall was a fitting climax. He thanked Birmingham for having backed him through the years; he urged them to uphold Empire, show greater sympathy for the colonies. Though his themes were familiar, and the words were not new, they caught at his hearers' hearts.

Joe and Mary drove home. Japanese lanterns flickered in the parks, there was a torchlight procession, and a crowd of thousands swept past the carriage. Still Joe's words were ringing in his family's ears: "England without an empire! Can you conceive it! England in that case would not be the England we love . . . it would be a fifth-rate nation, existing on the sufferance of its more powerful neighbors. We will not have it . . .

"I hope I may be able to live to congratulate you upon our common triumph, but in any case I have faith in the people . . . I look forward to the future with hope and confidence, and 'Others I doubt not, if not we, The issue of our toil shall see.' "[6]

Two days later Mary and Joe were back in London, dressing to go out to dinner. Huge copper cans of hot water were brought to Mary, for she bathed in her own room. The master of the house had his own bathroom, with tub and steam cabinet, installed next to the library. Mary was thankful the ceremonies were over, prepared to enjoy their evening out; she finished dressing first and started downstairs. There was a cry. Sidney, the footman, hurried on the scene. The bathroom door was open, and across the threshold lay Joe, the right side of his body stricken and paralyzed.

In those first dreadful moments Mary's head whirled. The same terror swept over her as when she had heard of his cab accident, only worse, far worse. Here Joe lay, helpless before her; but Mary took command of herself at once. She sat down and wrote a note to the doctor to come immediately. She wrote another to their hostess, explaining she was unwell, and they could not dine that evening. Though she could not know what the future held, she was determined no one out of the family should hear of Joe's illness. It had been seven-thirty when she heard Joe's call. In the next few minutes there was no time for thought. The carriage rolled away with her messages, she and Sidney made Joe as comfortable as they

could. Then the doctor came, with a grave diagnosis. Years of
strain and overdoing had had their way at last. The excitement of
the last week, coupled with Joe's previous fatigue, had made him
easy prey for this stroke. Now he must have complete rest; the
world would be told he was suffering from gout.

At the end of an anxious week Joe had improved enough to be
moved upstairs to their bedroom. Mother was at Highbury; Mary
did not see how she could have managed if she had been in America. She scribbled a note or two to William and Louise, letting them
think, with the public, that she was very busy, and Joe had had a
bad gout attack. But she could never have dissembled with Mother.

July 21st was Austen's wedding-day. It was hard to leave Joe,
but Mary went off to St. Margaret's, Westminster, with the rest of
the family; and Austen and Ivy stopped at the house to see Joe before leaving on their honeymoon. Though Joe was tired out by this
exciting day, he seemed none the worse for it.

Joe's progress was slow, in a hot and silent August. He began
massage treatments, walked from one room to another, then was
carried down to the drawing-room. And Mary marvelled: there she
was at her writing-table with her dear, dear husband lying on the
sofa just behind her. They had had tea together for the first time in
more than five weeks; she could hardly believe that he was really
there with her.

William wrote cheerily from America, under the impression still
that Joe was a victim to gout: "The 70th Birthday Celebration,
gratifying and moving and splendid as it all was, must have been a
trying ordeal. But I doubt not Mr. J. C. would refuse to think that
it had anything to do with the attack. All the same, anything so
emotional as that must have been, might have ignited a latent spark
of the old enemy."

He continued exuberantly about Austen's wedding, and urged
his sister to tell "that old bachelor Neville to come out here for a
part of a winter, and we'll send him home with an American wife
that will suit Ma and Pa. He apparently needs a smart American
girl who will let him know as only an American can . . . that she
thinks him wonderful. That fetches them always. The girls—well—
I have not entirely lost hope. Can't they get a beau? They won't if,

when you have house guests, they all three walk together 'because it is pleasanter'. It is too bad, for they would all make such splendid wives . . . I am convinced that anything (respectable of course) is better than being an old maid.''[7]

In September Joe was well enough to make the trip to Highbury; when she had seen him settled there, Mrs. Endicott returned to America. Mary's engagement calendar was full as ever, but instead of recording dinners and receptions it now showed such advances as ''Joe came to lunch and dinner for the first time'' or ''Joe walked and was in bath chair in the morning, while I took photographs. We drove in the afternoon.'' At first there had been two nurses; by the end of October there was only one, and she never went out with Joe. Mary would not have a sick-room atmosphere, either in London or at Highbury. When they walked she was the one beside Joe, one hand under his arm, ready to steady him if he should fall. Every day after lunch Joe had his cigar in the conservatory; if he were not going out he would walk slowly down to see the greenhouses. He could not read for himself, so Mary spent the mornings with the newspapers. She found it hard to keep him supplied with amusing books. Lady Dorothy Nevill had published some pleasant, though not very spicy, memoirs; when they had worked through these, Mary wrote to America for light but worthwhile reading. Austen and Ivy came often to visit, and little Hilda Mary would trot along with Grandpa and Grandma, and sometimes her puppy, when she came to visit. But Joe found other visitors a strain, and Mary, though it caused hurt feelings in Joe's family, kept them away.

Joe's children were amazed by Mary's gentleness and patience. She had been married for eighteen years to a man who drove himself constantly, smoked at all hours, and went to bed in early morning. Mary had called it reform when she and Joe got to bed before one a.m., and whenever Joe was without a pipe or cigar it was worth mentioning. Now he had an invalid routine, and the burden of entertaining him fell on her. To outsiders his speech was indistinct, and his facial expression rigid; but Mary loyally noticed every change for the better, and was cheerful about the future. To her, Joe was the patient one; he did not fret, but yielded to his illness without complaint. ''I look at him in wonder and admiration, and so he sustains me, as he ever has done, since first we met. Eighteen years of absolute and complete happiness! A record which comes but to those who are blessed by a love such as ours is . . . It makes sorrows easier to bear, if it sharpens the anxiety they bring when they touch one who is all in all . . .

"It is not strange that the strenuous life of unremitting work should have finally proved too much, and nature has taken her revenge. Still, I hoped he might have escaped."[8]

Mary, accepting in her heart that Joe might never recover, behaved to her family and the world as if she knew he would. It was a question of time and rest; perhaps a change of scene would help. His hardest times to bear were in London, in the dreary winter months when Parliament was in session. Mary arranged for them to go to the Riviera. At first she bothered a bit about making all the arrangements herself, but when her villa was rented and Joe heard of it, he reassured Mary, "Everything you do is right!" The winter was a success, and became an annual custom.

William and Louise came over in 1907 so Sargent could paint William's portrait. Louise had been done in 1903 in Boston; Mary had sat in London in 1902. William, grumbling at the bother and expense, climbed into a frock coat, and dutifully posed. Sargent's effort pleased Louise the most: "The eyes have such a nice, pleasant, interested expression—not the dreamy romantic look William hoped would be put into them—much better this way, I think."[9] After the picture was done they summered at Highbury with Mary, Mrs. Endicott, and "Mr. Chamberlain". Everyone pretended to be cheerful, but the three Endicotts were worried about Mary's health; they thought she was wearing herself out in the unsparing care of her husband.

Though Mary admitted she was tired, it was worth it if she could keep Joe's life happy and varied. She stayed up all one night that fall with Austen, walking the corridors, and waiting for Ivy's baby to be born. She soothed and encouraged, and all the time wondered if she should tell Austen the doctor feared for the baby's life as well as the mother's. Finally, early in the morning, a baby boy of nearly ten pounds arrived safely; his mother, though tired, was safe as well. Trembling with weariness and relief, Mary freshened up and went to say good morning to Joe, and tell him all about his new grandchild, "Little Joe" Chamberlain.

Two grandchildren in the house brightened Joe's winter. He managed the trip to Cannes well, and enjoyed the Villa Victoria Mary had hired. He had his library downstairs, next to Mary's boudoir; then upstairs he had a balcony opening off his bedroom. Mother and the girls could fit in quite comfortably; and the sunshine and flowers were wonderful.

That autumn Mary thought Joe needed stirring up intellectually. She read to him, and talked over politics. Austen wrote frequent letters which were an informal political diary, but still in Birmingham Joe lacked companionship. One welcome visitor was the Reverend William Hartley Carnegie, Rector and Canon of Birmingham Cathedral. He was attractive and urbane; his conversation ranged freely over religious and political topics. He, Mary, and Joe sat over tea; Joe held up his end of the talk, and spoke more fluently than at any time since his illness. Carnegie was stimulating to Joe; Mary was as enthusiastic about their visitor as her husband, and resolved not to lose sight of him.

A short trip to London stirred up Mary as much as it did Joe. Old friends came in for tea or a meal. One of the most welcome was Lord Milner, just back from a Canadian speaking tour. He had come out strongly in favor of Tariff Reform, and declared Joe's founding of the movement "the bravest, most unselfish, patriotic and historically memorable deed that has been done by a British statesman."[10]

Another year went by; again the Chamberlains wintered in Cannes. One fine day Joe managed to walk 280 steps alone, then rested and did 127 more, then after another rest walked 170 more. Sidney the footman was always about to help with the bathchair, and get Joe in and out of the carriage; the girls spelled her in reading and talking to Joe; but it was always Mary who bore the brunt of his illness. She was almost never away from Joe, but she had her reward in seeing his improvement.

Joe managed, in December, 1909, to dictate letters to his constituents, who loyally returned him for West Birmingham unopposed in the election which came the next month. In February, 1910, he went with Austen to the House and took the oath of office.

Mary was jubilant; she had feared the excitement might be too much for Joe. But he smiled and talked in the most natural way, and said he hoped he could go to hear some of the speeches sometimes.

While at Cannes they drove about sometimes in a motorcar. Joe disliked this, but Mary was fond of it. One day they watched five aeroplanes practicing dips and whirls through the sky. It seemed to Mary they marked a new age—how swiftly it was to sweep away the old one she could not guess.

On May 6th, 1910, came the news of the King's grave illness; that night he died. Austen hurried home from a holiday for the funeral; Mary and Joe returned at the end of the month, as planned. Though Joe seemed calm and composed, Mary knew the change of reigns had upset him.

In nine years England had shed Victorian dullness, and followed the King into an age of gay and elegant living. In these years Joe had reached the height of his powers. Though his opponents jeered, and called him changeable, he pursued his cause—the unity of Empire—unshakably. He might have been Prime Minister, for he was certainly the leader of Imperialism; but Joe had put that chance aside. He had many enemies, among Conservatives and Unionists alike. When he struck out on Tariff Reform there were those who said he had wrecked his party in pursuit of an idea. So had it been, twenty years earlier, when the Liberals split over Home Rule. The Imperial idea had guided Joe through most of his battles in intervening years; Mary, at his side had seen the issues clearly through Joe's eyes. Now, struck down, he was fretful, and anxious about the future.

Only a week after their return to London King George came to call on Joe, and stayed talking for an hour and ten minutes. He was sympathetic and interested in Joe's opinions. Joe urged him strongly to attend the great Coronation Durbar in India, which at that time the King's Ministers were reluctant for him to do.

In her own family, as in the Royal one, Mary found absorbing changes. She was unperturbed at reaching her middle forties, for unlike Louise Endicott, Mary inclined neither to stoutness nor grey hair. Worry, in fact, had had a slimming effect upon her; and though it changed her hair color, too, it was so gradual as hardly to be noticed.The best evidence of her youthful appearance came from a godson at school, to whom she had sent her photograph, "When I opened it there were several fellows in the room, and one of them said, 'Well, Gus, your girl is certainly charming, but she is too old for you, she must be 24 or 25.' "[11]

In the autumn Neville, whom all had feared a confirmed bachelor, suddenly, in good Chamberlain fashion, became engaged. Mary was overjoyed. Neville was forty-one: active in Birmingham business and good works he came to marriage late, but like his brother and father, completely happily. Joe could not come to his son's wedding to Anne Vere Cole in January, 1911, but its celebration did much to banish his gloom about political affairs.

Another General Election had been held in December, and Joe had been returned unopposed once more. Generally the Unionists lost many seats. To Mary's disgust Balfour had taken up the Liberals' challenge to submit Tariff Reform to a Referendum. When it had been before the people for seven years, and in three elections, this seemed absurd. The election results were disheartening, but Mary was thrilled that once more Joe could go himself to visit the House of Commons. "He took the oath quite audibly and clearly, kissed the Testament and touched the pen with which Austen signed the roll for him. Sitting on the Treasury Bench he looked exactly like his old self—so *clean cut*—as his appearance always was, the lines of his head just the same with the same look of youth."[12]

The signing of the oath had been a gesture; Mary knew that, but she accepted the best each day offered, and her cheerfulness never seemed forced. Joe's having left the battlefield did not mean the end of Tariff Reform; people were carrying on the fight, and turned often to Joe for his advice. Mary was glad when he could give it, but she played watchdog relentlessly, and would not let his visitors tire him. When a reciprocal American-Canadian trade agreement seemed about to be settled, Mary told her mother of the upset to Tariff Reformers. The unwelcome situation was "another proof of Joe's foresight. He always prophesied that if England did not treat the question seriously and meet it quickly something of this kind would occur."[13]

Mary went to the debates in the House sometimes; not only was there a new element, the Labour Party, but the whole atmosphere seemed different, "It gives the impression of being less intellectual . . . lacking in the power of criticism. One feels many of the members simply have no conception of anything beyond the subject of the moment, the special claims of their own constituencies, and have no care for the future . . . The character of the interruptions has changed. They are like the interruptions at a public meeting, and I came away feeling that the whole body was undergoing a transformation which added neither to its dignity nor its influence."[14]

Hard as it was not to rebel at the fate which had crippled Joe, Mary celebrated their twenty-third anniversary of being engaged with perfect happiness. They walked by the water, gulls arched overhead, and waves rippled softly on the sand. Even on cloudy days they could enjoy bird-song, palm trees swaying, and the blossoms all around.

Politically, they were disgusted with the Government. It was cheering that Canada rejected the American reciprocity agreement; otherwise the world seemed muddled and bungling. Railways' and coal miners' strikes meant endless conferences about wages, hours, and benefits; William was as agitated about affairs in America as the Chamberlains were in England. The Lawrence mill workers' strike had finally ended with the owners giving in to the workers' demands, after weeks of suffering and bloodshed. But "Bad as conditions are here, we seem to be better off than you are in England. Brooks Adams has a theory that in this age of the world the more democratic a country is the more trouble they have. England is certainly more democratic than we are, and to have a future that promises Heaven knows what!

"At any rate the old order is changing on all sides, and much as I disapprove of Mr. Roosevelt I do believe he is far ahead of his contemporaries in many ways, and has a following, even among decent people, that is impossible to estimate. If he should get the Republican nomination I am sure he would sweep the country. If we are to have a demagogue like Woodrow Wilson as Democratic candidate, I believe the country would be safer with Roosevelt than with him or his ilk."[15]

As things turned out Roosevelt and the Progressive Party lost out, and "the demagogue" had to face World War, as well as labor unrest. The Chamberlains, inveighing against Lloyd George, happily for their peace of mind, did not realize just how soon cataclysm would sweep over their horizon.

In 1913, though she enjoyed having Neville's and Austen's two baby daughters to visit, Mary insisted on getting off for their usual Cannes visit. She had been ill herself, but at first all went well on the Riviera. Then one night Mary woke with a terrible pain, which got worse; acute appendicitis was diagnosed, and immediate surgery advised.

Hilda took charge of the household at once; Mrs. Endicott, frightened as she was, sat quietly in the sunshine while the situation was explained. The surgeon had to act at once; a table was hastily prepared in an unused drawing-room, gaudy with Japanese fans. The appendix had perforated, and peritonitis had set in. Though Mary got through the operation there was grave concern for her life. The rest of the family had been summoned. Mary had been carried away from the improvised operating room; her mother and Joe saw her briefly that evening. But Hilda's great problem was whether to tell her father how ill Mary still was.

She thought it all over, and felt stronger just having Mrs. Endicott, so calm and collected, beside her. If, Hilda reasoned, her father didn't know, the news of Mary's closeness to death might kill him. Hilda suspected he did know, and that if Mary died he would surely die also. On the other hand, if she recovered, he would be all right. So Hilda took her decision, and her father was not told of the doctors' concern.

After five days the crisis was passed. Morning and evening Joe was wheeled into her room, and no matter how poorly Mary felt she always smiled and was cheerful. He, meanwhile, had been as self-controlled as Mrs. Endicott. Few households as filled with fright and anxiety could match the Villa Victoria for exterior calm. Soon Mary was well enough to be carried down to tea; within a week she managed little walks along the terrace. Then one day she surprised the family by coming to lunch. Joe came into the dining room all unconscious; just as he was sitting down he saw Mary sitting opposite him: "Well, I never! What will you do next?" he exclaimed.

What Mary did was to return immediately with Joe to England, and spend the next six weeks nursing him through two colds and a bad attack of gout. She had to have a nurse for herself still, but talked as little as she could about how she felt.

That summer 5000 of Austen's constituents gathered at Highbury to honour him for his twenty-one years of representing East Worcestershire. And Mary went out to Birmingham University to see the portrait of Joe, in his Chancellor's robes, properly installed. In the autumn came Mary and Joe's silver wedding anniversary. The King and Queen, and Queen Alexandra sent telegrams, the house was filled with flowers, and they had the whole family at lunch. What matter that Joe's speech was indistinct, and his movements slow—Mary was unfailingly optimistic about him. He had had his glasses changed and he could read for himself now. She greeted what he had to say almost as if he were an oracle. His mental vigour was undoubted. Once at Cannes Hilda was managing the house, and Joe asked what was for lunch. Being told cold veal pie, he retorted, "Cold veal is as insipid as sisters kissing!"

His interest in public affairs was unflagging. Mary felt the gaps in her education. She would mention Albania, and Joe would be off on the Balkan situation generally. Canon Carnegie had continued his calls at Highbury; since becoming Rector of St. Margaret's, Westminster, he now turned up in London, too. Mary was especially grateful to him, for his talk interested Joe, but did not tire him out, as that of his old political cronies was apt to do.

The next winter was a hard one, for in January, 1914, Joe made public his decision not to stand for Parliament again. Mary was sure he was right about this; Joe did not want anyone to say he had trespassed too long on his constituents' indulgence. But when the word was officially out it was hard for Joe; " 'I did not think I should feel it as I do,' he said to me last night, with that quiet pathos with which he always faces the inevitable and again today, 'it has cut me up more than I expected' to Mr. Collings. But he never wavers in his conclusion that the time has come—because he feels that the public interest demands it, and as ever throughout his political career he puts that before all thought of self . . .

"Friends and opponents alike express the conviction that he has had an influence rare in any generation, which must always give him a place in the first rank of English statesmen, whatever the future estimate of the part he has played."[16]

Their happiest moments came in just sitting quietly together in the garden at Cannes. The Irish situation was disturbing, so much so Mary preferred to write her mother about it, rather than sound off indignantly to Joe. Prime Minister Asquith, when the question of Home Rule came up, as it must do, being the price of Irish support of the Liberals, found the Ulsterites threatening civil war. Mary sputtered that the Government had committed the crime "of having ignored and made no serious attempt to meet the just fears of a loyal section of the people until they have been driven to contemplate armed resistance as their only hope of deliverance from the domination of the Nationalists."[17]

Though all the world was so troubled in 1914, the Riviera seemed bound to deny it. The peaches and apricots of March gave way to the roses and willows of April. Mary, promenading in white suit and sunshade along the front at Cannes, was slim and girlish in appearance. When they returned to England she went to Weymouth to unveil a plaque honouring her ancestor John Endecott. Otherwise she spent all her days with Joe and her mother. At Highbury Neville brought little Dorothy and Baby Frank to visit; in London Austen's little Joe and Diane came to amuse their grandfather.

London in late June was lovely and sunny. Mary was preparing as usual for their afternoon drive on the 30th when Joe suddenly felt faint, and had heart pains. The day was hot and brilliant; for Mary the minutes until the doctor came passed in slow, clear procession. It might be the weather, or indigestion, but she was not surprised to be told Joe had had a heart attack. He spent the afternoon downstairs, then they carried him up to bed where to her hopeful eyes he seemed better.

They were to have dined that evening with Lord and Lady Lansdowne, but Mary did not have to hide Joe's illness from a curious world this time. The dinner was postponed, because of the assassination of the Archduke Franz Ferdinand and his wife at Sarajevo. Next day Joe was uncomfortable and restless; the heat was oppressive, and Mary was not satisfied with the doctor's assurances. Another night, and Joe's pain increased.

War clouds gathered, but Mary never noticed them. Her world was ending as she watched her husband die. Joe was perfectly clear in his mind, but he grew steadily weaker. She hardly left his side, but on the evening of July 2nd her long watch came to an end. Briefly Mary wrote in her diary, "At 10.15 my darling died quite peacefully in my arms."

The days that followed were dream-like. So many times Mary had written to comfort those she loved, when a relative had died, and had calmed her own rebellious feeling, "Why?" Now Joe lay still before her, and she could not rebel; she was only thankful his suffering was over. Later would come the pain; now she sat beside him, and felt his spirit very near. He looked so peaceful, and Mary, in her calm, brought Joe's children to acceptance of his death. Austen felt that "To have seen her at my father's bedside and since is to have known faith so beautiful and courage so serene, that, once known, they can never be forgotten. I have never imagined anything so holy."[18]

On July 4th Mary looked on Joe's face for the last time, then placed a cross of roses and lilies of the valley in his coffin. For another day it rested in the library at Prince's Gardens, then was brought to Birmingham. A memorial service was held at St. Margaret's, Westminster, attended by the Cabinet, Members of Parliament, and other friends. In Birmingham the service was private, as Joe had wished, the Mayor and other civic figures being the only mourners outside the family. There were sorrowful crowds outside Highbury, all the way to church, and all the way to Key Hill Cemetery, in West Birmingham. All that day and the next they silently filed past Joe's grave. Letters and cables poured in, and the papers had columns of eulogy. It was impossible to realize that Joseph Chamberlain was gone. Austen spoke for the whole family when he wrote, "There is comfort in this great wave of sympathy, and above all in this world-wide recognition of my father's greatness of soul and character. And I think we can all feel and say that, though we must sorrow deeply, there is nothing we wish changed."[19]

CHAPTER XIV

"Others I Doubt Not, If Not We"

THE household arrangements rose up to haunt Mary. Every bit of furniture, at Highbury and in London, had its memories. She had to sort things out, and arrange for movingmen, for Highbury must be broken up. Austen could not live there, and Mary would be going to settle into Prince's Gardens.

She hoped her house would be a family centre. This would be difficult in war-time, but Mary, like thousands of others, believed the fighting would be over in a few weeks. Beatrice had found herself a small house in London; Ida and Hilda were settled in Hampshire, in the village of Odiham. Beatrice, with many friends, and committee work, would be happy, but Mary fretted a little about the other girls. Ida and Hilda had devoted themselves entirely to Joe; now their lives seemed almost as empty as her own. Neville was happily married, with two young children, and continued in business in Birmingham. For three years he had been on the City Council, where his outstanding interests were health, housing, and town planning.

Austen was in London with his family; though he had political disappointments recently, Mary felt at ease about him. Balfour had dealt Tariff Reform a bitter blow by pledging his party to submit it to a Referendum after the next elections. Again, in November, 1911, when Balfour resigned party leadership, and Austen might well have become Conservative leader, it had not worked out that way. He and his most obvious rival, Walter Long (former Chief Secretary to Ireland), both withdrew, so that Mr. Bonar Law might be unanimously chosen. When his father died, Austen had little time to brood. War was coming, and he must rally Conservative opinion. Mary watched Austen's courage in crisis, and it helped her through times of trouble, as Joe always had.

The house at Prince's Gardens now, crowded only with memories, seemed huge. Her old life seemed cut in two, as if with a knife, and the way ahead looked dark and bewildering. Through all her loneliness Mary had one comfort: there was no more pain and suffering for Joe, who had borne both so patiently for eight long years.

Friends coming to visit her helped take Mary out of herself. She also took up going to St. Margaret's each Sunday. Canon Carnegie was Rector there, and also Canon of Westminster Abbey. Quite often he would come for tea, or walk with Mary through the Abbey after services.

She missed having Joe's talk about the war. He had assured her that if world conflict should come, England's empire would rise as one man at the call to arms. He had been right, as her cousin Endicott Peabody observed: "The loyalty of the colonies, shown in their contributions of ships and money and men, is due in large measure to the inspiration of your husband."[1] But Mary felt adrift from the world of politics now; she spent more time pondering over her American letters. Uncle Augustus Peabody, still hale and hearty at eighty-four, delivered himself of some prophetic remarks about Germany, "There never has been such a war machine as the Prussian war office has built up, and the alliance of three powers may or may not break it down; at any rate, there is no possibility of any sudden collapse. Personally I hope that . . . if the allies are successful, something may be cooked up not too humiliating, for I dread beyond words a socialistic and anarchistic supremacy on the whole continent. A chastened Germany, yes; but a broken Germany, no. Barring Prussian militarism, she is in some respects the best example in the world giving ordered control, if not ordered liberty, and holding at bay a . . . license which is eating into the vitals of most modern countries."[2]

Mary, who was not strong enough for war work, admired the Chamberlains' efforts more than ever. In the Coalition Cabinet formed in May, 1915, Austen was Secretary of State for India. Neville carried on family tradition as Lord Mayor of Birmingham. Beatrice was making speeches and raising money for the sick and wounded. In the country Ida and Hilda did welfare work, raised poultry and vegetables, and billeted some officers. Mary managed not to be lonely. Her mother had advised her to get to know young people, and she had turned naturally to Canon Carnegie's lively family of five daughters. As a widower, the Canon understood Mary's problems more than academically. Besides talking, he did her the favour of helping re-arrange her library. Her mother had sent money to buy a new marble fireplace, and the Canon went shopping with Mary for just the right one.

As the Canon had been so kind and helpful it seemed only hospitable for the girls to ask him down to Odiham with Mary one weekend. He made himself most agreeable, and Mary was glad Ida and Hilda had such a good chance to get to know him.

Mary was cheered to be asked to tea at the Palace. Both King and Queen were sympathetic and friendly. The King, who in that spring of 1915 had so many crushing anxieties himself, talked at the tea-table for over an hour, while Queen Mary seemed more at ease than Mary ever remembered. Both of them spoke to her of Joe's courage and ability; both realized how out of things she now felt. Mary thought how pleased he would have been to think of their sending for her!

With the Canon Mary made several expeditions to Kew. The bluebells and young green leaves delighted her, but she found her companion's sympathy and encouragement as cheering. They talked of the war, politics, and religion. In less serious vein Mary and he pondered the pleasures of travel, and the upbringing of daughters. Each week the Canon fitted lunch, dinner, or tea with Mary into his schedule, sometimes all three. He and his eldest daughter joined her that summer on a holiday with Austen's family. Then Mary went with the Carnegies to Littlehampton, where they had taken a summer house. The salt air and sandy beach reminded her of Nahant, and Mary remembered how Joe always laughed at her when they got to the seashore. He said there was no place in the world where she was not sooner or later reminded of Nahant.

Feeling young again, Mary found the lightheartedness of the Carnegies refreshing. In London the Canon's tall figure often seemed stooped and anxious. Here in the open air, striding along the shore with his five lively girls, he seemed like a boy, and shared in all their enthusiasms.

Back in town Mary found fogs, long evenings, and bleak war news more bearable because of her friendship. The Canon's quick mind worked in different channels from what she was accustomed. Devoted to his work and family, he spoke of both with a light Irish touch quite new to her experience. Mary's memories of the past were increasingly happy ones. She could see Joe, striding up and down, eyes flashing and voice intense, and it was as if his years of illness had never intervened. Because he had never stopped growing, Joe had always seemed young to Mary. She felt that he would not have wanted her to stop growing.

It was 1916, and in a world at strife, Mary was astonished to find her friendship growing into love. She spent Easter with the Carnegies in their house at Dean's Yard; late in the day they watched the light fade on the Abbey towers and the Houses of Parliament. Next day she and the Canon walked through the Abbey, where she always felt at peace, and admired the newly-finished bust of Joe. She looked on it with pride and affection. That evening Mary wrote her mother, "your wish for me . . . of a 'Happy Easter' is being fulfilled in a way which I could not have believed could ever be again for me."[3]

On a country visit the following week Mary and the Canon made their decision. "We strolled through the fields and sat under a tree for a long time, watching the deepening tints of the branches and twigs, and the tender green tinging the trees, and listening to the larks singing in an ecstasy. The sheep were grazing and the lambs bleating after their mamas and the whole scene was so rural and peaceful and exquisite in its soft light that it was almost impossible to believe that within a hundred miles of us the horror and turmoil of war was going on."[4]

Mary was longing to talk to her mother; since Mrs. Endicott, now eighty-three, could not risk a transatlantic trip in war-time Mary decided to go to America herself. She should have taken as her own motto, "Damn the torpedoes! Full speed ahead," for Mary, once aroused was, like her mother, a summer whirlwind. In a week's time she was aboard the *Adriatic*, to carry the news in person of her engagement to the Reverend William Hartley Carnegie.

Mrs. Endicott knew and liked the Canon, and rejoiced in Mary's new-found happiness. Her great difficulty in the three weeks of Mary's visit was to keep the news a secret. Hard though it was, it was nothing like as difficult as it had been to conceal the Chamberlain engagement.

Mary waved aside all difficulties, and felt ready to "cope". This was fortunate, for when she returned to England she was deluged with activity. The Carnegie girls received the news of their father's engagement with pleasurable equanimity. Francie and May, the elder two, had seen more of Mary than the others, and had a fair suspicion of the romance. The younger girls, who had mostly been away at school, and were used to their handsome father's popularity with lady parishioners, had given no special thought to his friendship with Mrs. Chamberlain. Since their mother's death their aunt Geraldine had managed the household at 17, Dean's Yard. The atmosphere there was always one of hospitality and cheerful confusion. Though there was not much money to go around their aunt was a thrifty manager; if the Canon brought home unexpected company, the meal was somehow stretched for visitors. There were constant comings and goings, meal times were somewhat erratic, and the house tended to run itself. The girls saw their father cheerful and purposeful, and were happy for him. They were not too upset at the thought of a step-mother's changing the house around; rather, they expected she would want to change many things.

The Chamberlains had watched and worried over Mary for months after their father's death. What concerned them most was that she had no one to spend her energy upon. It was as if Mary were the mirror in a room lit by one candle. When the light went out she was alone in a darkened room. Mary had spoken bravely of her adjustment to the solitary life, and had quite convinced her American relatives, especially two unmarried cousins, Fanny Mason and Clara Sears. Consequently they were surprised and a little offended when they heard of her engagement. Unfortunately they saw the newspaper announcement before her carefully written notes reached them. It was all the harder for her cousins, who had constructed in their minds a picture of Mary's noble widowhood, to comprehend this abrupt turn in her fortunes.

Beatrice Chamberlain was able to explain the situation very well:

"The very devotion . . . that Mary gave to Papa left her life entirely empty when he was taken from her. She had kept up no occupations, no relations, nothing—except what could bring something into his life, and with one stroke she was left with nothing to spend herself upon—many loving her but no one needing her . . . It is with deep satisfaction that I see Mary once again making a home, and helping a man in his work. All personal relations—sympathy and wise counsel to individuals—are her job, and she does it best as the centre of a home.

"The Canon (I have not yet accepted with a good grace the fact that he is called Willy, and prefer to call him Canon) is very good in accepting, and more than accepting, us all, as part and parcel of Mary's life. Of course we can't expect the day to hold as many hours for our share as it did, but he does all he can to bring us in and make us at home."[5]

While Mary was in America the Canon had been appointed Chaplain to the Speaker of the House of Commons. St. Margaret's had traditional ties with the Members of Parliament; as Rector there, and Canon of the Abbey, the new House Chaplain would have a unique opportunity to bring politics and religion closer together. Mary was thrilled to think of scenes she had known and loved with Joe being part of her life once more. She was nearly swamped in a welter of household details, though; it seemed she had just settled Prince's Gardens, and now here she was settling about alterations to Dean's Yard.

The wedding took place on August 3, 1916, in the Henry VII Chapel of the Abbey. Early morning sunshine streamed down on Mary and Austen, who was giving her away. She wore a simple mauve dress, trimmed in pink and violet, and a soft black straw hat. There was a soft radiance in her expression, and her whole mood. As she walked up the aisle on Austen's arm the sun was so bright she could hardly distinguish the tall dark figure of the Canon awaiting her. When they were together and the scarlet-clad choirboys sang, they both felt drawn into the Abbey's traditions. After a family breakfast Mary and her Canon drove away on their honeymoon; the sun still streaming down seemed the best of omens for their new life.

After two weeks in the country they returned to Prince's Gardens. Mary promptly asked Austen and his cousin Norman Chamberlain, back on sick leave from the front, to dine. For Austen's special delectation she brought out 1834 port, and some of his father's cigars. He lingered on till nearly midnight, and talked so freely and unreservedly that it marked, Mary felt, his feeling that "Willie was in deed and in fact a member of the inner family circle."[6] It was a charming concept, and one to which the Canon gallantly offered no objection.

The Carnegie girls gave their father and Mary a rousing welcome when they reached Littlehampton. To her great pleasure they had decided to call her "Mother"; she hoped she would be able to make up to them in some way for all the years they had been without a mother. Beside Francie and May there were seventeen-year-old Kathleen, sixteen-year-old Jocosa, and Rachel, who was fourteen, for Mary to oversee. Willie took up where brother William was always leaving off, and said firmly that his bride must not "overdo". A houseful of young girls was quite different from the Chamberlain menage, and he would not have her worn down by them. She must have peace, quiet, and time for herself.

Mary, who never felt tired when she was usefully busy, started on a round of clerical luncheons and dinners when they returned to London. The stay in Prince's Gardens, while the Dean's Yard house was being renovated, made the transition in social life easier for her. Her new guests were at least in familiar surroundings; though she found that clergymen's conversation was more theoretic than what she was used to, Mary found them polite and agreeable, and had high hopes for the future. Though some of the clergy were dull, Willie himself was a delightful companion, and stirred them all up. Used to the rather heavy-handed Chamberlain wit, which relied heavily on sarcasm, Mary was enchanted with the Irish in her new husband: his engaging manner, and sense of humour so quick "the dull and prosaic might sometimes accuse him of flippancy."[7] Mary had dieted on sobriety for many years past; her new, light-hearted household did her good.

Mary kept up her interest in all the Chamberlains' affairs. Neville was asked by Lloyd George to serve as first Director of National

Service. He was reluctant to take the job, for in Birmingham he was busy inaugurating the War Savings Bank, founding the Birmingham Orchestra, and municipalizing the bus service. As there was no universal military service yet, Neville found the new post a thankless one. His responsibilities were ill-defined: the work of the National Service consisted in calling for labour volunteers to fill the spots of workers transferred to essential war-time industries. For seven frustrating months Neville stayed with this task; then resigned and returned to the Birmingham City Council.

Austen meanwhile was reaching another crisis in his career. An inquiry committee was studying the conduct of the campaign in Mesopotamia. Serious mismanagement, especially in medical services, was uncovered, and Austen felt he must resign. Even though no blame could possibly be attached to him as Minister, it was the Government of India which had been conducting the campaign, and therefore his Department which was concerned. In July, 1917, Mary went to the Speaker's Gallery to hear Austen's speech. She felt the House was sympathetic to him, and approved his sentiments, though regretted his decision. It was hard to have a break in the Cabinet in war-time, but Mary knew how strongly Austen felt, and wished Joe could have been there to hear him. The evening brought back old times; Austen was in fine spirits, and exclaimed over dinner, "*Now* I can have a holiday!" What pleased Mary most was to have Willie there with her "to see what it all meant—this close sympathy, and the stir and thrill of the House of Commons on a dramatic occasion."[8]

As St. Margaret's had come to be regarded as the parish church for Americans abroad, Mary found herself very busy after the United States entered the war. She gave dinners, teas, and "at homes" to groups of nurses, colonial officers, and theological students from abroad. These last, whose training in Serbia and Czechoslovakia had been cut off by the war, were finishing up at the Anglican School of Cuddesdon. They used to come for dinner, and an evening of good talk at Dean's Yard, but were apt to linger on till far into the night. The Chamberlains murmured to themselves that the Carnegies were rather exuberant, and might be wearing Mary out; but both the Canon and Mary saw that this did not happen. She had breakfast in bed, and generally had tea in her sitting-room, where she had her favourite books, her writing table, and, most important—the green damask-patterned wallpaper had been chosen to set it off—the Sargent portrait of Joe.

Mary brought order to the Carnegie routine. Meals were on time, and as she was particular about their being hot, and properly prepared and served, everyone, especially schoolgirls home on holiday, noticed better food. Mary was eager to chaperone the older girls at luncheons and teas, and to give them all the social training she could. She had won their affection readily, for she had persuaded the Canon to speak with them about their own mother, and she never was jealous of the easy-going rapport they shared with him. The girls' attitude to their father was quite different from the hero-worship in which the young Chamberlains had held Joe. Mary sat back and let Willie and the girls argue and debate such points of art, economics, or philosophy as they chose, even when they were of little interest to her. Mary tried to teach them such things as shopping wisely; she wisely sensed that "methods adapted to more methodical people must be carefully considered lest they do more harm than good. The Irish vein which is so attractive would easily make them restive if one held too tight a rein."[9]

Before Mary and her not inconsiderable means came into the Carnegies' lives they had had to manage most economically, and Mary wanted them to keep on in this way. The Canon heartily concurred with his wife's prudent management; though it was evident that his fortunes had appreciated when tax-time came around, and he found his half share of the tax due on their joint return amounted to more than his total income!

Mary did feel cut off from her former life sometimes, so it was a great thrill to be asked with Willie to Windsor. She walked about showing Willie just where she and Joe had walked and talked with Queen Victoria. Then she had a good talk with Queen Mary, in the drawing-room, found her much interested "in the Americans now here, and wanted to be told all I could about them and their point of view. As to the King, who talked to me all the rest of the evening, I wish you could have seen the light which came into his eye, and the feeling into his face as he described his meeting with General

Pershing and the other American officers when he received them on their arrival in England and what he said to them: how one of the dreams of his life was accomplished in seeing the two countries side by side, fighting the greatest of causes in the name of liberty and justice and humanity. I did not realize he had it in him to care in just that way, for it was with profound feeling that he spoke. The war has been a severe school for him . . . and he has risen to it splendidly."[10]

When they got back from Windsor, Mary felt the Carnegies had a new link with the Chamberlains. She was pleased to see how well Austen got on with Willie. He would pass over an important paper, Willie would read it through, and off they would go on an evening's discussion. His closeness was a great comfort to Mary in the bleak months following the Armistice; for only a few days after its signing Beatrice Chamberlain died of influenza.

Of all his children Beatrice had been most like Joe. From the very first she had made Mary feel at home in England. From her own visits to America she had grown to understand Mary's family and associations there better than any of the others. She had kept as close to Mary as ever, though her work for the Unionist Association was far removed from Anglican theology. Mary was dazed by her death; she could not share with others in the elation at the war's end.

When peace was finally signed at the end of June, 1919, Mary wrote: "Think of it! Nearly five years have passed since those anxious days when you and I waited in breathless wondering as to what was going to happen, and whether or not the British Government would respond to the call. Do you remember how we felt, and the intensity of the relief when Austen returned from the House of Commons and called to us as he came up the stairs, 'It's all right.' Happily, in this world no one ever realizes what is before them, and if we then had foreseen how long was the struggle to be, and how the whole world would be involved in it, there would not have been the same happy rush of loyal enthusiasm and light-hearted readiness."[11]

That summer Mary and Willie went to America, and he met all her friends and relations. Though it seemed such a short while they had been married, the Carnegie girls were growing up. Francie greeted Mary and her father on their return with the news of her engagement to Michael Peto, a young Guards officer.

They had a real family Christmas; Mary got up at six-thirty, and got herself in order for the Santa Claus ceremony at seven. Her husband stayed comfortably in bed; when the girls and Mick arrived with their stockings, the Canon looked benignly about, and felt Mary had brought them all from darkness and sadness into sunshine again.

M. Jean Worth, hearing of the engagement, murmured smoothly, "And I shall make her dress, of course," and would brook none of Mary's feeble complaints that she could not afford such an extravagance. He had his way and created a masterpiece in dull white satin, with a long court train falling from the shoulders. Followed by her bridesmaids in white and gold Francie, on a brilliantly sunny February day, made her way to the High Altar of the Abbey, where Mick in the full dress uniform of the Coldstream Guards, awaited her. Some nine hundred guests were there for the ceremony, and the bride was ferried, in a storm of orange blossoms, newsreel cameras grinding away, through an honor guard of Mick's brother officers. Mary described the luncheon at Dean's Yard afterwards as "simple and little", and so it seemed, for only two hundred gathered to celebrate and toast the bride.

About a year later Mary noticed that "one young man in particular was finding 17, Dean's Yard a sort of magnet; but in these days when young men are on such an easy footing that they drop in to tea with perfect camaraderie I felt I must not be too confident of my instinct."[12] It proved a sound one, for May announced she was engaged to Pen Slade, who was just beginning a law career. Mary was delighted with her choice, for the young man was a grandson of Alice Beale, one of Neville's, and his sisters' aunts, and thus he knew her already as "Aunt Mary". But she and Willie were dismayed to think of the long wait they would have before Pen was established, and the wedding could take place.

Mary presented Willie's daughters at the Garden Parties which were the post-war substitute for evening Courts. She was startled to find that Rachel and Hilda Mary, her oldest Chamberlain "grandchild" were both to be presented at the same time. She and Willie found their evenings full for "the modern fashion of going to a dance with a partner means so far as our ideas are concerned asking him to dinner first, so every week we have one or two or three young men to dine, sometimes several nights."[13]

The Duke of York's marriage in 1923 to Lady Elizabeth Bowes-Lyon gave Mary a chance for some political reflections. She was perched in the organ loft of the Abbey with young Joe Chamberlain by her side; she pointed out the important people as they came in. Neville, who had entered Parliament in 1918, now wore the gleaming gold lace of a Privy Councillor. It had been an eventful year for the brothers. Austen had gained leadership of his party, and was Lloyd George's chief lieutenant; he had had to follow the Prime Minister out when the Coalition Ministry dissolved. Thus he once again lost a chance at the Premiership, while Neville started on the ministerial career which would one day make him Stanley Baldwin's successor. In the year before the Baldwin Ministry fell he was Postmaster General, Paymaster General, Minister of Health, and Chancellor of the Exchequer. Now he sat only two seats from Austen, who looked equally splendid, but whose Privy Councillor's lace was tarnished with years of service.

Young Joe was thrilled to see both father and uncle in full regalia; Mary wished that her Joe could have been beside her. Then, with a start, she realized this was not just a family occasion, and bestirred herself to consider the bride and groom. She thought they looked a well-matched pair; it was nice to think the Duke was marrying for love, for Royal weddings had not always so happy a basis.

Mary was never one to be awed by Royalty; at a Garden Party that summer she thought the new Duchess of York had a sweet smile and charming expression. And her mother-in-law, whom for so long Mary had classified as "little Princess May" had emerged as really "a handsome woman. She looks just the same except that her hair is grey, which is most becoming, and in her own old-fashioned way which certainly suits her, she is an imposing figure."[14]

Mary herself became a mother-in-law anew that winter, when May and Pen Slade were married soon after she and Willie returned from America.

Austen returned to office as Baldwin's Foreign Secretary in 1924; he reached the pinnacle of his career in the following year. At Locarno he successfully negotiated the conferences held among Great Britain, France, Germany, Belgium, Italy, Poland, and Czechoslovakia, so that a series of non-aggression pacts were agreed on. It was believed that these documents were the foundations of a lasting peace; when they were signed on December 1, 1925, Austen won high honor. The King created him Knight of the Garter: not only was this unusual for a commoner, but it was bestowed without waiting for a vacancy, which was unprecedented. Ivy was awarded the Grand Cross of the British Empire for her share in creating the "spirit of Locarno". There was an air of hopefulness and trust, a mutual good-will which spoke well for the success of the League of Nations. Austen was awarded the Nobel Peace Prize for 1925.

In Baldwin's second administration Neville had returned to the Ministry of Health, where he remained until 1929. His outstanding activities were in the encouragement of private building, and expansion of the building societies, slum clearance, old age pensions, maternal and child welfare, and the strengthening of the local government structure.

As for the "roaring twenties" they made few inroads on the Carnegies' way of life. In his sermons Willie deplored divorce; at home Mary gave short shrift to the cocktail and the cigarette. Though firm in maintaining standards, Mary was well aware of changing customs. One used to go to proper dinner-parties, but the modern generation asked one to lunch. She realized with a start that she had joined the "older generation" though there were still many people she had known when first in London. She asked Lord and Lady Lansdowne, now in their eighties, to dine, and they were pathetically pleased to come. It seemed so recently Joe had stayed with them in Ontario, and she had followed his travels by newspaper. Now, wonder of wonders, when Austen addressed the Assembly of the League of Nations in Geneva, he could be clearly heard in London on a "crystal set" costing a guinea.

For all her interest in progress, Mary had wistful moments of brooding on the past. Queen Alexandra, whom she thought of as the beautiful Princess of Wales, was dead. Lord Milner was dead.

If Joe were alive he would be over ninety. And Mrs. Endicott, at ninety-four, was losing her hold on life. Mary journeyed to America in the summer of 1927 to be at her bedside. When she died, Mary brought back with her to London the thousands of letters she had written her over forty years; they were kept carefully in a locked tin trunk. Mary could not shake off the letter-writing habit, and continued to send lengthy bulletins to William and Louise.

The following year the Carnegie household shrank further, when Jo was married to Casper Swinley, a young naval officer. Mary was delighted with this, but soon afterwards had a bad bout of pneumonia. Willie shipped her off to Italy to convalesce; she was somewhat scandalized to find on her return, that without so much as a by-your-leave, he had hired a car for her.

To this agreeable tyranny she succumbed gracefully, and the following spring returned the compliment. Uncle Augustus Peabody had passed to his reward at the age of ninety-eight, and with his legacy Mary proposed to buy their very own motor-car. She and Willie felt quite giddy at the prospect, and planned it in every detail. The car would be a Daimler (for a Rolls would be too conspicuous, and if they should take it abroad, prices would surely rise) and it must not only accommodate the Canon's lengthy frame in comfort, but the seat must be high enough for Mary to look out the windows properly. When finished the Daimler was a wonderful "toy", and the Carnegies would drive out to Ranelagh, where the Canon would golf, then they would settle in the clubhouse there for a leisurely cup of tea.

To Mary's disgust Labour captured some of the seats in Birmingham in the general election of May, 1929. Austen and Neville had retained theirs, though, which was what counted. Austen had gone out of office as Foreign Secretary, and Neville as Minister of Health. Mary grumbled a good deal about "those men" in the Government, and not surprisingly most of her letters now dealt with family affairs. Rachel Carnegie was married in the autumn of 1929 to a young barrister, Drewett Chaytor. This was a cheering event in a world that was fiscally gloomy. Both Mary's English and American investments slumped drastically, and she thought and spoke a good deal of "living carefully" through the Great Depression. Yet in the bleak winter of 1931 she and Willie got off to Naples, where they had a happy reunion with William and Louise. The Endicotts, rotund and cheerful, had journeyed by private houseboat along the Nile. Mary laughed at a picture of William in a burnous, and the days were full of reminiscence.

The Labour Government collapsed, a National Government was formed in August, 1931, and both Chamberlains returned to office, Austen at the Admiralty and Neville at the Ministry of Health. At the General Election the following October Austen waived his claims to office, and wrote Stanley Baldwin he hoped Neville's accession to Chancellor of the Exchequer would be all the easier. Neville received the appointment easily. In the next five and a half years he faced a host of trials: restoring the country's finances meant drastic economies. He directed the balancing of expenditures with revenues with courage and sound judgment. His greatest satisfaction came, though, in the direction of Empire trade policy.

On February 4, 1932, Mary, Hilda, and Neville's wife and daughter were in the Speaker's Private Gallery to hear Neville propose a return to Protection. It was eighty-six years since the repeal of the Corn Laws had ushered in Free Trade, and almost twenty-nine since Joseph Chamberlain had evolved his campaign for Tariff Reform. On this historic day Neville proposed a general duty of ten percent on all goods not already dutied, or specifically exempt (such as wheat, meat, cotton, and wool). An independent Tariff Board would recommend additional duties on non-essential goods (luxuries, or goods produced in bulk at home). Goods from the colonies and mandates would enter duty-free; Dominion goods would not be dutied until an Imperial Economic Conference was held at Ottawa. This program was "Moderate Protection", as the Chancellor called it. It had taken the unemployment of two and one-half million people, and a huge surplus of imports over exports to bring the country round to share Joseph Chamberlain's vision. When the speech was done Austen rose from the seat which had been their father's after he left the Cabinet, came down on the floor of the House, and shook his brother's hand. It was a warm, spontaneous gesture; Mary, looking at Joe's sons, was proud of them both.

At the Ottawa Conference in July, though there was dissension

and disappointment over many tariff discussions, the basic principle of Imperial Preference was upheld. There was haggling and
jealousy, but Neville felt satisfied that the dangerous drifting apart
of the countries of the Empire was stopped. The better understanding and real liking that had sprung up among various delegations
would bear fruit in future. For Mary there was deep satisfaction.
Protection and Imperial Preference had been Joe's battle standards;
it was fitting to the Chamberlain tradition that Neville should carry
them on, and bring closer Joe's dream of a united empire.

Though Neville's budgets were austere, the Carnegies got to
America, and the Endicotts, after the pleasant weeks of visiting
were over, arranged a farewell tea on a scale that all of them took
for granted. Mary's friends and relations from Salem and the North
Shore were asked, and over four hundred turned up. The Canon,
getting over the flu, found the party just the tonic he needed. Mary,
of course, could never have enough of the hand-shaking and family
inquiry such an occasion demanded. She never forgot names, faces,
or the numbers of her friends' descendants; she and Willie returned to England refreshed and relaxed.

Though she had been operated on for a cataract, Mary had thus
far managed to avoid spectacles, which she intensely disliked. She
was a very youthful seventy in the fall of 1933, and a devoted grandmother. The following summer the Carnegies cheerfully undertook
a holiday which involved ten grown-ups, seven children, and a supporting cast of five dogs, a Shetland pony, four nurses, Mary's
maid, and the Daimler's chauffeur. Willie played golf with his sons-
in-law; Mary gossiped with the girls about the grandchildren, and
it was all a great success.

Christmas shopping for her extended family was one of Mary's
favourite pastimes, the buying and wrapping of presents being one
of the few things she did entirely for herself. Other people helped
her dress, cooked for her, cleaned for her, wrote letters, and did
errands. But Mary would spend hours pursuing the right present
for the right person, and wrapping it in appropriate ribbons and
paper. Setting out one November afternoon in the Daimler Mary
and the Canon went into a bookshop where they soon ran straight
into Queen Mary who was also Christmas shopping. While she and

the Queen were chatting, Mary wondered whether her husband realized who her companion was. He had been pottering about, picking up one book after another, but when the Queen turned to him Mary was relieved to see Willie's hat sweep off as he greeted her. Presently, their shopping done, the Carnegies departed. The Canon made a beeline for the Daimler in front of the door, just where theirs had deposited them. Mary had to snatch his coat tails and steer him off to the one behind. The royal Daimler had displaced their own, and they had just time to install themselves properly before the Queen came out. "Fortunately," observed Mary, "Her Majesty did not emerge in time to see his predatory instinct."[15]

She might have been talking to a small boy, instead of six feet of impressive churchman; but the similarity of the Daimlers would cause many people besides the Canon confusion in years to come. Mary, out driving in the Park, would notice people waving to the erect and white-haired figure they assumed must be Queen Mary. When she went into a store she might come out and find a crowd collected round the car. She rather enjoyed these incidents, but still found it hard to picture the shy young princess she recalled as the matriarch Queen Mary had become.

Mary went to the Silver Jubilee celebrations for King George. She had been told that he had dreaded the idea of the Jubilee, and the tributes paid to him came as a complete surprise. He said, "I do not understand it. I am just an ordinary man. I had no idea my people felt so much about me."[16]

Mary watched the Naval Review from Casper Swinley's destroyer *Express*; she mentioned this later in the summer to the King at a Garden Party. "His Majesty was a little rueful about the number of the ships. He contrasted the 280 ships with 80,000 men of his Coronation Review before the War, and the 160 ships and 40,000 men of his Jubilee; and yet there are people who still labour under the delusion that Great Britain has not reduced her Navy as much as they have theirs, and that she has gone on replacing the battleships which the Naval Treaties of recent years permitted. So far is this from the fact that she now possesses only a few obsolete ones, so busy has she been in trying to set an example of reductions to the world at large. The time has come when something will have to be done about it, for she has already passed the danger point now. To a certain extent of course, it has also been a question of economy, but like so many economies it has created a good deal of havoc."[17]

There were ominous hints of war that year. In March, 1935, Hitler had repudiated the parts of the Versailles Treaty limiting German armaments. He had also decreed universal military service. The following October Italy invaded Abyssinia. The League of Nations imposed economic sanctions upon Italy, the aggressor; by late November a League Committee was considering adding oil to the list of sanctions. Mussolini threatened that this would mean European war. It seemed likely that Britain might wind up fighting Italy, Germany, and Japan all at once, which she was in no position to do.

In these circumstances Sir Samuel Hoare, the British Foreign Secretary, meeting with M. Laval of France, evolved a proposal to give Italy outright a large portion of Abyssinia, and to give her economic control over another large area in return for the cessation of hostilities. On December 9th the details of this plan leaked out, the British Government accepted them, and a storm of public indignation arose. Opposition in the House, forwarded by Austen Chamberlain, led to the abandonment of the Hoare-Laval proposals; Hoare then resigned.

Mary felt very close to the Abyssinian Crisis, for Austen was staying at Dean's Yard and each evening would drop into her room to tell her what was going on in the House. It all reminded her of the old days at Prince's Gardens, when such late-night résumés were a matter of course. As House Chaplain the Canon was naturally in the House often enough to keep the run of what was going on, but his wife felt that was rather from the outsider's point of view. Austen, who had worked long and hard for Italian friendship, still hoped Mussolini would be brought round by sanctions. If the League were to exist at all, he was convinced it must be the medium for peace.

Mussolini swept on undaunted. Abyssinia was formally annexed to Italy on May 5th, 1936, after which both Austen and Neville saw the continuance of sanctions as both dangerous and futile. Meanwhile Hitler had swallowed up the Rhineland in March. Mary wrote to America, "We are anxiously awaiting the developments of the situation which Hitler has created by tearing up the Locarno Treaty, and at the same time suggesting a basis of negotiations between the European Powers. It is a curious way of paving the way for this by breaking his word, but it is true to type. The Germans are bullies, and I am afraid one comes to the reluctant conclusion that it is never possible to rely upon their word."[18]

Mary was saddened by King George's death in January, 1936, but felt confident about the new King; she thought "he has a high sense of duty and must thoroughly understand what the position of a constitutional monarch must be. His knowledge of the Empire is unrivalled, and his temperament has made it easy for him to mix with all sorts and conditions of men . . . It will be interesting to see how he adapts himself to the political world, of which I imagine he knows much less; but I am told that he likes Mr. Baldwin and the latter will therefore be in a position to help over the initial stages of taking up his duties . . .

"King George did a great work in consolidating his people and he saw the country through a crucial period after the Great War. Now comes the time when it is obvious that re adjustments have got to be made, and new developments must come . . ."[19]

One consequence of the new reign was the Canon's retirement from the House. His health had not been good for some time, and the change did him good. Many spare hours were spent with his grandchildren; Mary meanwhile became a great-grandmother with the birth of Austen's first grandchild.

That summer there were centennial celebrations of Joe's birth in London and Birmingham, which Mary found "hard to reconcile with his and my relation to each other, for . . . I never felt the difference in our ages and just ignored it always . . . I could not face going to Birmingham, [but] preferred to go to the great meeting at the Albert Hall where Joe himself had spoken on Tariff Reform on his birthday . . . It was decided that Neville should go to Birmingham and Austen be in London. They both were sorely tried at the prospect of the task before them, but . . . neither one of them could have spoken better, and as one read their tributes to their father one felt that it really was remarkable that his two sons should each be occupying positions so distinguished and be doing so much in these critical times to hold the scales straight."[20]

Mary left with the Canon for the Continent in excellent spirits. The "water cure" and some leisurely cathedral-viewing seemed to banish Willie's ill health; both gout and grippe were behind him when they reached home in the autumn. 17, Dean's Yard had been freshly papered and painted; they were planning how to arrange books and pictures, and went driving in October sunshine. Then in the middle of the month Willie was laid up. A cold became bronchial pneumonia; the doctor said he had little strength with which to fight it, and Mary sent messages to his children. On Sunday evening, October 18th, only a few minutes after he had talked with Mary and Kathleen, the Canon slipped into unconsciousness. With them beside him he died.

Carnegies and Chamberlains gathered for the funeral service; Mary stood in the sunlight, on October 21st, beside her husband's grave. It was placed in the nave of the Abbey; Mary thought how appropriate it was that Willie should rest in the church where for so many years he had played such a part. She was thankful he had had a short illness, but more than this Mary could not bear to think about her husband. As she had when Joe died, she plunged at once into practical details. After the first, worst weeks were over she would have strength for reflection.

For the first time in her life Mary had the choice of a house. She was bound she would stay in London, and brother William, anxious from afar, wrote Mary, urging her to spend as much as she needed in order to be comfortable. Prince's Gardens and Dean's Yard had been waiting for her; she rather enjoyed picking a house for herself. London was changing rapidly into a city of flats; Mary was firm in wanting a house, and moreover, it could not be in an ordinary street, for she had never lived where she could not see trees and an open space. Finally in a quiet square she found a well-built house she could afford, and wrote enthusiastically of 41, Lennox Gardens to William. He never had the letter, for the day after it was mailed, November 28th, William Endicott died of a heart attack.

In six short weeks Mary had lost both husband and brother, but though she was exhausted, her courage did not fail her even now. They both still seemed so close. William, her bluff, impatient, charming older brother, who laughed at her Salem foibles, but understood them, shared her love of family and possessions. He knew that old ways were good ways, and cared about preserving them. His life had taken a different turn from hers. Genial host and careful trustee, William Endicott spent his energies (and frequently his righteous indignation) in managing New England institutions: the Essex County Agricultural Society, Boston Museum of Fine Arts, Peabody Museum of Salem, and Massachusetts Historical Society were only a few of his interests. Mary's concern with politics and the Church he could understand; but he much preferred to talk about gardening with her. She had always been his "little sister" and he had never been quite sure the English were treating her right.

Then Mary thought of Willie, who brought her sympathy and understanding, but also a light heart. He loved and found peace in traditions, as she did, but he was so sociable and lively-minded he could not be hide-bound by them. His conversation rambled, and he was distinctly absent-minded; Mary, besides looking up to, had looked after him. William had said when she married the Canon, "Well, at least Mary can talk in her own house now!" And it was true: at Highbury, though she had unmistakably made her way felt, Mary had been speech critic, listener, and peacemaker, far more than conversationalist. She could find nothing to regret in her life as Mrs. Chamberlain; as Mrs. Carnegie she felt there was still work for her to do. Now that Willie was gone she must be the family centre; at the same time keeping on with her "inner circle" of Chamberlains, and, in America, comforting Louise and writing to her cousins.

Mary was shocked at the Abdication Crisis, which came in the midst of her own private troubles; but she felt its outcome was the only possible one. Meanwhile her packing, dividing of possessions, and sorting things out went on. Mary admired the fortitude of the British in enduring large trials, in politics and war; but she had never seen why they put up with the discomforts of weather and plumbing. At Lennox Gardens she had electric wiring done, put in

central heating, and installed three bathrooms. She tried to repro-
duce the Dean's Yard decorative atmosphere. She even found the
same green damask wallpaper, and had her Grandma Peabody's
brocade curtains carefully darned and hung. The marble fireplace
her mother had given her when she married Willie was also carefully moved.

It was as well household business kept her free from brooding,
for Fate had one more blow for Mary still to bear. In March of 1937
Austen Chamberlain suffered a sudden, fatal heart attack. Austen
had been her closest link with politics. Mary had always discussed
the important matters in her life with him; it was he who dropped
in to chat, or sat late at her table over his father's cigars. When
Mary married Joe, Neville had been a shy and awkward youth, destined for business; while Austen was a man grown, embarked on his
political career. She had known him forty-nine years, and Mary
could recall no friction or misunderstanding between them. More
and more she had come to depend on Austen's advice. Neville, she
knew would be badly shaken; Mary did not think he realized how
much he depended on Austen "and now he feels deprived of the
possibility of his wise counsel and support, just when in his own
life moments may easily come when he would have found in him the
only person to whom he could unburden himself . . .

"For myself . . . our intimacy touched every possible point of interest—politics, art, literature, all that made him such a good companion. I have been so accustomed all my life to find in men the
stimulus and purpose which have helped me to meet in some small
measure the claims of it that instinctively I have turned to the
rather unusual and remarkable ones who have been so close to me
in both countries, and after the loss of the three who have shared
most closely everything, in the three periods of which my life has
been made up, so near together in five short months, I am like a
ship without a rudder—or rather with the rudder out of action till
I can regain my hold on it."[21]

When the helmsman in Mary took control, it was with a firm grip
she would never relinquish. She was seventy-three when she moved
to Lennox Gardens that spring, but she was too absorbed to think
of growing old. Fate had kept both Joe and Austen from their

"promised land"; a third Chamberlain now had the chance. In May, 1937, George VI, who had not wanted to be King, was crowned, while Neville Chamberlain, who only entered Parliament at fifty, became Prime Minister of England.

CHAPTER XV

"Je Tiens Ferme"

MARY saw little of Neville before she left for America, but she spoke of the Prime Minister's problems with great vigour. Having a Chamberlain in the thick of things seemed to give her a new lease on life. Louise Endicott, lonely and bewildered by widowhood, found the intricacies of British politics hard to follow, but her sympathy and kind heart were unmatched. Louise sorted through her possessions and picked out things given to Endicotts by Chamberlains over the years; she tied tags on them and despatched them to England. Neville had a pair of silver candlesticks, Ida and Hilda, too, had presents.

Neville was pleased with the interest Mary's American family showed in British affairs. He wrote on January 16, 1938, to Mary's cousin, Fanny Prince: "I believe that Americans and British want the same fundamental things in the world, peace, liberty, order, respect for international obligations, freedom for every country to devote all its resources to the improvement of the conditions of its own people . . . I believe that these things must be wanted too by Germans, Italians, Russians, and Japanese. But those people are in the grip of their governments and in some cases the Governments are so constituted that they must maintain their prestige or die . . . They pay no heed to reason but there is one argument to which they will always give attention and that is force. U. S. A. and U. K. in combination represent a force so overwhelming that the mere hint of the possibility of its use is sufficient to make the most powerful of dictators pause . . ." But he was aware of isolationist sentiment in America, and also saw France weakened with internal disorders, "Therefore our people see that in the absence of any powerful ally and until our armaments are completed we must adjust our foreign policy to our circumstances and even bear with patience and good humor actions which we should like to treat in very differ-

210

ent fashion . . . I am about to enter upon a fresh attempt to reach a reasonable understanding with both Germany and Italy and I am by no means unhopeful of getting results."

Anthony Eden, the Foreign Secretary, resigned on February 20, 1938, opposing Chamberlain's determination to open talks with Italy. The same day Hitler had addressed the Reichstag with a violence that boded ill for reasonable conversation. It was only a few weeks before the end of Austria, on March 11th. On the 14th Mary sat in the House listening to Neville's résumé of events; next day she wrote Louise of the great clarity with which he had spoken. "The House was responsive to the note he set, and showed a quiet determination and sense of the imperative need of avoiding excitement—and of the necessity for us to be ready for emergencies—the first reaction will be a further speeding up of the various branches of our re-armament policy, and probably an enlargement of it."

Neville wrote to Ida and Hilda each week; Mary, talking over his bulletins with the girls felt that he must be right; appeasement really did seem the only means of averting war. She lunched at 10 Downing Street, and there met Ambassador and Mrs. Kennedy for the first time. They were friendly and pleasant, and evidently passed her severest scrutiny for Mary resolved to ask them to a meal. This was a tradition with Mary; in almost fifty years in London, "only one ambassador, I think, I deliberately neglected, and that was Colonel Dawes. I could not face the possibility of his bringing out his pipe in the middle of dinner, and asking for coffee with the soup! These peculiarities may have been a libel, but I could take no risks after I saw him smoking his pipe in the corridor of Buckingham Palace while waiting for his motor."[1]

The early summer passed off pleasantly; young Carnegies and Chamberlains came in and out of Lennox Gardens just as Mary had hoped. Late in August she sailed for America, letting it be known as usual that she was going to "cheer up Louise". So she was on hand when the terrific September hurricane swept across New England. Though dismayed by the damage it did to the landscape, Mary was otherwise undaunted. Neville Chamberlain, meanwhile, had flown into the eye of a much more sinister and long-lasting storm.

The Prime Minister had a businessman's mind. While seeing that Hitler was a bully and a fanatic, he still believed that, with so many millions of lives at stake, the Fuehrer would be amenable to reason. If given an advantage, he would come to terms. In September, 1938, the Sudetenland was the advantage. While the Prime Minister flew back and forth to Germany, German troops were massed, awaiting orders to invade Czechoslovakia. But, said Hitler, if the Sudetenland were handed over, it would be the last of his territorial claims in Europe. Neville Chamberlain, a man of peace, flew home from Munich in the belief he had averted catastrophe. ". . . In spite of the hardness and ruthlessness I thought I saw in [Hitler's] face, I got the impression that here was a man who could be relied upon when he had given his word."[2] Thousands in England were prepared to agree with their Prime Minister; they cheered him for relief "from a war which they had not feared, but on the merits of which they were divided, and the prospect of which they abhorred."[3]

Mary came home to find a seething political confusion. She only saw Neville one day at tea-time for five minutes, and they could not cover anything significant in their talk; Mary, as she had been wont to do with Joe, simply let Neville know her confidence in him. The country was still at peace, and Mary tried to make Christmas the happiest in years. At Chequers, the country retreat of Prime Ministers, Neville was deluged with telegrams and cards thanking him for having prevented a war. At Lennox Gardens Mary got out the gold plate she had kept in the bank since 1914; besides the glittering dinner table, she had a Christmas tree. She hunted up coloured balls, garlands, and stars; she even turned up some strings of popcorn Beatrice had made at Highbury forty-five years before. They were as pretty as ever; she could not help laughing at what William always called her "old maid qualities". Salem had made Mary a careful preserver; the Christmas celebration was filled with souvenirs, and Mary wrote triumphantly, "The hoarding instinct in me never dies."[4]

Mary hoped Louise might come abroad that summer, but that hope was dashed. On March 17th, 1939, she sadly reported: "The gobbling up of Czechoslovakia has created an intolerable situation, and of course for Neville it is a bitter blow . . . [His] hopes have been high, though he has never concealed from himself the possibility that Hitler would ignore what had passed at Munich if it happened to suit his purpose. Fortunately, being a realist, and cautious, all his efforts when he returned from Munich were directed to placing the country in a stronger position, and in the last six months this has been gathering momentum . . ."

Italy's seizure of Albania was next; Mussolini's adherence to the Rome-Berlin Axis was painfully clear. Hitler would turn to Poland next, Mussolini to Greece. The only heartening thing was the Prime Minister's assurance that England would assist Greece and Roumania, as well as Poland, should they be attacked, and wish help in defending themselves.

Mary's sons-in-law had received their war-time assignments; Kathleen had trained as an air-raid warden. The Prime Minister was called back from his August holiday; Mary returned from a round of family visits to black out fifty windows and four sky-lights at Lennox Gardens. Hitler's forces rolled into Poland, and on September 3, 1939, the Prime Minister told the House, "everything that I have worked for, everything that I have hoped for, everything that I have believed in during my public life, has crashed into ruins." Mary saw the tragedy as a personal one. It mattered most to her that Neville's conscience was clear. "He spared no effort to settle these matters, as they could have been settled, by negotiation, and keep the Peace of Europe. That he failed is not his fault, and it is very satisfactory that that is universally recognized."[5]

As the Second World War opened, Mary realized she was actually old. At seventy-five, though, she did not propose to bury herself in the country, or to go to America. By keeping her London house open, she might ease the strain on those of her family actively at war. Michael Peto was at the Ministry of Transport, Pen Slade was at the Admiralty, Casper Swinley in command of a destroyer. Mary wanted to give them, or any other relatives in town a meal, or bed for the night. She could see it would be hard, for the Lennox Gardens house demanded a large staff; and she was only sure of the help of Pink, her butler, and his wife, who cooked. Never since she came to England had Mary stayed in one place as long as she now stayed in London: seven months of the "phoney war" wore on, months of waiting and worrying about the war.

The Opposition spoke loudly about unpreparedness, lack of equipment. There were chafings at war-time restrictions and delays. Then in early May came the fall of Norway, the evacuation of British troops. And almost immediately the Germans attacked and over-ran the Low Countries. On May 10, 1940, having found he could not form a National Government, Neville Chamberlain resigned as Prime Minister. He had tried his best to prevent war; when it seemed imminent he tried to prepare for it; and when it came he pushed it forward with all the forces at his command. Now he stood aside, though he remained in the War Cabinet; and Winston Churchill, First Lord of the Admiralty, took office.

Mary, like other Londoners, did business as usual during the Battle of Britain. She and Kathleen cheered wildly one day when they saw a German bomber shot down; night after night of air raids only confirmed her view that Hitler was a "perfect nuisance". Three or four nights a week she would have people in to dinner: thuds, cracks, and shattering glass were simply an unwelcome counterpoint on her conversation. She and Pen Slade read the Victorian poets aloud to each other; one night when a raid kept her guests with her late Mary suggested that they compose limericks.

Though she thrived on the confusion herself, she worried about Neville. His health was failing fast; following a severe operation in the summer, he had had to resign from the War Cabinet early in October, and retire to Hampshire. Mary went down to Odiham, and drove over to see him. Neville, hearing she had come, said "That is perfect!"; his whole face lighted up as she came in the room, and he said it was lovely to see her. They talked for a few minutes, and then a change came over his face. Quickly the rest of the family were summoned. Then, on November 9th, 1940, so quietly and peacefully the watchers could hardly tell when he stopped breathing, Neville Chamberlain fell into his last sleep.

Of Joe's children, only Ida and Hilda now remained, and with Neville gone, their link with politics was broken. He had always confided in them freely; sharing his father's dedication to politics,

Neville had always wanted to be in close touch with his sisters. Supremely happy in his marriage, he bitterly regretted that they had never found the same happiness. Somehow at Highbury a pattern had been set which kept them in the family circle. Mary had brought their father closer to them, had shared him with his children as few step-mothers would or could. Yet in society she was bride, and they the bridesmaids. Whether she would or not, Mrs. Chamberlain outshone the Misses Chamberlain. Politics, as pursued by their father and brothers, was more absorbing to the girls than potential suitors. Now that Neville, closest to his sisters' hearts, was gone, Mary saw that she must comfort them, remind them of their family motto, "Je tiens ferme."

At Lennox Gardens she had made a haven from storm. Whether she entertained "properly" in the drawing-room, or (more practically) less formally in the downstairs library, she could banish the war completely. Her fan collection, and Joe's china, she had sent away for fear of bomb damage; but the remaining silver and crystal were as highly polished as always. Every clock, decorative box, and stick of furniture had a story of its own. Joe's portrait was upstairs, Governor Endecott's in the library; sitting beneath them one gained in perspective, felt reassured. Pink presented an imperturbable front. Casper Swinley, going into a dangerous operation, warned him about it; when he returned forty-eight hours later, "with no seat to his pants", he managed a jaunty "Morning, Pink"; to which Mary's butler returned, "Your bath, sir."

Mary, whose eyesight was failing, looked raptly at her guests. Her hair was dressed high on her head in the same style she had always had. Her dresses, though of pre-war vintage, sat becomingly on an almost-girlish figure. In a roomful of strident gestured talk, Mary's voice was low and musical, unhurried, controlled. Her conversation, whether concerning the conduct of the war, Mr. Chamberlain's orchids, or her grandchildren's schooling, all seemed important, and directed especially to her companions. She was as skillful and beguiling a hostess as always.

Mary had worried, though, that when she died Kathleen might be left alone. So she watched, with considerable restlessness, the progress of Kathleen's friendship with a distant cousin, Raymond

Gibbs. As both were in their forties she felt she could hardly inter-
fere; finally when she had begun to despair came the news she had
hardly dared hope for. Writing of Kathleen's engagement, Mary rejoiced, "So now my galaxy of sons-in-law is complete."[16]

On May 10, 1941, when London had more than two thousand
fires started by incendiary bombs, and the House of Commons
turned to rubble, Mary had her closest brush with catastrophe. The
tide was low, and bombs had smashed many water mains, so many
fires blazed for hours. All over London the skyline glowed pink;
then an excited shout came from the street and Mary found her
own roof was on fire.

There was water in the bath-tubs; Pen Slade and Pink, with two
pumps, and the household passing them buckets, managed to dis-
lodge and put out the fires from two bombs lodged just above the
top-floor bathroom. Floods poured through the holes in the roof,
and the housemaids, barefooted, stood below swabbing down the
bathroom. Aside from charred rafters, there was little damage
done. Just as everyone was congratulating everyone else, the fire-
fighters arrived on the doorstep, eager for the fray.

Pink, all butler once more, stood barring the way. "Excuse me,
but you must not run up the front stairs. You'll ruin Mrs. Carnegie's carpets!" They would have poured on water, but once more
Pink intervened, "You mustn't run any more water, there won't be
enough for Mrs. Carnegie's bath!" At length they departed, and
Mary settled gratefully in bed, a fine sense of accomplishment in
her heart. She had said she would stay in London and see to her
property, and she had. Later on her private battle with the blitz became family legend. Mary's dinner guests would glance from her,
exquisite in chiffon, with bits of lace at wrists and throat, to Pink,
white-tied and silver-haired, hovering behind her chair. They wondered if such a night really could have happened.

Mary was overjoyed when America finally saw the light, and entered the war. Her house was quiet now, for Pen Slade was gravely
ill, and had returned to the country with his family, and Kathleen
was married. So Mary delighted in welcoming American visitors:
some were cousins in uniform, like James Lawrence, Jr., and Minturn Sedgwick; some were friends, or friends of friends—Mary rus-

tled round and enjoyed them all. For a soldier, the shining order
and comfort at Lennox Gardens were almost incredible. One of
them recalled "what it meant to a man, who had recently spent
fourteen months in a tent in an oat field in Italy, to enjoy such a
unique hostess and such a pleasant meal. The charm with which
she entertained us will never be forgotten."

Though the meals she could manage were skimpy, Mary entertained as often as she could. She loved to sit late with her guests in
the firelight; when one of them mischievously asked how it felt to
be sitting there with two handsome young men, Mary smiled and
replied "Just the way it always did!" She even managed a small
dinner for the new American Ambassador, Mr. Winant. Enthralled
by his hostess, he afterwards exclaimed, "She is the one woman in
London I should like to run away with!"

Mary, distressed by the aging of her contemporaries, took great
care of her own appearance. She loved going to the theatre, or a
really good movie like *Gone With the Wind*. But she was startled to
realize that to young people the American Civil War seemed like
ancient history: Mary, aged seven, had once been kissed by General Grant! Caught on the street by air raid sirens, Mary exclaimed
"Certainly not!" when asked if she did not wish to take shelter.
She tripped along with Jim Lawrence in tow, for all the world like
a girl on a special date. Mary could still sit, stand, and walk straight,
which, she observed with satisfaction, was more than many people
near eighty could manage.

There were many breaks in the family circle. Austen's widow,
Ivy, died early in 1941, Pen Slade in the fall of 1942, and Ida Chamberlain in the spring of 1943. Of all Joe's children Ida had needed
most a mother's affection. Mary remembered her, eighteen and
eager, but desperately shy. Ida had taught herself shorthand, and
as Mary's helper and secretary conquered some of her reserve.
Without that early training she could never have done all the work
she did in Hampshire on the District and County Council. Ida had
been a worrier; if one of the girls had to be left alone, Mary was glad
it was Hilda; but all the same, it was hard to have another link with
the past broken.

Mary's household still ran much as ever. She heard that a bottle of Chartreuse had brought £15 at a Red Cross auction, so despatched Pink to her cellar to see what could be found. Two similar bottles turned up: they had migrated from Prince's Gardens to Dean's Yard to Lennox Gardens; now, labelled with their history, they went off to help the war effort. At Thanksgiving, 1943, Mary's guests were regaled with goose and plum pudding, but had to do without the blue flames on the pudding. Mary felt she really could not sacrifice her only brandy: cognac of 1848! Pink had a proper respect for history also. At one of Mary's dinners, after a lady guest had refused port he whispered urgently, "Does the lady know it is the *Chamberlain* port, sir?" Casper Swinley, playing host, passed this word along and, chastened, the lady accepted the wine.

Mary would have thought it wrong to abandon the possessions and habits of a life-time. Part of her New England heritage was a feeling for continuity and the importance of standards. Salem people still possessed the fiery spirit of Puritan ancestors, but it mostly burned within; showing itself chiefly as reverence for the past, a zeal for property and family history. Mary had all these traits, but also she had an eagerness and spontaneity which kept her from being bound to tradition. The wine, food, and accessories mattered very much at a dinner-party, but really they were only accessories to the conversation.

Some accessories, she thought, could be dispensed with. Mary asked Pink to keep china compotes on the table instead of silver. He was no longer young, and she wanted to spare him the polishing, but days went by, and still, in sparkling condition, the silver appeared. London lay in ruins, thousands ate in cellars and shelters, but while the walls of 41, Lennox Gardens stood, Pink did not favour compromise. "Madam," he reminded Mary gravely, "we must keep up our standards."

Mary's spirits only faltered when she was alone. The Doodle-bugs, robot bombs which came over regularly from D-Day until March, 1945, did not bother her. The idea that she and her household might cease to be useful, did. She never felt tired when she was busy, but she was quite annoyed when the newspapers heard about her eightieth birthday. "Since then I am constantly congratulated, or condoled with, or told how wonderful I am, or offered an armchair I do not want, or asked if I really can walk . . . and I find it very tiresome . . . It is one of the penalties a long life brings, and I now sympathize with Grandpa Peabody's irritation when Dr. Holmes [the Autocrat of the Breakfast Table] came to see him, and would talk about the 'sere and yellow'.

" 'Cat's Toe!' said Grandpa, 'why can't he talk about something one wants to hear!' "[7]

There was so much Mary wanted to hear about: politics, the war, and all three of her families. She could trace out the intricate relations of Endicotts, Peabodys, Gardners, and Crowninshields with the greatest of ease; she was equally competent with Chamberlains and Carnegies. Pink, who had been with her over forty years, and remembered parents, cousins, and grandparents of her present callers, was apt to break in on Mary's table talk, and supply missing details. He, too, enjoyed the comings and goings of young men in uniform, and had his own store of anecdotes to recall.

Mary took her family legends rather seriously. Pink had the more humourous view. There was the elderly Peabody cousin who had arrived by cab, years before, and practiced New England thrift when it came to a tip. Pink, opening the door for the new arrival, saw the Irish cabby shake his fist, and heard him shout disgustedly, *"They calls ye Mr. Pay-body, I calls you Mr. Pay-No-Body!"*

On V-E Day Mary went to a special Thanksgiving Service at St. Margaret's; at Lennox Gardens she had her Union Jack flying in the breeze, as it had flown for the Diamond Jubilee, and the Armistice of 1918. Soon it flew again, to celebrate victory over Japan.

The war's end brought new farewells. Mary's American friends and relations went home, Roosevelt was dead, and Churchill turned out of office. Mary took the darkest possible view of the Labour Government; she tiraded about "those men" with their meddlesome, bungling ways for hours. The nationalization of services and industries brought down her especial wrath. Though the world outlook was troubled, Mary's own view of life was greatly aided by a long-deferred eye operation. Then at Thanksgiving, 1946, despite austerity rations American food parcels helped Mary give a dinner with turkey, cranberry sauce, plum pudding, and mince pie. She revived a black evening dress, and pink-cheeked and smiling, received her guests in the drawing-room.

Christmas was less happy, for just after dinner on December 24th, Mary suffered a heart attack. A defective valve, which had complicated her recovery from illness twice in previous years, now saved her life, for it allowed a clot of blood to pass through the heart. Dimly Mary was aware of her maid Dance settling her on the library sofa, and the doctor saying she must not move. Then she fell into a troubled sleep, from which, in the small hours, she awoke, feeling somewhat better, but restless. If only she were in her own bed she was certain she would be more comfortable. Like a child conspiring to be naughty, Mary insisted that Dance lift her and help her to the stairs. She would not call Pink, for fear he would try to carry her himself, or else forbid her the climb. Slowly she struggled up two flights of stairs, wondering at the end if she would make it. Settled in her room at last, Mary was quite happy to lie still, and when the doctor sternly ordered six weeks in bed, his patient, who had gained her point, did just as she was told. Her recovery was complete, and to her family's watchful eyes Mary looked more rested than before her attack. She took two grand-daughters to a Royal Garden Party, planned a trip to America, and talked over plans for the long-deferred fourth volume of Joe's biography.

She was alternately amused and indignant at the arrangements for the American trip. The doctor had approved it, but Mary found there were numerous other officials involved. At the U. S. Consulate she had to present her weight and fingerprints, as if she were a wanted criminal. Then she had to see "those men" at the Treasury, who seemed to have the idea that £75 would be all she needed in America, at any rate all they would allow her to have. Long wranglings with bankers ensued, but Mary won. In the matter of jewellery she did not come off so well. Fearful that British subjects might export their valuables for sale abroad the Government had limited the jewellery a person could take out of the country to one brooch, one necklace, one bracelet, etc. To Mary, for whom every ring and pin she owned had sentimental value, and who could not have conceived of selling them, this was insufferable. Formerly she might have worn four or five pieces of jewellery at once; now, though less elaborately garbed, she had certain favourite pieces she liked to keep at hand. In vain she evoked the spectre of Mr. Chamberlain, insisted she needed more jewels, and had no intention of disposing of those she took. The compromise she finally reached was strictly unofficial. She gave Dance, who would accompany her, a favourite emerald ring, which she never wore but liked to have about, with the injunction, "If anyone asks, it is your engagement ring!"

On July 31, 1947, Mary, Dance, and thirty pieces of luggage boarded the *Queen Mary* for its first civilian voyage to New York since the war. Every pin, ruffle, and petticoat was perfectly packed by Dance; suitcases were labelled for the voyage, needed in New York, or to go direct to Danvers. It was rather a large-scale departure from austerity England; but considering that Mary and the Canon had once arrived for a weekend stay with twenty-one pieces of luggage following them in a hand-cart from the station, thirty pieces for a three-month stay was almost modest. Fireboats turned out to spray a welcome for the returning *Queen*. When Mary debarked in New York, her own journey continued like a Royal Progress. The Cunard Line bowed her off, she was met by a cousin with flowers, and the Ambassador Hotel sent an emissary to guide her through the intricacies of an over-night stay there. Next day, arriving at Danvers, she was reunited with Louise and her household.

It was nine years since they had met, and there had been many changes. Friends of Mary's childhood were dead, small children had grown up, and young relatives grown middle-aged. Only the year before, the last of Mary's mother's servants, kept on by Louise, had died. The Farm itself was still the same; Mary went through each room with delight, and found the gardens lovelier than ever. When she left England, Mary put behind her all fretting about her house, taxes, shortages, and servants. She maintained she would be quite quiet, and did not wish to put Louise out in any way. Nevertheless, she visibly pined when there were no afternoon callers, or they did not go out for a drive. It was a busy time for Mary's kindly sister-in-law.

Large and amiable, Louise Endicott presided over tables-full of guests. At luncheon, tea, and dinner she had served successions of rich and delicious meals. After lunch she was quite content to settle in a basket chair on the verandah, the smell of flowers and new-mown hay heavy in the afternoon. Considering the garden drowsily, she was soon happy to steal away, loosen her stays, and settle down to an afternoon nap. For forty years she had cheerfully obliged her mother-in-law, deferred to her taste, and consulted with her or William about every step she took. Now, widowed for ten years, and growing deaf as well, she often felt painfully alone. It hurt that the vivacious Mary should at once attract such legions of admirers, young and old; but Louise was too good-hearted to admit this. Mary in her turn was too tactful to complain when she found the Danvers household sedate and silent. So these two dissimilar ladies accommodated to each other, and spoke of their mutual past, dear William, Mr. Chamberlain, and the Canon in affectionate terms.

Late in October Mary and Louise, with their impedimenta, proceeded to Boston. There, with the silver lion doorknobs screwed firmly onto the great front doors of the Marlborough Street house (Louise had them removed each spring for fear of burglars), they organized themselves for life in town.

In Boston Louise frankly relaxed, and cautioning Mary not to get too tired, left her pretty much to pursue her own way. The fewer days there were of her visit, the more that Mary seemed to fill them. She shopped for clothes and presents, marvelled over children's toys and nylon stockings. She lunched out, went to exhibitions and the theatre, and showed no sign of strain. Louise, dozing in the library, would fret as the evening wore on, and peer through the curtains from time to time till her giddy sister-in-law was safely home.

Though she wept at leaving America, Mary was glad to be home; she got there just in time to enjoy Princess Elizabeth's wedding, the first ceremonial of post-war years. It was pleasant to be in command of her household again, and Mary revived a custom of being "at home" on Sunday afternoons. When alone, Mary was rather absent-minded about tea, but on Sundays she went up to change her clothes, and from five to seven, received in the drawing-room. There were plates of cucumber sandwiches about, and she was quite disappointed if they were not all eaten. To her sorrow, what had been a thriving occasion was dwindling as the weekend out of London gained in popularity. Her family, especially grandchildren, tried especially hard to come, for they knew how Mary loved her "At Homes".

Austen's daughter Diane and her husband persuaded her to resume her "silver, candlelight, and champagne" dinners. She maintained she could not afford them, but was so cheered by the thought of a few formal dinner-parties that she did so anyway. She ordered a good dinner, put on her best dress, and was quite shocked if her gentlemen guests did not understand they were to wear white tie. The war had been one thing—she had not minded any odd uniform or costume; but peace-time was quite different. If she had meant to be informal, Mary might, like Louise, have helpfully advised, "Don't bother to dress, dear, just black tie!" Even when she had settled details of food and service, there was a guest problem. "Dinners are really difficult to organize just now so far as men are concerned, for so many of my stand-bys are Members of Parliament, and with the Labour Government I feel I cannot be responsible for luring away any Conservatives who might enable them by their absence to secure larger majorities than they deserve."[8]

However much it cost, Mary was determined to maintain her Daimler. She recalled how the Canon enjoyed it, and though it was prey to various ailments, and devoured petrol, the ancient car still took Mary about on afternoons and Sundays.

Mary felt closer than ever to the Dowager Queen Mary. Swiftly on her husband's death had come the Abdication Crisis, then the war and the death of the Duke of Kent. Queen Mary had never flinched; she had dutifully, though reluctantly, spent the war years in the country; now she was in anxiety over the illness of the King. Mary, like many others, thought the weariness in King George's face came from the strain of years past; he had got over an operation well, and she was shocked to hear, in February, 1952, of his death.

From the roof of St. Margaret's Mary watched the arrival of the gun-carriage bringing the King's body to lie in state in Westminster Hall. The Dukes of Edinburgh and Gloucester walked behind; waiting at the entrance of the Hall were the young Queen Elizabeth, the Queen Mother, Queen Mary, and Princess Margaret. Two days later Mary watched the silent thousands pass through the Hall; wintry sunshine fell on the great oak rafters and stone walls. Mary watched till the scene was clearly in her mind. She had a gallery of ceremonials, covering five reigns; a photographic memory allowed her to review them, at the merest mention of a name or occasion. So she felt she need not watch the funeral procession through London, or the service at St. George's Chapel, Windsor. She could imagine them perfectly; royal rituals were comfortingly the same. Far from being depressed by them, Mary found they served as landmarks to her happy recollections of the past.

At St. Margaret's, when she heard "God Save the Queen", Mary suddenly realized how many in the congregation must be hearing it for the first time. The words were thrilling to her, for they recalled her earliest days in England. Mary thought the new Queen was doing very well; she admired also Queen Mary's "usual fortitude"; but in the year after the King's death, her strength slowly ebbed away. She instructed her grand-daughter firmly that if she should die, Court mourning should not delay the Coronation. It was as she had wished. On March 24th Queen Mary died, and on June 2, 1953, Queen Elizabeth was crowned.

These years of a new reign were happy for Mary. Considering her car must be at least as dependable as herself in weathering the years, she ordered it round to take one great-granddaughter and twin grand-daughters to be presented. The girls were in their prettiest dresses for the Garden Party, the car was on time, and all went well until, in the line of cars in Palace Yard, the Daimler drew reluctantly to a halt. It had to be pushed to the door by a group of tall guardsmen; then, when the girls were out, wheeled off to be revived. Mary was crestfallen.

She had given a wedding reception for May's eldest daughter, and an eightieth-birthday celebration for Hilda Chamberlain. Then Casper and Jo Swinley had their silver wedding, and soon after another grand-daughter was to be married. Mary felt very happy and useful planning all these parties, but she was quite overwhelmed when her own turn came, and Diane arranged a ninetieth-birthday party for her. It was a dinner for thirty-six to which came Chamberlains and Carnegies, and three American cousins as well. After dinner other friends, Pink proudly among them, came by to pay their respects. It was two in the morning before Mary thought of going home to bed. For the whole next month she was writing to thank for the forty-eight baskets of flowers, and over a hundred letters sent by well-wishers.

Her trips to America were always happy. As they grew older she and Louise were increasingly thoughtful of each other. Louise, on getting out from a car, would turn fussily and urge that someone take care of Mrs. Carnegie, who could hardly see; while Mary, in turn, whispered conspiratorially that you must be sure to speak up, for Mrs. Endicott could hardly hear. Mary once shook her head and confided, "You know, Louise is aging fast; she can't really go about the way I want her to." Louise, aware of these sentiments, cherished an ambition to outlive her busy and bustling sister-in-law. Each year she held a farewell party for "Cousin Mary", who smiled and shook hands with any quantity of relations, and each year Mary returned. Both ladies spoke often about the past, but Louise kept on sorting cupboards and passing out possessions to her family; while Mary, it seemed, was always too involved to tidy up. She was as meticulous in appearance as ever, but would have felt quite lost if she had ever had all the letters written, or desk drawers sorted out, that she meant to do.

Mary thought with increasing pleasure and perfect recollection of life in Salem, Washington, and Victorian England. Though sometimes forgetful of present-day matters, she insisted on being in command of her household. She was apt to misplace her handkerchiefs, or even her steamship tickets, but those around her tactfully kept her supplied. In her own, and many other New England families Mary had seen cases where a person lived on and on, health only gradually failing, but with mind long outworn. It was a fate that she dreaded. She used to maintain that if you rode upstairs in a lift, you lost the use of your muscles. Now that she had some trouble with her legs, as well as her heart, she was a bit more willing to climb the easy way. But she would not let go of household details; she was determined her mind should continue to manage her affairs.

There was one disturbing change at Lennox Gardens. Pink, after fifty-five years in Mary's service, and his wife, after thirty-five, retired in 1956. Mary had not realized how much she depended on them until they had gone. In the next six months she ran through seven cooks and three butlers. She was more thankful than ever to get to America.

Life itself was no chore to Mary; it was merely that the mechanics grew difficult. She delighted in new hats and Worth dresses still. She had been on a Thames River excursion boat, and she never missed a Garden Party. There were not hours enough for all she thought she should do, and Mary scoffed at the suggestion of composing memoirs. "Why, if I spent all my time looking backwards at the past, I'd have no time left for living in the present and future."

Her ninety-third birthday was spent at the theatre, and when asked if she wouldn't like to go straight home afterwards she replied, "I should hate that! I want to be taken to a large, loud, gay restaurant for supper!" So often people tried to consider her years, when she was feeling liveliest. Half a dozen young Conservative M.P.s came round to dine, and after an agreeable evening got up to go at eleven o'clock. Mary exclaimed, "You are not leaving now? I am at my best till two a.m.!"

She continued to give dinner-parties until two weeks before her death. Early in May, 1957, Mary had a heart attack, and for thirteen days lay in her own bed at Lennox Gardens. She had always disliked nurses and nursing homes; now, though she slept a lot, and when she woke was restless and uncomfortable, she was grateful for familiar surroundings. She knew quite well she was going to die, and so she did not really listen when told she would soon be downstairs again.

Mary's thoughts turned back. She spoke of her very first day in London, and the drive she had taken with her cousin William Endicott. She recalled perfectly the sights and sounds of seventy-five years before, and looked so pretty and excited in the telling it was easy to picture her as a girl of eighteen. She had another heart attack; after the doctor had done what he could, she settled peacefully to rest. At eleven-fifteen on the evening of May 17, sighing a little in her sleep, Mary died.

She was buried in Westminster Abbey, beside the Canon, and

only a few steps away from the bust of Joseph Chamberlain. So London, her home for nearly seventy years, became Mary's final resting place. It was what she had wished, for she had always found peace in the Abbey, the sense that life continued, traditions would endure. Within its walls was something great and strong, without regard for time.

While she lived, she gave to time new meaning. So vividly could she describe what she had seen and heard that Mary made the past and present merge. Exquisitely dressed, with eyes that sparkled as she spoke, she was perennially charming. In her presence, even dull men felt distinguished. It was hard to believe she was true; but sitting in her drawing-room, hearing her speak of what one reads in history books as if it had been yesterday, one *did* believe. One saw a little girl in Salem, spirited and strong, and almost heard her mother's voice, "And mistress of herself, tho' China fall."

NOTES

CHAPTER I: THE MARRIAGE OF TRUE MINDS

1. Quoted in Appendix to *Beatrice Webb's Diaries, 1924–1932*, ed. by Margaret Cole, London, 1956, p. 315.

2. She was unrelated to the author of children's books. She later married Sidney Webb, and with him pursued a brilliant career of social investigation.

3. Cole, ed., *op. cit.*, p. 316.

4. *Ibid.*, p. 315.

5. Letter of Mary Crowninshield Endicott, hereafter MEC, to Fanny Peabody Mason, hereafter FPM, December 27, 1887, in collection of Massachusetts Historical Society, hereafter MHS.

6. MEC to FPM, February 24, 1888. MHS.

7. MEC to her mother, Ellen Endicott, hereafter EE, January 10, 1914, in the Chamberlain Papers at Birmingham University, hereafter B'ham.

CHAPTER II: SALEM LIVERPOOL

1. Eliza Endicott Perry, a widowed aunt of Endicott's who served as family nurse in moments of emergency.

2. Diary of William Crowninshield Endicott, in Endicott Papers, MHS, March 15, 1864.

3. MEC, Diary, November 16, 1876. MHS.

4. MEC to Fanny Prince, sometime in 1937. MHS.

CHAPTER III: LONDON MEN AND ENGLISH MEN

1. MEC, Diary, May 29, 1882. MHS.

2. MEC, Diary, June 11, 1882. This Second Coercion Act (the first was in 1881) struck back at Irish nationalists following the murder of the Chief Secretary, Lord Frederick Cavendish, and Under Secretary, Mr. Burke, in Phoenix Park, Dublin. It empowered the Government to put in jail without trial any person suspected of intending to commit or promote crime.

3. MEC, Diary, July 10, 1882. MHS.

4. MEC, Diary, January 6, 1883. MHS.

5. MEC, Diary, January 31, 1883. MHS.

6. MEC, Diary, May 22, 1883. MHS.

7. MEC, Diary, July 13, 1883. MHS.

8. *Ibid.*

9. MEC, Diary, July 21, 1883. MHS.

10. MEC, Diary, September 8, 1883. MHS.

11. MEC, Diary, September 20, 1883. MHS.

CHAPTER IV: AT HOME IN WASHINGTON

1. *New York World*, June 14, 1885.
2. William Crowninshield Endicott to MEC, April 24, 1891. MHS.

CHAPTER V: THE LION RAMPANT

1. Maycock, Willoughby, *With Mr. Chamberlain in the United States and Canada*, London, 1914, p. 34.
2. Mary's pocket diaries, Chamberlain's *Diary in America*, and letters to his daughter Beatrice, hereafter BC, are all to be found in the Chamberlain Papers at Birmingham University.
3. *Town Topics*, November 15, 1888.
4. Henry Adams to Elizabeth Cameron, October 23, 1887, in *Letters of Henry Adams, 1858–1891*, Boston, 1930, Vol. I, p. 386.
5. Joseph Chamberlain, hereafter JC, to BC, December 2, 1887. B'ham.
6. JC, *Diary in America*, December 6, 1887. B'ham.
7. Hay, who had been Lincoln's Private Secretary, and was subsequently employed in diplomacy and journalism, was chiefly occupied in 1887 in writing, with his colleague John Nicolay, a life of Lincoln.
8. JC to BC, December 9, 1887. B'ham.
9. JC to BC, December 6, 1887. B'ham.
10. JC to BC, December 15, 1887. B'ham.
11. Newspaper clipping, quoted in Maycock, *op. cit.*, p. 87.
12. Cecil Spring-Rice, British Ambassador to Washington before and during World War I, was at this time Third Secretary at the Legation; quite a beau of Mary's, and affectionately known to his friends as "Springy".
13. JC to BC, January 13, 1888. B'ham.
14. JC to BC, January 18, 1888. B'ham.
15. Maycock, *op. cit.*, p. 147.

CHAPTER VI: "AND LEAVE THEE FOR AWHILE"

1. MEC to FPM, April 21, 1888. MHS.
2. BC to MEC, March 12, 1888. MHS.
3. Austen Chamberlain to MEC, March 11, 1888. MHS.
4. Neville Chamberlain to MEC, April 9, 1888. MHS.
5. George Augustus Peabody to EE, October 12, 1888. MHS.
6. MEC to FPM, October 22, 1888. MHS.
7. MEC to EE, November 16 and 17, 1888. MHS.
8. JC to EE, November 16, 1888. MHS.
9. MEC to EE, November 18, 1888. MHS.
10. Mrs. George Peabody to EE, November 18, 1888. MHS.
11. *Punch*, November 16, 1895, p. 231.

12. William Crowninshield Endicott, Jr., hereafter WCE, to Mrs. George Peabody, November 24, 1888. MHS.

13. John Hay to JC, November 14, 1888. B'ham.

14. MEC to EE, December 8, 1888. B'ham.

15. MEC to EE, December 25, 1888. B'ham.

16. *Ibid.*

17. JC to EE, January 4, 1889. B'ham.

CHAPTER VII: "DEAR LADY, WELCOME HOME"

1. MEC to EE, January 11, 1889. B'ham.

2. MEC to EE, January 15, 1889. B'ham.

3. MEC to EE, January 24, 1889. B'ham.

4. *Ibid.*

5. MEC to EE, March 15, 1889. B'ham.

6. MEC to EE, March 26, 1889. B'ham.

7. MEC to EE, March 23, 1889. B'ham.

8. MEC to FPM, March 27, 1889. MHS.

9. MEC to EE, March 9, 1889. B'ham.

10. JC to EE, March 15, 1889. B'ham.

11. Mrs. George Peabody to MEC, January 9, 1889. MHS.

12. MEC to FPM, March 27, 1889. MHS.

13. Clipping, headed *Talk of the Town*, enclosed in EE to Mrs. George Peabody, May 4, 1889; and Mrs. Peabody's reply. MHS.

14. William Crowninshield Endicott to WCE, May 5, 1889. MHS.

15. EE to Mrs. George Peabody, May 20, 1889. MHS.

16. EE to Mrs. George Peabody, May 26, 1889. MHS.

17. EE to Mr. George Peabody, August 10, 1889. MHS.

18. Cornwallis-West, Mrs. George, *The Reminiscences of Lady Randolph Churchill*, New York, 1908, pp. 119–120.

CHAPTER VIII: THE ROAD TO OFFICE

1. WCE to MEC, May 5 and June 15, 1890. MHS.

2. MEC to EE, July 26, 1890. B'ham.

3. See Garvin, J. L., *The Life of Joseph Chamberlain*, London, 1933, Vol. II, pp. 452–455, for his account of "Joseph in Egypt". (Hereafter cited as Garvin, *Life*.)

4. Unheaded newspaper clipping, in Endicott family scrapbook. MHS.

5. EE to MEC, July ?, 1890. MHS.

6. Hayes, C. J. H., *A Political and Cultural History of Modern Europe*, New York, 1939, Vol. II, pp. 359–360.

7. MEC to EE, April 11, 1893. B'ham.

8. MEC to EE, April 22, 1893. B'ham.

9. MEC to EE, July 28, 1893. B'ham.

10. This story was told to me by both Mrs. Carnegie and Miss Hilda Chamberlain, though neither lady fixed a date for the incident, but referred to a visit to the Farm "after the Irish disturbances". I have placed it here, as following Chamberlain's opposition to the Second Home Rule Bill. The 1890 visit of the Chamberlains was leisurely, and largely spent in Salem; there is a possibility the assassin's attempt may have been made on an 1896 trip, when the Colonial Secretary was meeting with Secretary of State Olney to try to settle the Venezuelan crisis; none that it was in 1898, when their trip was planned as a brief holiday in the first place, since Chamberlain could not leave his work for more than a few weeks.

11. MEC to EE, September 7, 1894. B'ham.

12. JC to MEC, February 26 and 28, 1895; quoted in Garvin, *Life*, Vol. II, pp. 625–626.

13. JC to the Duke of Devonshire, April 19, 1895; quoted in *ibid.*, p. 630.

14. Quoted in *ibid.*, p. 595, fn. 2.

CHAPTER IX: "TO VISIT THE QUEEN"

1. Hilda Chamberlain to EE, July 16, 1895. MHS.
2. MEC to EE, August 9, 1895. B'ham.
3. MEC to EE, November 23, 1895. B'ham.
4. MEC to EE, November 13, 1895. B'ham.
5. MEC to EE, December 7, 1895. B'ham.
6. MEC to EE, December 10, 1895. B'ham.
7. MEC to EE, December 21, 1895. B'ham.
8. FPM to MEC, December 24, 1895. MHS.
9. See Garvin, *Life*, Vol. III, pp. 65–68, 163–165.
10. Quoted in *ibid.*, p. 89.
11. MEC to EE, January 8, 1896. B'ham.
12. MEC to EE, April 3, 1896. B'ham.
13. MEC to EE, June 17, 1896. B'ham.

CHAPTER X: "TO THY JUBILEE THRONG"

1. Quoted in Garvin, *Life*, Vol. III, p. 145.
2. MEC to EE, May 28, 1897. B'ham.
3. MEC to EE, June 28, 1897. B'ham.
4. MEC to EE, July 2 and 6, 1897. B'ham.
5. Ida Chamberlain to EE, June 29, 1897. MHS.
6. MEC to EE, July 9, 1897. B'ham.
7. MEC to FPM, January 5, 1898. MHS.
8. BC to EE, April 5, 1898. MHS.

9. Clara Endicott Sears to MEC, April 24, 1898. MHS.
10. JC at Birmingham, May 13, 1898; quoted in Garvin, *Life*, Vol. III, p. 302.
11. JC to Lord Salisbury, November 30, 1898, quoted in *ibid.*, p. 380.
12. MEC to EE, January 4, 1899. B'ham.
13. Milner to JC, quoted in Garvin, *Life*, Vol. III, pp. 395–396.
14. MEC to FPM, August 31, 1899. MHS.
15. MEC to EE, September 20, 1899. B'ham.
16. President Steyn to Milner, October 11, 1899, quoted in *The Times History of the War in South Africa*, London, 1900, Vol. I, p. 373.
17. Steyn's manifesto to his burghers, quoted in *ibid.*, p. 375.

CHAPTER XI: "WE ARE MARCHING TO PRETORIA"

1. MEC to EE, October 11, 1899. B'ham.
2. MEC to EE, October 20, 1899. B'ham.
3. Eva Holland to MEC, November 25, 1899. This letter, written from Admiralty House, Chatham, is now, with other souvenirs of the launching of the *Venerable*, in the possession of Captain Casper Silas Balfour Swinley, D.S.O., D.S.C., Royal Navy.
4. See Garvin, *Life*, Vol. III, pp. 324–343.
5. MEC to EE, November 24, 1899. B'ham.
6. *Ibid.*
7. MEC to EE, February 2, 1900. B'ham.
8. JC in speech to House of Commons, February 5, 1900.
9. MEC to EE, February 7, 1900. B'ham.
10. MEC to EE, March 2, 1900. B'ham.
11. JC to MEC, September 19, 1900, quoted in Garvin, *Life*, Vol. III, p. 594. See pp. 593–605 for an account of the Khaki Election and other extracts from JC's letters to his wife.
12. Quoted in *ibid.*, p. 616.
13. Quoted by MEC to Louise Endicott, February 3, 1901. MHS.
14. MEC to EE, January 6, 1901. B'ham.
15. *Letters of Queen Victoria*, ed. by George Earle Buckle, London, 1930, 3rd series, Vol. I, p. 498, April 30, 1889.
16. MEC to EE, February 7, 1901. B'ham.
17. *Ibid.*
18. MEC to EE, November 29, 1901. B'ham.
19. WCE to MEC, February 23, 1904. MHS.
20. JC at Birmingham, January 11, 1902.
21. MEC to EE, February 18, 1902. B'ham.
22. MEC to EE, October 7, 1902. B'ham.
23. MEC to EE, November 10, 1902. B'ham.
24. MEC to EE, November 29, 1902. B'ham.
25. JC at Birmingham, November 17, 1902.
26. MEC to EE, November 29, 1902. B'ham.

CHAPTER XII: ''MUCH HAVE I TRAVELLED IN
THE REALMS OF GOLD''

1. MEC to EE, December 13, 1902. B'ham.
2. MEC to EE, December 20, 1902. B'ham.
3. MEC to EE, December 25, 1902. B'ham.
4. MEC to EE, January 13, 1903. B'ham.
5. *Ibid.*
6. MEC to EE, January 26, 1903. B'ham.
7. *Ibid.*
8. MEC to EE, February 5, 1903. B'ham.
9. JC, Business Diary, Vol. i, p. 190, January 30, 1903. Quoted in Amery, *Life,*
Vol. IV, p. 349.
10. MEC to EE, February 12, 1903. B'ham.
11. JC, speech of February 8, 1903. Quoted in Amery, *Life*, Vol. IV, p. 356.
12. MEC to EE, February 12, 1903. B'ham.
13. MEC to EE, March 2, 1903. B'ham.
14. *Ibid.*
15. *Ibid.*
16. JC, speech at Mansion House, March 20, 1903.

CHAPTER XIII: IN SIGHT OF THE PROMISED LAND

1. EE to WCE, September 18, 1903. MHS.
2. WCE to MEC, September 20, 1903. MHS.
3. JC, speech at Birmingham, November 4, 1903.
4. JC to EE, January 30, 1906. B'ham.
5. Austen Chamberlain to EE, February 20, 1906. B'ham.
6. JC, speech at Birmingham, July 9, 1906.
7. WCE to MEC, August 26, 1906. B'ham.
8. MEC to FPM, December 6, 1906. MHS.
9. Louise Endicott to MEC, May 14, 1907. MHS.
10. MEC to EE, November 14, 1908. B'ham.
11. Augustine Gray to MEC, January 8, 1910. MHS.
12. MEC to EE, February 4, 1911. B'ham.
13. *Ibid.*
14. MEC to EE, February 12, 1911. B'ham.
15. WCE to MEC, March 25, 1912. MHS.
16. MEC to EE, January 10, 1914. B'ham.
17. MEC to EE, March 23, 1914. B'ham.
18. Austen Chamberlain to FPM, July 20, 1914. MHS.
19. *Ibid.*

CHAPTER XIV: "OTHERS I DOUBT NOT, IF NOT WE"

1. Endicott Peabody to MEC, December 14, 1914. MHS.
2. George Augustus Peabody to MEC, October 5, 1914. MHS.
3. MEC to EE, April 24, 1916. B'ham.
4. MEC to EE, April 27, 1916. B'ham.
5. BC to FPM, October 30, 1916. MHS.
6. MEC to EE, August 18, 1916. B'ham.
7. MEC to FPM, October 7, 1916. MHS.
8. MEC to EE, July 13, 1917. B'ham.
9. MEC to EE, January 1, 1918. B'ham.
10. MEC to EE, April 21, 1918. B'ham.
11. MEC to EE, June 30, 1919. B'ham.
12. MEC to EE, April 22, 1921. B'ham.
13. MEC to EE, January 1, 1921. B'ham.
14. MEC to EE, July 27, 1923. B'ham.
15. MEC to WCE, November 9, 1934. MHS.
16. MEC to WCE, May 31, 1935. MHS.
17. MEC to Mrs. Morton Prince, July 26, 1935. MHS.
18. MEC to WCE, March 17, 1936. MHS.
19. MEC to Mrs. Morton Prince, February 12, 1936. MHS.
20. MEC to WCE, August 12, 1936. MHS.
21. MEC to Louise Endicott, March 30, 1937. MHS.

CHAPTER XV: "JE TIENS FERME"

1. MEC to Mrs. Morton Prince, May 2, 1938. MHS. Charles G. Dawes, former Vice-President of the U. S., and a Chicago banker, caused a fearful uproar in Court circles when as the newly-arrived Ambassador, he insisted on appearing in long black evening trousers, instead of knee breeches at an evening Court. See H.R.H. Edward, Duke of Windsor, *A King's Story*, New York, 1947, pp. 232–237.
2. Quoted in Keith Feiling, *The Life of Neville Chamberlain*, London, 1946, p. 367.
3. *Ibid.*, p. 383. Duff Cooper resigned as First Lord of the Admiralty in protest at the Munich Agreement. In his memoirs (*Old Men Forget*, London, 1953, p. 200) he said of Neville Chamberlain: "He had never moved in the great world of politics or of finance, and the continent of Europe was for him a closed book. He had been a successful Lord Mayor of Birmingham, and for him the Dictators of Germany and of Italy were like the Lord Mayors of Liverpool and Manchester, who might belong to different political parties, and have different interests, but who must desire the welfare of humanity, and be fundamentally reasonable, decent men like himself."
4. MEC to Mrs. Morton Prince, January 20, 1939. MHS.
5. MEC to Mrs. Morton Prince, September 16, 1939. MHS.
6. MEC to Mrs. Morton Prince, May 1, 1941. MHS.
7. MEC to FPM, July 10, 1944. MHS.
8. MEC to Louise Endicott, June 27, 1951. MHS.

BIBLIOGRAPHY

The Endicott Papers, in the Massachusetts Historical Society, Boston, Massachusetts, and *The Chamberlain Papers*, in the University of Birmingham, Birmingham, England, provided the vast majority of the written sources for this book. Letters, diaries, photographs, invitations, scrapbooks, and engagement calendars were all scrupulously preserved by the Endicotts, and presented by them to the Historical Society. Mary's letters to her mother (written approximately twice a week from the time of her marriage in 1888 until Mrs. Endicott's death in 1927 whenever they were apart) were returned to Mary, and kept by her in England for the rest of her life. She left them, after her death in 1957, to the University of Birmingham, together with Joseph Chamberlain's papers, to form the nucleus of the Chamberlain Room in the Library there. Mary's engagement books, guest books, photograph albums, and other mementoes of her life as Mrs. Chamberlain are also in this collection. Generally Mary covered ten or fifteen sides of paper in a letter; but sometimes she had time for only a "note" of five or six; and at other times she would write steadily for two or three hours and produce one of thirty to forty sides in length. Mrs. Endicott's answers, though of less formidable proportions, were as regular; Mary wrote frequently to William and Louise, and her numerous cousins, so that her correspondence would be impressive for its bulk, quite apart from its contents.

I consulted a great many memoirs, biographies, and miscellaneous essays covering Mary Endicott's lifetime; only the most useful and pertinent ones are listed below.

Asquith, Margot, *Autobiography*, London, 1920. Two volumes.
Balsan, Consuelo, *The Glitter and the Gold*, New York, 1952.
Chamberlain, Rt. Hon. Sir Austen, *Politics from Inside*, London, 1936.
Choate, J. H., *Memoir of William Crowninshield Endicott*, Cambridge, Mass., 1904.
Churchill, Sir Winston Leonard Spencer, *Great Contemporaries*, London, 1937. *The Gathering Storm*, Boston, 1948. *Their Finest Hour*, Boston, 1949.
Cornwallis-West, Mrs. George, *The Reminiscences of Lady Randolph Churchill*, New York, 1908.
Edes, Mary Elizabeth and Frasier, Dudley, *The Age of Extravagance*, London, 1955.
Eliot, Elizabeth, *Heiresses and Coronets*, New York, 1959.
Feiling, Sir Keith, *The Life of Neville Chamberlain*, London, 1946.
Garvin, J. L., *The Life of Joseph Chamberlain*, Vols. I–III, London, 1932–1934. Vol. IV by Julian Amery, London, 1951.
Hadley, W. W., *Munich Before and After*, London, 1944.
Jeyes, S. H., *The Right Hon. Joseph Chamberlain*, London, 1896.
Laver, James, *Edwardian Promenade*, Boston, 1958.
Lawrence, William, *William Crowninshield Endicott, 1860–1936*, reprinted in *The Saturday Club, A Century Completed, 1920–1956*, Boston, 1958.
Marris, N. Murrell, *The Right Honourable Joseph Chamberlain*, London, 1900.
Maycock, Sir Willoughby, *With Mr. Chamberlain in the United States and Canada, 1887–1888*, London, 1914.

Nevill, Lady Dorothy, *Reminiscences*, ed. by R. Nevill, London, 1906.

Pakenham, Elizabeth, *Jameson's Raid*, London, 1960.

Petrie, Sir Charles, *The Life and Letters of the Right Hon. Sir Austen Chamberlain*, London, 1940. Two volumes.

Pope-Hennessy, James, *Queen Mary, 1867–1953*, London, 1959.

The Times History of the War in South Africa, 1899–1902, ed. by L. S. Amery, London, 1900–1909. Six volumes and index.

Webb, Beatrice Potter, *My Apprenticeship*, London, 1926.

Beatrice Webb's Diaries, 1924–1932, ed. by Margaret Cole, London, 1956. Appendix.

Wheeler-Bennett, Sir John, *King George VI*, New York, 1958.

Edward, Duke of Windsor, *A King's Story*, New York, 1947.

INDEX

Abdication Crisis, 207, 223

Abercromby, Lady, 70, 75

Abyssinia, 119, 204

Achmet Effendi, 82

Adams, Brooks, 182

Adams, Henry, 39, 55

Albert, Prince of Saxe-Coburg-Gotha (1819–1861), 137–138

Alexandra, Queen (Alexandra, Princess of Wales; 1844–1925), 26, 70, 71, 99, 116–117, 140, 143–144, 148–149, 167, 184, 199

Alix, Princess of Hesse, 91

Alphonso XIII, of Spain, 97, 120

Andros Fibre Company, 86, 89–90, 92, 94, 109

Angell, James, 37

Anglo-American relations, 100–101, 121, 129, 210

Anglo-French relations, 119, 125, 210

Anglo-German relations, 104–105, 118–119, 127–129, 143, 205, 210–211, 212–213

Arnold, Matthew, 30

Asquith, Herbert Henry, 185

Australia, 96, 115, 120, 126, 132, 138, 144

Baden-Powell, General Robert Stephenson Smyth, 132, 162

Baldwin, Stanley, 198, 201, 205

Balfour, Arthur J., 93, 94, 136, 144, 145–146, 166, 168, 169, 172, 173–174, 181, 187

Baring, Evelyn, first Earl of Cromer, 150, 171

Bayard, Thomas F., 37, 38, 45, 101, 108

Bayard, Mrs. Thomas F., 108

Beale, Alice, 197

Beatrice, Princess, 118

Bechuana Chiefs, 98, 101–102

Bedford, Duchess of, 69

Bell, Alexander Graham, 39

Bergne, Henry, 37, 38, 43, 44

Birmingham: JC as mayor there, 15; welcomes MEC, 65–66; JC's famous speeches there—Jewellers' Dinner (January 11, 1902), 143, "Two Loaves" (November 4, 1902), 170–171, Bingley Hall (July 9, 1906), 175; in 1906 election, 172–173; JC's seventieth birthday celebration, 174–175; JC's burial, 186; JC's centennial, 205

Birmingham, University of, xi, 141–142, 184, 236

"Black Week", 129

Blaine, James G., 33

Bloemfontein, 123–124, 162–163

Boer War (1899–1902), 125–137, 138, 142–143, 145

Boers, 102, 103, 122–125, 127, 130, 132, 136–137, 142, 146, 157–158, 160, 167

Bonar Law, Andrew, 187

Bond (Dutch Nationalist party), 156–157, 163, 164, 165

Botha, General Louis, 146, 157–158

Bowes-Lyon, Lady Elizabeth (Duchess of York, later Queen Elizabeth, and Queen Mother), see Elizabeth, Queen

Brodrick, (William) St. John (Fremantle), 137

Browning, Robert, 30

Buller, General Sir Redvers, 129, 130–131

Bülow, Prince Bernhard von, 128–129, 143, 144

Burger, General Schalk W., 159

Burke, Charles, 85, 229

Bute, Marchioness of, 71

Cambridge, George Frederick, Duke of, 93, 108

Cameron, Elizabeth, 39

Campbell-Bannerman, Sir Henry, 93, 172

Camperdown, Lady, 75

Canada, 36, 37, 42–43, 109, 129, 146, 168, 181, 182, 201–202

Cape Colony, 96, 101, 102, 111, 123–124, 127, 129, 131, 147, 158, 161–166

Cape Town, 106, 130, 134, 147, 163, 164–166

Carnegie, Andrew, 141–142

Carnegie, Frances, see Peto, Lady

Carnegie, Jocosa, see Swinley, Mrs. C. S. B.

Carnegie, Kathleen, see Gibbs, Mrs. Raymond

Carnegie, May, see Slade, Mrs. G. P.

Carnegie, Rachel, see Chaytor, Mrs. A. Drewett

Carnegie, Reverend William Hartley (1860–1936), ix, xi, 179, 184, 188–191, 193; Chaplain to Speaker of House of Commons, 192; marriage to MEC, 192; life at Dean's Yard, 194–206; Windsor visit, 195–196; American visits, 196–197, 198; death, 206; MEC's recollections of, 207

Carnegie, Mrs. W. H., see Endicott, Mary Crowninshield

Cavendish, Lord Frederick, 85, 229

Chamberlain, Arthur, 62, 63

Chamberlain, Mrs. Arthur (Louisa Kenrick), 62, 63

Chamberlain, Rt. Hon. Sir Austen, K. G. (1863–1937), xi, 16, 38, 39, 51, 61, 62, 67, 72, 74, 83, 84, 91, 95, 96–98, 107–108, 114, 115, 128, 135 136, 171, 172–173, 174, 177, 178, 179, 183, 185, 186, 187, 192, 193, 194, 196, 200, 201, 204, 205, 223; meets MEC, 61; member for East Worcestershire, 86; maiden speech, 87; Civil Lord of Admiralty, 94; Postmaster General, 166; marriage, 176; honoured for twenty-one years as M. P., East Worcestershire, 184; Secretary of State for India, 188; Foreign Secretary, Locarno Pact, K. G., 199; death, 208

Chamberlain, Mrs. Austen (Ivy Dundas), 174, 176, 177, 178, 199, 217

Chamberlain, Beatrice, 45, 50, 51, 62, 63, 72, 74, 75, 83, 84, 88, 108, 136, 172, 187, 188, 191–192, 196, 212

Chamberlain, Diane, see Maxwell, Mrs. A. T.

Chamberlain, Dorothy, see Lloyd, Mrs. Stephen

Chamberlain, Ethel (Mrs. Lionel Richards), 62, 64, 86, 133, 134, 147, 171–172

Chamberlain, Frank, 185

Chamberlain, Hilda, xi, 62, 64, 86, 106, 129, 136, 172, 183, 184, 187, 188, 189, 201, 210, 211, 214–215, 217, 224, 232

Chamberlain, Ida, 62, 64, 74, 83, 86, 108, 140, 172, 187, 188, 189, 210, 211, 214–215, 217

Chamberlain, Rt. Hon. Joseph (1836–1914), ix, x, xi, 13, 14, 16, 37, 42–44, 50, 51, 52, 64, 66–67, 68, 69–70, 73–74, 75, 76, 77–78, 80–81, 82, 83, 84, 85, 92–93, 95, 96, 97, 118–119, 119 120, 122, 123–126, 130, 131, 132, 133, 136, 138, 139–140, 141–142, 143–144, 192, 194, 195, 196, 198, 199, 200, 201, 202, 206, 208, 227, 236; Member for Birmingham, early years in Parliament, 15; Chief Plenipotentiary to Fisheries Conference, 36; meets MEC, 38; Washington life, 39–41, 47–49; courtship and engagement to MEC, 44–47; return to America, 53–54; marries MEC, honeymoon, 55–61; life at Highbury, 62 64, 91; Birmingham's welcome home, 65–66; life in London, 70–73; visits to Windsor, 73–74, 86, 87, 91, 99, 128, 143, 171; meets emperor William II, 77; talks with MEC on politics, 79; trips to America, 83–84, 89–90, 101, 109, 121–122; opposes second Home Rule Bill, 87–88; Secretary of State for the Colonies, 94; "Moatlodi", 98, 102; Venezuela crisis, 100–101, 105; Jameson Raid, and his repudiation of it, 103–105; interviews Rhodes, 106; question of Colonial office's prior knowledge of Raid raised, 106; painted by Sargent, 106–107; reception for Empire Chambers of Commerce, 108–109; failure of sisal investment, 109; honorary degrees, 109, 129; Milner appointment, 111; Colonial Premiers' Conference and Jubilee activities, 111–118; cleared of complicity in Jameson Raid, 117; keeps England from protesting Spanish-American War, 121; talks with Kaiser and Bülow, 127–129; Khaki Election, 134–135; last Minister to see Queen, 137; cab accident, 145; plans South African trip, 146; Sandringham visit, 147–148; tribute to MEC, 149; South African trip, 150–167; Tariff Reform Campaign, 168–175; resigns from Cabinet, 169; 1906 election, 172–173; seventieth birthday celebrations, 174–176; illness and last years, 175–186; death, burial in Birmingham, 186; MEC's widowhood, 187–192

Chamberlain, Mrs. Joseph (Florence Kenrick), 63

Chamberlain, Mrs. Joseph (Harriet Kenrick), 63

Chamberlain, Mrs. Joseph, see Endicott, Mary Crowninshield

Chamberlain, "Little Joe", 179, 185, 198

Chamberlain, Neville (1869–1940), xi, 16, 51, 62, 74, 81, 82, 94, 98, 133, 172, 176, 183, 185, 187, 197, 200, 204, 205, 208, 235; visits Bahamas, 84; sisal plantation on Andros, 86; plantation progress, 89; crop failure, 92; speaks for father in 1895 election, 95; failure of Andros venture, 109; marriage, 181; Lord Mayor of Birmingham, 188; Director of National Service, 193–194; offices in Baldwin ministries, 198–199; Chancellor of Exchequer, 201–202; Prime Minister, 209–214; Munich Agreement, 212–213; World War II begins, 213; resigns as Prime Minister, 214; illness and death, 214–215

Chamberlain, Mrs. Neville (Anne Vere Cole), 181, 201

Charles, Prince of Denmark (afterwards Haakon VII, King of Norway), 116

Chaytor, A. Drewett, 200

Chaytor, Mrs. A. Drewett (Rachel Carnegie), xi, 193, 197–198, 200

Christian, Princess (Princess Helena), 70

Churchill, Lady Randolph, 78, 79, 128

Churchill, Lord Randolph, 79

Churchill, Sir Winston Leonard Spencer, K. G., 128, 132, 214, 219

Clarence, Albert Victor, Duke of (1864–1892), 89

Clarke, General Stanley, 117

Cleveland, President Grover, 33, 40, 47, 53, 56, 59, 100

Cleveland, Mrs. Grover (Frances Folsom), 40, 56

Coercion Act, 26, 84, 229

Colcraft, Mr., 66

Colenso, 129, 156

Collings, Jesse, 95, 172, 184

Colonial Nursing Association, 99, 142

Colonial Office, 96, 103, 104, 106, 107, 113, 117, 120, 121, 127, 139, 142, 166, 171

Colonial Preference, 118, 146, 168–175, 201

Colonial Premiers, 111–116, 146

Connaught, Prince Arthur, Duke of, 118

Coolidge, Marian, 22

Cromer, Lord, see Baring, Evelyn

Cronje, General A. P., 131

Cronje, General Piet A., 157

Crowninshield, Jacob, 32

Czechoslovakia, 212

Dance, 220, 221

Davitt, Michael, 84

Dawes, Charles G., 211, 235

17, Dean's Yard, 190, 191, 193, 206, 208, 218

De La Rey, General J. H., 146, 157, 160–161

Devonshire, Duchess of, 66–67, 113

Devonshire, Duke of, see Hartington, Spencer Compton Cavendish, Marquis of

De Waal, Mr., 164, 165

De Wet, General Christiaan Rudolph, 146

Diamond Jubilee, 111–118

Dover House, 28

Dundonald, Earl of, General Douglas Mackinnon Baillie Hamilton Cochrane, 131

Durban, 147, 155

Eden, Anthony, 211

Edgar incident, 122

Edinburgh, Prince Philip, Duke of, 223

Education Bill of 1902, 147, 168

Edward VII, King (Albert Edward, Prince of Wales; 1841–1910), 71, 108, 115, 116–117, 118, 137, 138, 143, 145, 146, 148–149, 166, 167, 180

Edward VIII, King (Prince Edward, Prince of Wales, later Duke of Windsor), 99, 205, 207

Edward, Prince, see Edward VIII, King

Edwardes, Henry, 41

Eliot, Sir Charles Norton Edgecumbe, 152

Elizabeth, Princess (later Queen Elizabeth II), 222, 223, 224

Elizabeth, Queen (Lady Elizabeth Bowes-Lyon, later Duchess of York, Queen Elizabeth, and Queen Mother), 198, 223

Endecott, John, Governor, 14, 19, 40, 74, 141, 185, 215

Endicott grandparents, 21, 54, 61

Endicott, Mary Crowninshield (later Mrs. Joseph Chamberlain, Mrs. W. H. Carnegie; 1864–1957), ix–xi, 14, 15, 16, 17, 18, 19, 20, 21, 22, 23, 39, 40, 66–67, 74–79, 80, 85, 88, 92–95, 96–98, 107–110, 111, 120, 125, 126, 127, 129, 130, 131, 132, 133, 136, 139–140, 141, 142, 146–147, 193; first trip to Europe, 24–31; debutant, 32; Washington life, 33–35; meets JC, 38, early comments on JC, 41–42, courtship, 44–47, engagement to JC and family reactions, 47–49, wedding preparations, 50–55, marriage to JC and honeymoon, 55–61; first weeks at Highbury, 62–64; Birmingham's welcome, 65–66; presentation to Queen

Victoria, 68–70; life in London, 70–73; Windsor visits, 73–74, 86, 87, 91, 99, 128, 143, 171, 195–196; meets the Kaiser, 77; growing used to political life, 78–79; painted by Millais, 81; trip to Egypt with JC, 81–82; trips to America, 83–84, 89–90, 101, 109, 121–122, 196–197, 198, 200, 202, 210, 211, 220–222, 232; Colonial Nursing Association, 99; Sandringham visits, 99, 148–149; indignation over Venezuela crisis, 100; Jameson Raid, 104–106; plans party for Colonial Premiers, 112; Diamond Jubilee activities, 113–118; Osborne visit, 122–123; indignation at Paul Kruger, 124; travels with mother, 134–135; Queen's opinion of her, 137–138; as "grandmother", 144–145; JC's Birmingham tribute to her, 149; South African trip with JC, 150–167; tariff reform campaign, 169–175; JC's illness and last years, 175–186; widowhood, 187–191; marriage to Canon Carnegie, 192; life at Dean's Yard, 194–206; celebration of JC's centennial, 205; death of Canon Carnegie and first years of widowhood, 206–213; World War II, 213–219; last years, 220–226; death, burial in Westminster Abbey, 226–227

Endicott, William, 25, 55, 226

Endicott, William Crowninshield (1826–1900), 14, 16, 18, 19, 21, 34, 35, 38, 40, 44, 50, 52, 53, 54, 56, 57, 59, 121–125, 141; appointed to Massachusetts Supreme Court, 20; journey to Europe, 1882–1883, 24–31; runs for governor of Massachusetts, 32; appointed Secretary of War, 33; gives MEC Worth trousseau and diamond crescent, 55; visits England, 74–79, 86, 91–92, views on international marriages, 83–84; health failing, 109; death, 133

Endicott, Mrs. William Crowninshield (Ellen Peabody) (1833–1927), 18, 19, 21, 23, 38, 40, 44, 50, 52, 53, 54, 56, 57, 59, 62, 64, 71, 84, 121–122, 171,

178, 183, 190–191, 236; trip to Europe, 1882–1883, 24–31; Washington life, 34–35; visits to England, 74–79, 86, 91–92, 134, 168–169, 176–177; pleased with JC as son-in-law, 75; painted by Sargent, 140–141; death, 200

Endicott, William Crowninshield, Jr. (1860–1936), 18, 19, 20, 23, 29, 31, 51, 59, 74, 120, 121, 169, 176, 178, 182, 193, 200, 202, 236; sends flowers to debutante MEC, 32; takes MEC to British Legation reception, 38; dismayed by JC as MEC's suitor, 46–47; marriage, 67; indignant at British climate, 80; move to 163 Marlborough Street, 109; on the Nile, 201; death and MEC's recollections of him, 206–207

Endicott, Mrs. William Crowninshield, Jr., (Marie-Louise Thoron), ix, x, 67, 109, 121, 176, 178, 180, 200, 201, 202, 207, 210, 211, 221–222, 223, 225, 236

Evarts, Senator, 49

Fairchild, Charles S., Secretary of the Treasury, 38

"The Farm", Danvers, Massachusetts, x, 89–90, 101, 121

Fashoda, 119

Fawkes, Admiral, 150, 153

Fisheries Conference (British-American), 15, 35, 36–38, 39, 40, 42, 45

Fisheries Treaty, see Washington, Second Treaty of

Fitzpatrick, Sir Percy, 159

Franco-Prussian War, 19, 143

Franks, Reverend J. P., 21

Free Food League, 169–170

Gardner, Augustus Peabody, 20

George V, King (Duke of York, later Prince of Wales; 1865–1936), 91, 99, 108, 116, 131, 144, 148, 180, 184, 189, 195–196, 203, 205

George VI, King (Prince Albert, Duke of York; 1895–1952), 198, 209, 223

Gibbs, Raymond, 215–216

Gibbs, Mrs. Raymond (Kathleen Carnegie), xi, 193, 206, 214, 215–216

Gladstone, William Ewart, 15, 29, 84, 87–88, 90, 93

Gladstone, Mrs. William Ewart, 69, 100

Gloucester, Prince Henry, Duke of, 223

Gordon, General C. G., 82

Graaff Reinet, 163–164, 165

Grace Episcopal Church, 21

Grahamstown, 163

Grant, General Ulysses S., 19, 217

Guildhall, 144, 166

Hamilton, Lord George Francis, 169

Harcourt, Sir William George Granville Venables Vernon, 95, 130

Hardwick Hall, 66–67

Hartington, Spencer Compton Cavendish, Marquis of (later eighth Duke of Devonshire), 66, 76, 86, 92, 93, 94, 145, 166, 169–170

Hatfield House, 76, 77, 148

Hay, John, 39, 60, 121, 230

Herschel, Sir Farrar, 29, 30, 39

Hertzog, James Barry Munnik, 163

Highbury, 62, 63–64, 73, 74, 76, 78, 80, 83, 91, 92, 94, 104, 106–107, 121, 124, 134, 140–141, 146, 169, 172, 176, 177, 178, 184, 185, 187, 212

Hitler, Adolf, 204, 211, 212, 213

Hoare, Sir Samuel, 204

Hofmeyr, Jan Hendrik, 165–166

Holmes, Oliver Wendell, M.D., 219

Howard, Lady, of Glossop, 71

Imperial Preference, 118, 146, 168–175, 201

Ireland, 84, 129, 185

Irish Home Rule, 15, 79, 80, 84, 85, 86, 87, 90, 92, 180, 185, 232

Italy, 135, 171, 204, 210, 211

James, Mrs. (Lina Chamberlain), 62, 63

Jameson, Leander Starr, 102–106

Jameson Raid, 103–106, 107, 117, 126, 130, 131

Jefferson, President Thomas, 32

Johannesburg, 102–103, 106, 122, 133, 158–160

Joubert, Piet, 102, 157

Kennedy, Ambassador and Mrs. Joseph, 211
Kenrick, Florence, *see* Chamberlain, Mrs. Joseph
Kenrick, Harriet, *see* Chamberlain, Mrs. Joseph
Kenrick, William, 63, 95
Kenrick, Mrs. William (Mary Chamberlain), 63
Kent, Prince George, Duke of, 223
"Khaki Election", 134–135, 233
Kimberley, 127, 129, 131, 162–163
Kitchener, General Horatio Herbert, 82, 119, 129, 130, 136–137, 142, 143, 146
Knole, 86
Kruger, Paul, 102–103, 104–106, 122, 123–125, 133, 136, 157–158, 159

Labour Party, 182, 200, 219, 223
Ladysmith, 127, 129, 131, 156
Lansdowne, Lord, 42, 127, 128, 137, 185, 199
Laval, Pierre, 204
Lawley, Sir Arthur, 156–158
Lawrence, James, Jr., 216, 217
League of Nations, 199, 204
41, Lennox Gardens, 206, 207–208, 211, 212, 213, 215, 216, 218, 219, 225, 226
Leopold, King of the Belgians, 99, 139–140
Lichtenburg, 160–161
Livermore, Colonel, 21–22
Lloyd, Mrs. Stephen (Dorothy Chamberlain), xi, 185, 201
Lloyd George, David, 136, 183, 193, 198
Locarno, 16, 199, 205
Lodge, Senator Henry Cabot, 39
London Convention (1884), 102, 122
Long, Walter Hume, 187
Louise, Princess, 143
Low Countries, German attack on, 214

Mafeking, 127, 132, 133, 135, 161–162, 163
Magersfontein, 129
Mahdi, 82, 119

Majuba, 102
Manchester, Duchess of, *see* Devonshire, Duchess of
Mandeville, Viscount, 66
Margaret, Princess, 223
Maria Christina, Queen Regent, of Spain, 97, 120
Marlborough, Duke and Duchess of, 58–59, 142
163 Marlborough Street, 109, 122, 222
Mary, Princess, of Teck, *see* Mary, Queen
Mary, Queen (Princess Mary of Teck, Duchess of York, and Princess of Wales; 1867–1953), 89, 91, 99, 108, 116, 145, 184, 189, 195, 198, 202–203, 223, 224
Mason, Fanny Peabody, 41, 46, 48, 49, 58, 100, 191
Mason, William Powell, 24, 136
Mason, Mrs. William Powell, 58
Mason College, Birmingham, 141
Massachusetts Historical Society, x, 207, 236
Maxwell, A. T., xi, 223
Maxwell, Mrs. A. T. (Diane Chamberlain), xi, 185, 223, 224
Maycock, Willoughby, 37, 42, 43–44, 49, 53
McKinley, President William, 120, 121
Methuen, Paul Sanford, third Baron Methuen, 129
Middleburg, 164
Milner, Alfred, 111, 122–124, 126, 134, 142, 156–160, 163, 179, 199
Mombasa, 151–153
Monkbretton, Lord, 165
Morgan, Pierpont, 26, 28, 55
Mugwumps, 33
Munich, 212, 213, 235
Mussolini, Benito, 204, 213

Nairobi, 151–153
Natal, 96, 102, 124, 127, 131, 147, 155, 156, 158
Nettlefold, Mrs., 67
Nevill, Lady Dorothy, 70, 71, 177
Newfoundland, 96
New Zealand, 96, 129

Nicholas II, of Russia, 91
Norway, fall of, 214

O'Connor, Dr., 95
O'Shea, Captain W. H., 84–85
O'Shea, Mrs. W. H., 85
Olney, Richard, 100, 109, 232
Olney Doctrine, 100, 105
Orange Free State (later Orange River Colony), 102, 123, 125, 162
Osborne, 96, 122–123, 137
Ottawa Conference (1932), 201–202

Paardeberg, 131
Paarl, 165
Parnell, Charles Stewart, 84–85
Patti, Adelina, 31
Payson, Clara, 58
Peabody, Reverend Endicott, 30, 188
Peabody, Fanny, see Prince, Mrs. Morton
Peabody, George, 19, 21, 27, 219
Peabody, Mrs. George (Clarissa Endicott), 19, 21, 22, 58, 72, 74, 208
Peabody, George Augustus, 52, 136, 188
Peabody, Joseph, 20, 89
Peabody, S. Endicott, 26
Perry, Eliza Endicott, 18, 229
Pershing, General John J., 195–196
Peto, Lady (Frances Carnegie), xi, 191, 197
Peto, Sir Michael, xi, 197, 213
Phillips, Jenny, 21
Phoenix Park murders (1882), 85
Pietermaritzburg, 155–156
Piggott, Lady, 98
Pink, Sidney, xi, 175, 179, 213, 215, 216, 218, 219, 220, 225, 226
Playfair, Sir Lyon, 101
Poland, invasion of, 213
Port Elizabeth, 163–164
Portugal, King of, 139
Potchefstroom, 160
Potter, Beatrice, 13–14, 45
Pretoria, 106, 128, 133, 156
Primrose, Archibald Philip, fifth Earl of Rosebery, 87, 88–89, 90, 93
Prince, Mrs. Morton (Fanny Peabody), 22–23, 210

40, Prince's Gardens, 61, 75, 78–79, 96, 99, 104, 107–108, 139–140, 145, 166, 187–188, 193, 206, 218
Putnam, William, 37

Rayleigh, Lord and Lady, 93
Reid, George Houstoun, 115–116
Rhodes, Cecil John, 101–104, 106, 162
Richards, Hilda Mary, 144, 147, 171, 177, 197
Richards, Lionel, 133
Richards, Mrs. Lionel, see Chamberlain, Ethel
Ritchie, Charles Thomson, 168, 169
Roberts, General Frederick Sleigh, first Earl Roberts, K. G., 129, 130–131, 133, 136–137
Robinson, Sir Hercules, 103, 104, 106, 111
Roosevelt, President Franklin Delano, 219
Roosevelt, Theodore, 182–183
Rosebery, Lord, see Primrose, Archibald Philip
Rothschild, Ferdinand, 76
Ryland, Mrs. (Clara Chamberlain), 63

Sackville-West, Sir Lionel, 37, 38, 59, 86
Salisbury, Lady, 69
Salisbury, Robert Cecil, third Marquis of, 15, 76, 87, 90, 92, 93, 118, 125, 137, 138, 145; Prime Minister, 94; Venezuela crisis, 101; Jameson Raid, 103; Colonial Premiers' Conference, (1897), 111–112; "Two-Headed government", 119
Samoa, 119, 127–128
Sandringham, 99, 148–149, 171
Sarajevo, assassination at, 185
Sargent, John Singer, 106–107, 140–141, 178, 195
Sargent, Lucius Manlius, 22
Sears, Clara, 22, 41, 42, 191
Sedgwick, R. Minturn, xi, 216
Selborne, Lord, 29
Seymour, Admiral Sir Edward Hobart, 27
Shah of Persia, 76

Shea, Sir Ambrose, 84
Slade, G. P., 197, 198, 213, 214, 216, 217
Slade, Mrs. G. P. (May Carnegie), xi, 191, 197, 198, 224
Smith, Reverend Elias, 20
Smuts, Jan Christian, 158
South Africa, Chamberlains' tour of (1902–1903), 150–167
South Africa Company, 101, 106
South African Committee, 110, 111, 117
South African Republic, see Transvaal
South African War, see Boer War
Spanish-American War, 120–121
Spion Kop, 156
Sprigg, Lady, 114
Spring-Rice, Cecil, 41, 67, 230
Stanhope, Hon. Philip, 126
Steyn, Marthinus Theunis, 123, 125, 133
St. John's Church, Washington, 55
St. Margaret's, Westminster, ix, 184, 186, 188, 194, 219, 223, 224
Stormberg, 129
Sturgis, Russell, 27
Sudetenland, 212
Swinley, C. S. B., xi, 200, 203, 213, 215, 218, 224, 233
Swinley, Mrs. C. S. B. (Jocosa Carnegie), xi, 193, 200, 224

Tariff Reform, 167, 168–175, 179, 180, 181, 182, 187, 201–202, 205
Teck, Duchess of, 108
Teck, Duke of, 108
Teck, Princess Mary of, see Mary, Queen
Thoron, Marie-Louise, see Endicott, Mrs. William Crowninshield, Jr.
Toski, Battle of, 82
Transvaal (South African Republic), 102, 103–106, 110, 111, 122–125, 126, 131, 133, 156–161, 162
Tropical Medicine, London School of, 142
Tupper, Sir Charles, 37
Turner, Lady, 114–115

Uganda Railway, 151–153
Uitlanders, 102, 111, 122, 123
Unionists, 15, 66, 68, 69, 79, 80, 90, 92–93, 95, 133, 134–135, 147, 168, 172–174, 180, 181, 196

Vanderbilt, Consuelo (Duchess of Marlborough), 58–59, 142
Venezuela Crisis, 100–101, 105
Ventersdorp, 160
Vereeniging, Treaty of (1902), 145, 158
Versailles, Treaty of (1919), 196, 204
Victoria, Princess, 116, 143
Victoria, Queen (1819–1901), 16, 70, 83, 89, 96, 110, 122–123, 128, 131, 132, 195; Diamond Jubilee, 113–118; death, 137; opinion of MEC, 137; funeral, 138–139
Volksraad, 157–158
Volksrust, 157

Wales, Prince of: Albert Edward, see Edward VII, King; George, see George V, King: Edward, see Edward VIII, King
Wales, Princess of: Alexandra, see Alexandra, Queen; Mary, see Mary, Queen
Wanderers' Club, 159
Washington, Second Treaty of (1888) (Fisheries Treaty), 47, 48, 53
West, Victoria, 58, 59
Westminster Abbey, 28, 138, 190, 192, 206, 226–227
White, General Sir George, 129
White, Mrs. 75
Whitehouse, Sir George, 151–152
Whitney, Dorothy Payne, 55
Whitney, William C., Secretary of the Navy, 33, 39, 46, 50
Wilde, Lady, 30
Wilde, Oscar, 30
William II, Emperor, 77, 96, 119, 127–129, 138–139; Kruger telegram, 104–105; talks with MEC at Sandringham, 148
Williams, Powell, 95
Wilson, Lady Sarah, 132
Wilson, President Woodrow, 182–183
Winant, Ambassador John, 217
Windsor Castle, 73–74, 86, 87, 91, 99, 128, 138–139, 143, 171, 195–196

Witwatersrand ("The Rand"), 102

World War I, 187, 188, 190, 193–194, 195–196, 205

World War II, 213–219; Neville Chamberlain's effort to avert, 210–213

Worth, House of, 52, 55, 68–69, 76, 83, 112, 226

Worth, M. Jean, 197

York, Duchess of: Princess Mary, *see*

Mary, Queen; Elizabeth, *see* Elizabeth, Queen

York, Duke of: Prince George, *see* George V, King; Prince Albert, *see* George VI, King

Yznaga, Consuelo, 66

Zanzibar, Sultan and Sultana of, 154–155